Anti-discriminatory
Practice

Related titles from Continuum

Good Practice in Childcare: Janet Kay
Observing Children: Carole Sharman, Wendy Cross and Diana Vennis
Protecting Children: Janet Kay
Teaching 3–8: Mark O'Hara

Anti-discriminatory Practice

Second edition

Rosalind Millam

continuum
LONDON • NEW YORK

Continuum

The Tower Building
11 York Road
London SE1 7NX
www.continuumbooks.com

15 East 26th Street
New York
NY 10010

First published 1996 by Cassell

Second edition published 2002 by Continuum

Reprinted 2004

British Library Cataloguing-in-Publication Data
A catalogue record for this book is available from the British Library.

ISBN: 0–8264–5475–5 (hardback) 0–8264–5476–3 (paperback)

Typeset by Keystroke, Jacaranda Lodge, Wolverhampton
Printed and bound in Great Britain by Bath Press.

Contents

Acknowledgements

I should like to thank all the individuals who read and commented on the first edition of this book and gave permission for photographs to be used. Thank you also to those people who used the first edition and gave feedback on it.

Preface

The first edition of this book was published in 1996. It was written in line with the National Occupational Standards in Child Care and Education to provide workers with a source of information surrounding the issues of anti-discriminatory practice. Many changes have taken place in the early years care and education field since then. For example, there has been a great deal of new legislation relating to anti-discriminatory practice; the National Vocational Qualifications (NVQs) in Child Care and Education have been revised and are now NVQs in Early Years Care and Education; there is now an NVQ for individuals working in fostering and residential care settings, namely the NVQ in Caring for Children and Young People; new research and publications into issues concerning anti-discriminatory practice are constantly being brought to our attention; and, of course, individuals continue to attend training sessions, take part in development opportunities and reflect on their practice.

This new edition contains new and updated material which builds on and enhances the original edition of the book. For example, Chapter 1 contains information on the new legislation that has come into being since 1996 together with greater detail on the issues for male workers and their employers and most other issues covered in the original book. Chapter 5 contains information on the Early Learning Goals. Chapter 6 contains greater detail on communication and identity. New publications have been listed and there is an updated list of useful addresses at the end of the book.

Individuals who have worked with children and families have acknowledged for many years the need to respect and value people and to treat them as individuals. One of the underlying principles of the Children Act 1989 includes the acknowledging of a child's racial, religious, cultural and linguistic background. Subsequent legislation, including the Disability Discrimination Act 1995, the Human Rights Act 1998, the Schools Standards and Framework Act 1998 and the Care Standards Act 2000, all require workers to work within an anti-discriminatory framework with children, young people, families, adults, colleagues and other professionals. Legislation affects and impacts on all day-to-day work, from planning activities, recruiting and selecting staff, working with colleagues, through to the language we use, the attitudes we hold and all aspects of the environment in which we work.

When we work with children it is important to recognize and take into account the important role that everyone has in another person's life. People are not isolated individuals. They have a birth family that they may or may not live with; they have friends and a peer group; there are significant adults with whom they come into contact, such as key workers and teachers as well as people they meet on a daily basis. All these, together with people's living environment, have an effect upon them and their development.

Addressing issues of anti-discriminatory practice can sometimes feel threatening or worrying to workers, particularly given the current great changes in both legislation and day-to-day practice. Some people are not sure what it entails; others feel that they are already working in a way that encompasses these changes; and some workers do not know where to start.

Anti-discriminatory practice acknowledges, values and addresses the needs of the various groups and individuals that go to make up the society in which we live. These include gender, age, disability, sexual orientation, economic background, race, religion, culture and language, among other factors. Of course, it is important to recognize that one individual will be made up of many parts, and that we are all individuals. We may be seen by others as belonging to, or being part of, a specific group, and we may be labelled accordingly, for example in terms of our age. Anti-discriminatory practice actively takes account of the many different facets of individuals and groups and acknowledges them in all aspects of work. This book addresses the need to be aware of and use an anti-discriminatory framework in all areas of one's work. It looks at what the legislation requires of workers, it examines research to show why this is good practice, and it provides practical suggestions on how this can be achieved. The most important aspect of working in this way is a person's own attitude towards anti-discriminatory practices. This is the one issue that this book addresses throughout. Reading a book will not change anyone's attitude, but it will, I hope, address issues that will cause individuals to examine the opinions and attitudes they hold and how they can affect their work.

This book is designed to give workers an understanding of anti-discriminatory practice and a starting point for addressing the issues involved. I hope it will give workers confidence to explore issues of good practice and to carry out good practice on a practical level. Some workers may feel that they need to follow up some of the issues raised in this book with further reading or training.

Whom the book is for

This book will be useful for individuals working towards NVQs in Early Years Care and Education and NVQs in Caring for Children and Young People. It will also be useful for people undertaking related training and courses as well as workers who need up-to-date information. It can be used as a point of reference for anyone who may need it, including early years educators, foster carers, residential workers, teachers, social workers and trainers.

How to use the book

The six chapters in this book address different issues, starting with the importance of working within an anti-discriminatory framework. Each chapter examines the theoretical issue being discussed, so that workers have an outline of background information.

All chapters have in them boxes titled 'A Chance to Think'. These provide an opportunity to stand back from the theory and look at how issues can be incorporated into everyday practice. All the 'chances to think' are based on real examples. Some ask workers to write down answers, and these can be used by NVQ candidates for their portfolios. Those workers not working towards an NVQ may wish to use them as a starting point for discussion with colleagues or at staff meetings. Answers are given in the appendices at the end of the book for people wishing to compare their answers with some already provided by workers in the childcare and education field.

A list of publications (books for further reading as well as video titles) is given at the end of each chapter. There is a list of useful addresses at the end of the book.

The same terminology has been used throughout the book. Frequently used words include *workers* (any individual who is working with children on a paid or voluntary basis or as a trainee), *setting* (the place where workers are working) and *parents* (people who are parents or who have parental responsibility).

Chapter 1

Introduction

In Britain today there are many different types of childcare services. These include day nurseries, nursery schools, playgroups, nurseries, childminders, nannies, family centres, schools, foster care, residential settings, breakfast clubs, after-school clubs and playschemes. Each type of provision will offer a different type of service, with children and families making their own use of the provision as required. Services may be run by a variety of organizations, including private and voluntary organizations, registered charities, and education and social services departments. Moreover, children may attend for a variety of reasons. Their parents may work or study. They may be over 5, when by law they must have educational provision. Some children may be defined as 'children in need', a definition used in the Children Act 1989 and meaning that the children need some kind of childcare provision. Children may be 'at risk'; or they may have a special need such as speech therapy; or their parents might need a break. Other children may be defined as being 'looked after' by the local authority, which means that the local authority has responsibility for those children as set out in the Children Act. Some children attend a childcare setting in order to socialize and mix with other children. Some children and families may make use of more than one type of provision. For example, a child may live with foster parents and also attend a nursery school. Another child might go to a childminder in the morning, then go to school and subsequently attend an after-school club. Yet another child might have a nanny. But whatever the type of provision or the reason for a child's attending, all childcare provision has three things in common: children, parents and staff.

In this chapter we will be examining the necessity to work with children, families and colleagues within an anti-discriminatory framework. This is important in whatever setting we work. It does not just apply to particular settings or only in particular places such as large towns. We will look at why this is important and examine research into how young children see colour and gender in particular. We will see that very young children can have discriminatory attitudes; for example, they can be racist. We will look at how workers can begin to try to challenge such attitudes by working within an anti-discriminatory framework, and at the benefits this brings to children, parents and colleagues. We will look at what is meant by anti-discriminatory practice and how this may differ from a multicultural approach. An anti-discriminatory framework is required by law, and this chapter will examine the legislation that workers need to be aware of and to work within.

Sometimes, when we start to talk about things like culture, race, religion, gender, disability, age, discrimination, stereotyping and the need to work within an anti-discriminatory framework, people feel uncomfortable. This may be for a variety of reasons. Some adults do not really understand the concept of anti-discriminatory practice or know the difference between, for example, discrimination and stereotyping. Later in this chapter we will try to define some of the terms commonly used, so that people can feel less uncomfortable with them. It might be that people feel uncomfortable because they do not think that this is an issue that needs addressing with young children; they believe young children are not capable of having discriminatory attitudes, and they do not want to shatter this illusion. Other people will want to start addressing these issues but do not know where or how to start; and other individuals are aware of the need to work within an anti-discriminatory framework but are so worried about getting it wrong or upsetting people that they are too frightened to do anything about it. It is important to recognize that, no matter how hard we try, no one can get it right all the time, but that should not stop people from trying. Some people will be worried about beginning to address these issues, because they will have to examine their own attitudes towards the various groups that go to make up the society in which we live. Some people feel uncomfortable about doing this because it can focus on things they would rather not admit to, or cause them to question the attitudes they hold.

Everyone will have some sort of attitude or opinion about the different groups that make up the society in which we live. The *Concise Oxford Dictionary* defines 'attitude' as 'a settled opinion or way of thinking and behaviour reflecting this', and 'opinion' as 'belief or assessment based on grounds short of proof – a view that is held as probable'.

Having various attitudes and opinions is a natural part of life. Triandis (1971) says that people have attitudes for a variety of reasons because they: (a) help them to understand the world around them by organizing and simplifying a very complex input from their environment; (b) protect their self-esteem by making it possible for them to avoid unpleasant truths about themselves; (c) help them adjust to a complex world by making it more likely that they will react so as to maximize their rewards from the environment; and (d) allow them to express their fundamental values. People also have values that are important to them. Values emanate from one's own principles or standards, one's judgement

---

A Chance to Think 1
The society in which we live is made up of many different individuals, who are sometimes classified into groups, e.g. according to the religion to which they belong, or as being of a particular age, sex or sexual orientation, or because of their racial or cultural background. Think about two different groups in society and the way you view them. One group should be people you have daily contact with and the second group people you have little contact with. Write down your thoughts about the two groups.

What is your attitude to the group of people you have daily contact with?

What is your attitude to the group of people you have little contact with?

What has influenced your thinking about these two different groups of people?

of what is valuable or important in life. A person's attitudes, opinions and values are influenced and formed by many things, including the attitudes and values of parents and other significant adults, religious and cultural background, images in the media, the influence of friends, that person's own experiences and day-to-day things happening in the world around them. A person may have to juggle several different sets of values. They will have personal values – that is, those values that are important to them as an individual. They may then have professional values that have been influenced and formed by the profession they work in. A third set of values may derive from the organization in which they work. These various value systems may lead to a conflict within individuals when they have to balance them on a day-to-day basis. Here it is important to recognize that some of the attitudes people hold towards some individuals and groups can be stereotypes or prejudices.

The *Concise Oxford Dictionary* defines 'stereotype' as 'a person or thing that conforms to an unjustifiably fixed, usually standardized, mental picture'. Its definition of 'prejudice' is 'a pre-conceived opinion or (followed by *against, in favour of*) bias or partiality'. Therefore, stereotypes and prejudices are not based on what actually is, but are views that people have gained from the images or attitudes around them, which may be inaccurate. Stereotypes and prejudices can lead to discrimination. This is defined as 'unfavourable treatment based on prejudice'. Discrimination may in turn lead to oppression, which is defined as 'the act or instance of oppressing, the state of being oppressed, prolonged harsh or cruel treatment or control'.

It is how those attitudes are expressed through a person's behaviour, actions and language that is important, and this will play a part in influencing how young children develop their own attitudes. It is important for people working with children to have a positive attitude about themselves and an understanding of who they are. Workers are seen as role models by children, parents and colleagues, and will have to answer what may be potentially difficult questions or challenge unacceptable behaviour. It is important that workers are willing to deal with this and, if necessary, say that they do not have all the answers but are prepared to try to find out. This chapter will not change people's attitudes, but it will, I hope, get people thinking about the attitudes they hold about themselves and the groups that make up society, why they hold them, how they are expressing them and the effects this may be having on the children, parents and colleagues in the settings.

A Chance to Think 2
Think about yourself. Martians have landed from outer space and you have to describe yourself to them. Some of the things they want to know are: how you look, where you come from, what your background is, what you believe in, where you fit in your family, what you like and dislike about your job and what you think about yourself.
   Write down what you would say to them.
   How do you feel about what you have said?
   Now describe one of your colleagues to them. Are there any similarities or differences between the two of you?
   How do you feel about this?

The ways we feel about ourselves and other people develop very early on in life. Sometimes workers like to think that young children are unable to be unkind or have negative attitudes towards people. It is often easier to believe that young children cannot notice, for example, disabilities or the colour of a person's skin and have an attitude towards them. Workers using colour tables and colour matching games know that children recognize the difference between red and green, but still find it hard to believe that children notice the difference in skin colour. This may be because it can be uncomfortable to acknowledge the fact. When we acknowledge it, something has to be done about it and the way people work, and, as we have said, this can be threatening to some people. We shall now look at some of the research that has been undertaken on how children develop attitudes to colour and gender in particular.

Research

It is not possible to examine all the research that has taken place in the childcare field, but the main areas of research will be examined here to provide an insight into how children develop attitudes towards colour and gender. We will show that children do develop attitudes early in life and, if they have attitudes to colour and gender, then it follows that they will be developing attitudes to other groups, such as people with disabilities, languages other than English and people from perceived minority cultural groups.

One early piece of research conducted in the USA by Vaughan in 1964 showed that white American children as young as 3 were showing signs of racial prejudice. More recent studies, including one by Millner in 1993, support Vaughan's findings. Millner found that by 2 years of age children are noticing the difference in skin colour and between 3 and 5 years they are beginning to attach values to it, meaning that they perceive that people with white skin are generally seen as having the most powerful place in society.

A Chance to Think 3

Research tells us that children as young as 3 years old notice differences in skin colours and that they have clearly defined attitudes about them.

What do you think some of these attitudes may be?

Where do you think children learn these attitudes from?

How do you think awareness of skin colours may influence all children's behaviour?

Compare your answers with the sample answers in Appendix 1.

How do children gain these attitudes? The people who generally have most influence on the development of young children's attitudes are their parents. Parents are role models to children, and children will copy what their parents do. This is known as 'modelling'. One example of how young children model their parents' attitudes is illustrated in an article that appeared in the *Sunday Times* in 1995, headed 'Racism and Asian youth; whose life is it anyway?'. In it a 15-year-old Asian boy was talking about an experience he had of a young child's racist remarks. He said:

> 'Last week I was walking to school when this 5-year-old boy started shouting "Paki" at me. I know his parents because they come in the shop and they seem really nice. I can't believe they've taught him to be racist: maybe he learned that from school. I've grown up being called names and I just ignore it now; but that was the first time I've seen a kid that young act like a racist.'

Children's attitudes are also developed from the images they see around them: on the television, in comics and books and from what they hear being said. Television plays a particularly powerful role, as most families now have access to television and videos. Some children have their own television and video in their bedroom. Gerbner and Gross in 1976 found that by the time children reach the age of 12 most of them have spent more hours in front of the television than they have at school. The things children don't see also play a part in how they perceive the world to be. For example, if children don't see images of people with disabilities or of black people in positions of power then they may assume that people with disabilities do not have an important place in society or that it is not possible for black people to have positions of power.

The word 'black' is being used here to encompass all the perceived minority groups who experience discrimination owing to race or ethnic origin. It is acknowledged that this is a simplified way of classifying those people who are not perceived to be white, and that some individuals would not wish to use this general classification.

We have seen that very young children can have racist attitudes. This has negative effects on the development of both black and white children. If people feel discriminated against, their self-esteem will be damaged. The development of self-esteem is discussed in more detail in Chapter 6. All children need to feel

A Chance to Think 4
Ask children what their favourite television programmes
and videos are. Try to watch them. Look at them carefully
to see what sort of visual images they are portraying and
what sort of language they are using. See if they feature
black and white children and families in leading roles, or if
any of the characters are what could be considered to be
in stereotypical roles.
What sort of images do you see?
What sort of language is being used?
What messages do you think children are getting from
this?
If you cannot watch the programmes, ask the children
about them, who are in them, what happens and why they
like them.

valued and respected and to have the chance to fulfil their full
potential. Often this is not the case. We have seen how parents'
attitudes are passed down to their children. The same happens
with the attitudes of people who work with children. Sally
Tomlinson, in her book *Home and School in Multicultural Britain*
(1984), talked to teachers and found that they held negative
or stereotypical attitudes about children. To give an example,
children of Asian or West Indian parentage were perceived to
be disadvantaged. West Indian children in particular were seen
to be 'less keen on education' and to lack 'ability to concentrate'
(p. 40). The way teachers or workers with young children expect
children to behave has an effect on the way they do actually
behave. This is known as a 'self-fulfilling prophecy'. Rosenthal
and Jackson (1968) and Rubovits and Maehr (1973) found that
white teachers have lower expectations of black children and
that they underestimate their ability. Children then live up to (or
down to) the teachers' expectations. This was also confirmed by
Ashmore (1970), who said that because of the subtle discrimination that minority members of a school face they have the odds
stacked against them. Rotter (1966) found that if people feel that

they are not going to succeed they will not try. If they don't try, they cannot fail.

Much research has also taken place into exclusion (e.g. the Commission for Racial Equality, 1985; Cohen *et al.*, 1994; Parsons *et al.*, 1994). This research shows that even very young children at nursery can be excluded. The Commission for Racial Equality found that pupils most at risk of exclusion were Afro-Caribbean boys. This is worrying, as many of the children who have been excluded from school may be out of school for long periods of time, or never return to school, and thereby miss out on vital parts of their education. Does what was shown by this research still hold true? The Commission for Racial Equality (CRE) said in a press release in June 2001:

> Exclusion and under-achievement by particular groups of pupils is an urgent and deeply worrying challenge for everyone involved in education. Afro-Caribbean boys, Pakistani and Bangladeshi boys and girls, and white working class boys from deprived areas have been shown as the losers in a school system that is failing them, and all these groups deserve a radical change in the way they are treated.

What can be done to ensure that exclusion does not continue to occur? One suggestion put forward is that of segregated schools, where children are taught separately in community or faith-based schools. In the same press release, the CRE said that it did not see segregated schools as a way forward. The press release went on to say:

> First, the creation of black only schools can only ever educate a minority of black pupils. There will never be enough to provide for every black pupil in the country and so there will still be children missing out on the chance to succeed and reach their potential. Second, in creating separate education systems for one ethnic group, all ethnic groups miss out because children are denied the chance to mix and share experiences naturally. Finally, the solutions to the problems of under-achievement and exclusion do not lie in separation but in getting every school to take action on racial equality and on genuinely meeting the needs of pupils from every background.

Another group of children who may experience difficulties with their education because of other people's attitudes towards them are those children who are 'looked after'. The document *Education of Young People in Public Care* (DfEE, 2000b) sums up the research in this area and identifies some of the possible barriers to educational success:

- Children experience numerous and often unplanned moves of home.
- They experience unnecessary moves of school or are out of school for prolonged periods.
- Low self-esteem, and perhaps a justifiable mistrust of adults from pre-care and care experiences, can act as a barrier to enjoyment of schooling and educational success.
- Some children experience bullying, racial abuse or harassment.
- Schools and carers display lower expectations of young people in public care, which contribute to underachievement and failure.
- Pupils in public care are over-represented among pupils excluded from school.
- The needs of black and ethnic minority children are not always adequately considered in the care placement or educational placement.

Research and its outcomes have important implications for workers, for, as has been demonstrated, they hold powerful positions in the children's lives. Workers need to examine their own attitudes and to evaluate constantly how these attitudes may be transmitted to the children. It is possible that people do not consciously realize that they hold discriminatory attitudes or that they may be treating some children less favourably than others. It is often useful for workers to spend some time trying to assess the expectations they have of children in their particular setting, to think why they hold those expectations and, if necessary, to re-evaluate them.

As well as noticing colour and making judgements about it, young children are also making judgements about gender and sex role issues. Much research has taken place in this area. Some people expect males and females to behave in what they consider to be appropriate sex role ways, in the light of what society considers to be masculine and feminine behaviour. In the USA, Rosenkrantz *et al.* (1968) found that men were seen as more independent, logical, active, knowledgeable, ambitious, aggressive and objective than women. Women were seen as gentle, quiet, tactful and talkative. Male characteristics were seen by the majority of those taking part in the study to be preferable to female characteristics.

What is considered masculine and feminine behaviour varies between societies. Margaret Mead, an anthropologist, studied three tribes in New Guinea, where she found that among the Araspesh, men and women exhibited the same sort of gentle and nurturing behaviour. The Mundugumor adults both behaved in the same way, but this time they both exhibited assertive and independent behaviour, whereas the Tchambuli men behaved in what Western society would consider to be a feminine way, and the women behaved in a way that Western society would consider to be masculine. The way children behave is not due to the sex they were born to, but relates to the gender role in which they are brought up. Sex typing and gender identity are different. Sex typing is when a person takes on the characteristics and behaviour that are caused by the environment and are considered to be appropriate for males and females. Gender identity is the degree to which people consider themselves to be male or female. There continues to be great debate about heredity and environment, including sex and gender, in particular about how much children inherit from their parents and how much they learn from the moment of birth on. This is known as the nature/nurture debate. From nature we know that males and females are genetically different. Males have an X and a Y chromosome and females have two Y chromosomes. Their genetic make-up affects their reproductive physiology and genitalia, but does it affect anything else? From research we can see that nurture and the context and environment in which an individual is brought up have an effect on them. Both nature and nurture play a large part in how an individual develops.

By 3 years old most children are able to say whether they are boys or girls and have noticed that males and females are anatomically different. They know that men have penises and stand up to urinate and that women don't and sit down to urinate. By the age of 5, boys are placing more value on being male than female.

A Chance to Think 5

We have seen that young children have opinions about appropriate gender. These attitudes have to come from somewhere and, like opinions about skin colour, they may be influenced by the adults around them. Everyone has opinions about some of the toys they think children should play with, whether they want to admit to them or not. Think about the toys you have in your setting or toys you have seen young children playing with. Write down three lists:
- one containing the toys that you think appropriate for boys to play with;
- one containing the toys you think appropriate for girls to play with;
- one containing toys you think appropriate for both boys and girls to play with.

These lists may give some indication as to your attitude towards children's toys. Everyone has an attitude to children's toys but the most important thing is how this translates into a person's behaviour. Now think about your behaviour and how you use these toys in your setting.

What messages do you think you are giving to the children in the way you encourage them to play with toys?

Miller (1987) conducted research into children's toys. She began by trying to find out whether adults did classify children's toys according to gender-appropriate lines by asking psychology students to classify 50 toys according to whether they considered them to be appropriate for girls or appropriate for boys. Of the 50 toys, they considered 24 as significantly appropriate for boys, including guns, doctor sets, tricycles, remote control cars, microscopes and blocks. Only 17 of the toys were considered to be significantly appropriate for girls, including teddy bears, telephones, dolls and dolls' houses. The toys considered to be appropriate for both boys and girls included paints and a chalkboard. We can see that these have been rated according to very traditional gender stereotypes. Miller then asked the students to say what kind of development they felt the toy promoted. She found that boys' toys were thought to promote sociability, symbolic play, constructiveness, competition, aggressiveness and handling, whereas the girls' toys were thought to promote creativity, nurturance, attractiveness and manipulative skills. This means that if boys and girls are playing with different toys they may be developing different skills. Maccoby and Jacklin (1974) found that boys and girls do tend to have different intellectual and cognitive skills. On average, girls have better verbal skills and boys have better mathematical and spatial skills.

We saw earlier in this chapter that children model the behaviour they see around them. So if adults classify toys along gender-appropriate lines, then children may also do this. Research conducted by Blackmore *et al.* (1979) shows that this does happen. They found that by the age of 2, boys are choosing gender-appropriate toys. Girls, on the other hand, did not choose gender-appropriate toys until the age of 4, when they were showing a strong preference for feminine toys. By the time all children were 6 they could say which toys were for girls and which toys were for boys. This has implications for all childcare workers. If children as young as 2 or 3 are choosing to play with gender-appropriate toys and developing different skills, then workers need to ensure that all children have the opportunity to, and are encouraged to, play with all toys.

We have seen how children develop attitudes about colour from the things they see in the environment around them. The same things that influence how a child develops these attitudes also influence the attitude a child develops toward gender roles. In the way that children are portrayed by the media, in advertising and even in displays in shops, very strong messages are being given about gender roles. A childcare worker went into a store to buy a present for his niece. There were two displays, one labelled as 'toys for girls' and one labelled as 'toys for boys'. The computers were in the boys' display, so the worker asked the shop assistants if he could buy a computer for his niece, and he was told that he could, that they were not intending to imply that only boys could use computers and that they had not realized that this was the message they were giving out.

Resources that are used with children also give out important messages. How resources can be evaluated and used will be looked at in more detail in Chapter 5. One piece of research that illustrates how young children get messages about children from the books they are reading is that of Women on Words and Images (1972). This study analysed 2750 children's stories and found that there was a 5:2 ratio of boy-centred stories to girl-centred stories and a 3:1 ratio of adult male to adult female main characters, showing that males are more visible, with more central characters, even in children's stories.

A Chance to Think 6

Find the children's books that are in your setting. Read them to yourself and look at the visual images they are showing of male and female roles. See who the central characters are and what role they are playing.

What sort of activities are females shown to be doing?

What sort of activities are males shown to be doing?

What sort of messages do you think this is giving to all the children in the setting?

See if you can find some books that you would recommend, that show both females and males in positive non-stereotypical roles. Write a list of these and keep it in the setting, so that you can borrow them from the library.

We saw earlier in this chapter that research into black children's education and that of 'looked-after' children showed that workers can have a profound effect on a child's educational experiences. The same can also be seen of children's experiences as defined by their gender. Recent research into the experiences of nursery children by Sax quoted in *The Sunday Times* in 2001 shows that since girls develop language skills earlier in life, it is claimed they are favoured by women teachers and this 'discrimination' may leave boys aged 4–6 feeling foolish and inferior. Boys in nursery school should be taught some classes separately from girls to compensate for the near absence of male teachers and 'boyish' activities in their education. The predominance of women in nursery education is making boys feel inferior and devalued.

We can see from the research mentioned that children are getting some pretty powerful messages about the roles people are allocated in society, either because of their colour or because of their gender. This is also true of people with disabilities, homosexuals, elderly people and anyone who is part of a perceived minority group. Such messages can lead people to develop prejudiced or negative attitudes. People who work with young children need to be aware of this and make a concerted effort to combat the effects of discrimination.

Legislation

In Britain today there are various laws that people working with young children and families need to be aware of and work within, because what is contained in these laws affects many of the different aspects of work with children, families, colleagues, adults and other professionals. Legislation is constantly being reviewed and new legislation is coming into force all the time. It is essential that workers are aware of the changes and development in legislation and that they keep up to date with them. There is a great deal of legislation that workers need to know about, and work within, regarding anti-discriminatory practice. Although some of the legislation will relate to all workers wherever they work, other legislation may relate to particular areas of work and specific organizations. Some legislation may affect workers in the four countries of the United Kingdom differently, particularly as Scotland's and Northern Ireland's legal frameworks are slightly different from that of England, and Wales now has a National Assembly legislating for the Principality. Workers also need to be aware of European laws and other conventions, e.g. the United Nations Convention on the rights of the child, as these may have an effect on their work.

While legislation is important because it protects people, the one thing it cannot do is change people's attitudes. We have seen with research that people do have attitudes to issues, and it is important that those attitudes do not spill over into discrimination. Legislation is in place to ensure that people are clear about what is legally acceptable and what is not. For childcare workers, good practice should ensure that workers are constantly able to evaluate practice and to receive appropriate support and training, particularly in the area of anti-discriminatory practice, to ensure that practice goes above and beyond what is required by law. The following is an overview of the major points with regard to anti-discriminatory practice contained in the legislation that affects childcare workers. For workers requiring more detailed information, an information list is given at the end of the chapter.

Equal Pay Act 1975

This act says that women must be paid the same as men when doing equal work.

Sex Discrimination Act 1975

We have seen how discrimination can have a negative effect on the development of both girls and boys, and this Act ensures that neither women nor men suffer discrimination on the grounds of their sex. Despite the Sex Discrimination Act, the positions of women and men in society are still unequal. The Equal Opportunities Commission is responsible for administering the Sex Discrimination Act.

Race Relations Act 1976

The Race Relations Act came into being to ensure that people do not suffer discrimination on racial grounds. The Act defines discrimination in four ways: direct discrimination, indirect discrimination, segregation and victimization. Racial grounds are defined as those of colour, race, nationality (including citizenship) or ethnic or national origins. I will define these words, as they can be unintentionally misused. The following are all from the *Concise Oxford Dictionary*.

- race: each of the major divisions of humankind, having distinct physical characteristics; a tribe, nation, etc. regarded as of a distinct ethnic stock;
- nationality: the status of belonging to a particular nation; a nation; an ethnic group forming part of one or more political nations;
- citizen: a member of a state or commonwealth, either native or naturalized citizenship;
- ethnic: (of a social group) having a common national or cultural tradition; denoting origin by birth or descent rather than nationality; relation to race or culture (ethnic group, ethnic origins).

Direct discrimination occurs when a person is not treated in the same way as someone else on racial grounds, and is illegal. Some people may not realize that they are being discriminatory, but this does not make their behaviour acceptable. It is unlawful whether people realize they are doing it or not. An example of direct discrimination in childcare settings would be where a setting would not admit traveller children.

Indirect discrimination may not be intentional, and again the person who is doing it may not realize that it is happening, but it is still unlawful. It occurs when settings have rules, regulations or practices that some groups are unable to fulfil owing to racial grounds. An example of indirect discrimination in childcare settings would be where cooking ingredients were always used that meant a child could not do cooking (for example, a Jewish child would not be able to take part in a cooking activity that involved pork products).

Segregation means to separate people or keep them apart. The Race Relations Act makes it unlawful to segregate people on racial grounds. An example of segregation in childcare settings would be where black children had outside play at a different time from white children.

Victimization takes place when a person is in the process of taking action under the Act and receives different treatment from other people in the same situation. An example of victimization in a childcare setting would be where a setting refused to take on a particular student because in the past, when the student had a child in the setting, she had complained about racial discrimination within the setting.

The Race Relations Act does allow positive discrimination, such as where there is a need in the setting to have a bilingual speaker, or when race is a genuine occupational qualification. The Commission for Racial Equality is responsible for administering the Race Relations Act. Workers need to ensure they have an overview of the Race Relations Act and how it affects them. The information list at the end of this chapter gives some useful publications that provide a more detailed description of the requirements of the Act.

A Chance to Think 7

You have just started work in a setting that has a morning session and an afternoon session. You have noticed that the majority of the children in the morning session are white and the majority of the children in the afternoon session are black and younger than the morning children. When you ask the manager why this is, she says, 'That is just the way it is.'

What do you think of this situation?

Why do you think this may be happening?

What do you think you could do about it?

Compare your answers with the sample answers in Appendix 1.

Education Reform Act 1988

The Education Reform Act brought about major changes to the education system, with one of the most significant being the introduction of the National Curriculum. This stipulates that schools must offer a curriculum that is balanced and broadly based and that it should: (a) promote the spiritual, moral, cultural, mental and physical development of pupils at the school and in society; and (b) prepare such pupils for the opportunities, responsibilities and experiences of adult life.

The National Curriculum introduced the term 'Key Stage'. There are four Key Stages, at ages 7, 11, 14 and 16 respectively (Table 1.1). At the end of Key Stages 1, 2 and 3 children will sit national tests and tasks (often called SATs). At the end of Key Stage 4 children take national exams.

Table 1.1 Key Stages and national tests

Age	Stage	Year	Tests
3–4 4–5	Foundation		
5–6	Key Stage 1	Year 1	
6–7		Year 2	National tests taken in English and maths
7–8	Key Stage 2	Year 3	
8–9		Year 4	
9–10		Year 5	
10–11		Year 6	National tests taken in English, maths and science
11–12	Key Stage 3	Year 7	
12–13		Year 8	
13–14		Year 9	National tests taken in English, maths and science
14–15	Key Stage 4	Year 10	Some children take GCSEs
15–16		Year 11	Most children take GCSEs, GNVQs or other national qualifications

Source: DfEE parents' Web site, 2001.

The Act also says that state schools must provide religious education that is of a broadly Christian nature. This has implications for all schools as society today is made up of many different religions. These are discussed in greater depth in Chapters 2 and 3.

Children Act 1989

The Children Act 1989 has had a huge impact in the field of childcare. It affects all areas, including childminding, nurseries, foster care and residential care. It has introduced many new principles. These include the following:

- The welfare of the child must come first.
- Social services and education departments are required to provide for children in need.
- Organizations must work together in the best interests of the child.
- Childcare provision must take into account the religious, racial, cultural and linguistic needs of the child.
- People working with children must work in partnership with parents and those who have parental responsibility.

As mentioned at the beginning of this chapter, the Children Act brought into use two phrases: 'children in need' and 'looked-after' children. The Act says that a child should be taken as being '*in need*' if

> (a) he is unlikely to achieve or maintain, or have the opportunity of achieving or maintaining, a reasonable standard of health or development without the provision for him of services by a local authority under this part; (b) his health or development is likely to be significantly impaired, or further impaired, without the provision for him of such services; or (c) he is disabled.

A child is defined as being '*disabled*' if 'he is blind, deaf, or dumb or suffers from mental disorders of any kind or is substantially and permanently handicapped by illness, injury or congenital deformity or such other disability as may be prescribed'. The term '*looked after*' is defined as follows: 'A child is looked after by the local authority if he is in their care by reason of a court order or is being provided with accommodation for more than 24 hours by agreement with the parents or with the child if he is aged 16 or over.'

The Act is complex and comprehensive. It contains twelve parts as follows:

  I Introductory issues;
 II Orders with respect to children in family proceedings;
III Local authority support for children and families;
IV Care and supervision;
 V The protection of children;
VI Community homes;
VII Voluntary homes and voluntary organizations;
VIII Registered children's homes;
 IX Private arrangements for fostering children;
  X Childminding and day care for young children;
 XI The Secretary of State's supervisory functions and responsibilities;
XII Miscellaneous and general.

Workers need to be familiar with the parts of the Act that relate specifically to their area of work. The Act covers many areas involved in working with children and has many requirements, including:

- record-keeping;
- court orders;
- ratios of children to adults;
- the environment;
- children's rights;
- protection of children;
- staffing and who can work with children;
- parental responsibility.

Workers need to ensure that they have an overall knowledge of the Act and how it affects their day-to-day work. Following the Act came Regulations, which are additions to the Act, and which workers need to be aware of. Guidance manuals have been issued by HMSO which relate to the various areas covered by the Act.

Disability Discrimination Act 1995

The Disability Discrimination Act 1995 covers three areas where disabled people have been given new rights: (a) employment; (b) getting goods and services; and (c) buying or renting land or

*Disability Disc
Act 1995*

property. The Act defines a disabled person as someone who has 'a physical or mental impairment which has a substantial and long term adverse effect on [their] ability to carry out normal day-to-day activities'.

Part 2 of the Act relates to employment. In terms of employment, an employer discriminates against a disabled person if (a) a disabled person is treated less favourably than a person who is not disabled, and (b) the treatment cannot be shown to be justified. The Act states that in terms of disability and employment some discrimination may be 'justifiable'. Employers have a duty to make adjustments to enable disabled people to take up employment, and the Act gives twelve examples of steps employers are expected to take. These include making adjustments to premises and altering working hours. Employers with fewer than 20 people are exempt from this part of the Act.

We saw that both the Sex Discrimination Act and the Race Relations Act brought into being organizations (the EOC and CRE respectively) that have enforcement powers to oversee and administer the Acts. The Disability Rights Commission Act 1999 brought into being the Disability Rights Commission, which will have similar powers to those of the EOC and CRE in implementing the Disability Discrimination Act.

Education Act 1996

The Education Act 1996, like many Acts of Parliament, is long and complex. It covers practically all aspects of education. Its ten parts include sections on the statutory system of education, local authority schools, grant-maintained schools, special educational needs and the curriculum. It is essential that workers are familiar with any parts of the Act that relate to them. Part 4 concerns special educational needs. It states that a child has 'special educational needs' if he has a learning difficulty that calls for special educational provision to be made for him. It goes on to say that a child has a 'learning difficulty' if: (a) he has significantly greater difficulty in learning than the majority of children his age; (b) he has a disability that either prevents or hinders him from making use of educational facilities of a kind generally provided for children of his age in schools within the area of the local education authority; or (c) he is under the age of 5 and is, or would be if special educational provision were not made for him, likely to fall within paragraph (a) or (b) when over that age. A child must not be regarded as having a learning difficulty solely because the language (or form of language) in which he is, or will be, taught is different from the language (or form of language) which has at any time been spoken in his home.

The Act also states that a child with special educational needs should normally be educated in a mainstream school. The Secretary of State is required to issue a Code of Practice giving guidance concerning special educational needs. This refers to important principles, including ensuring that a child with special educational needs has those needs met; seeking the views of children; recognizing that parents have a vital role to play in supporting their children; meeting special educational needs in mainstream schools; and ensuring that children with special educational needs are offered full access to a broad, balanced and relevant curriculum. Schools and settings must have regard to the Code of Practice and should have a written special educational needs policy laying out the roles and responsibilities of everyone involved, including the SENCO, a Special Educational Needs Coordinator. It is essential that workers have access to a copy of this document and are aware of their role in working within it.

School Standards and Framework Act 1998

The School Standards and Framework Act 1998 covers educational provision from nursery education through to further education. Part 5 of the Act relates to nursery education, which it defines as 'full or part time education suitable for children who have not attained compulsory school age'. It was this Act that required local education authorities to establish Early Years Development Partnerships (EYDPs). The functions of EYDPs are to work with the authority to (a) review the sufficiency of the provision of nursery education, and (b) prepare an early years development plan, which must be submitted to the Secretary of State for approval. The School Standards and Framework Act also states that nursery education must comply with the Code of Practice relating to Children with Special Educational Needs in the Education Act 1996.

The School Standards and Framework Act is the Act that governs exclusions from school and lays down the legislation about inspection of schools. It also outlaws corporal punishment for all pupils and requires headteachers to take measures to prevent all forms of bullying.

Human Rights Act 1998

The Human Rights Act 1998 is based on the European Convention on Human Rights. This is a European charter that deals with civil and political rights. Because of this charter, people in Britain have been able to take human rights issues to the European courts. Now that the Human Rights Act has been incorporated into the legal systems of the United Kingdom, individuals no longer need take their cases to the European Court of Human Rights in Strasbourg; they can now be heard in British courts. The Act came into force on 2 October 2000.

The Act is based on a series of articles listing the various rights, including:

Article 2 Right to life;
Article 3 Prohibition of torture;
Article 4 Prohibition of slavery and forced labour;
Article 5 Right to liberty and security;
Article 6 Right to a fair trial;
Article 7 No punishment without trial;
Article 8 Right to respect for private and family life;
Article 9 Freedom of thought, conscience and religion;
Article 10 Freedom of expression;
Article 11 Freedom of assembly and association;
Article 12 Right to marry;
Article 14 Prohibition of discrimination;
Article 16 Restrictions on political activity of aliens;
Article 17 Prohibition of abuse of rights;
Article 18 Limitation on use of restrictions on rights.

The Act also states under Part II of the First Protocol:

Article 2 Right to education.

This Act affects all public authorities and states that 'It is unlawful for a public authority to act in a way which is incompatible with a Convention right'. A public authority is defined as 'a court or tribunal and any person certain of whose functions are functions of a public nature'. Public authorities could include health authorities, central and local government agencies, social service departments and private agencies if they are carrying out a public function.

Care Standards Act 2000

The Care Standards Act 2000 is in nine parts as follows:

Part 1 Introduction;
Part 2 Establishments and agencies;
Part 3 Local authority services;
Part 4 Social care workers;
Part 5 The Children's Commissioner for Wales;
Part 6 Childminding and day care;
Part 7 Protection of children and vulnerable adults;
Part 8 Miscellaneous;
Part 9 General and supplemental.

The Act has established the National Care Standards Commission as the registering authority in England responsible for registering, among others, children's homes, residential family centres and fostering agencies. The NCSC has the power to draw up and apply national minimum standards. The Act also established the General Social Care Council and the Care Council for Wales, which are responsible for maintaining a register of social workers. Part 6 of the Care Standards Act 2000 becomes Part 10a of the Children Act 1989, bringing with it additions and changes. Registration and inspection of early years settings is the responsibility of the Early Years Directorate within OFSTED (the Office for Standards in Education). National Standards have been issued for full day care, sessional day care, crèches, out-of-school care and childminders. There are fourteen National Standards, with relevant annexes where appropriate, which represent a baseline of quality below which no provider may fall. The fourteen National Standards cover the following areas:

Standard 1 Suitable person (for caring for children);
Standard 2 Organization;
Standard 3 Care, learning and play;
Standard 4 Physical environment;
Standard 5 Equipment;
Standard 6 Safety;
Standard 7 Health;
Standard 8 Food and drinks;
Standard 9 Equal opportunities;
Standard 10 Special needs (including special educational needs and disabilities);
Standard 11 Behaviour;
Standard 12 Working in partnership with parents and carers;
Standard 13 Child protection;
Standard 14 Documentation.

Annexes cover babies/children under 2, overnight care, nursery schools and alternative criteria for open access schemes. Guidance documents are issued for each standard.

Standard 9, concerning equal opportunities, states: 'The registered person and staff actively promote equality of opportunity and anti-discriminatory practice for all children.' This is further qualified in the guidance document for sessional day care:

> Children need to feel valued and be free from discrimination. Where the registered person and staff are committed to equality they recognise that children's attitudes towards others are established in these early years. They understand relevant legislation and plan to help children learn about equality and justice through their play. The provision is carefully organised and monitored to ensure all children have access to the full range of activities. Family members and staff work together to share information, for example about cultures, home languages, play activities and children's specific needs.

Standard 10, on special needs (including special educational needs and disabilities), states:

> The registered person is aware that some children may have special needs and is proactive in ensuring that appropriate action can be taken when such a child is identified or admitted to the provision. Steps are taken to promote the welfare and development of the child within the setting in partnership with parents and other relevant parties.

This is further qualified in the corresponding guidance document:

> Children with special needs are most likely to have their needs met where the registered person and staff have secure knowledge and understanding of individual needs of every child in their care. Staff work together with parents and other relevant parties to organise the environment and plan activities to ensure all children take part at an appropriate level to their needs.

As with all legislation, it is essential that workers become familiar with the part of the Act relevant to their work and have access to the National Standards and guidance documents.

A Chance to Think 8

As part of the inspection process of your setting, the inspection officer is coming to your staff meeting. One of the questions she wants to address at the meeting is how the setting provides for the religious, racial, cultural and linguistic needs of the children.

You have been asked to prepare a list of what you are doing to take to the meeting.

Compare your list with the sample answers in Appendix 1.

Race Relations (Amendment) Act 2000

The Race Relations (Amendment) Act 2000 says that it is 'an Act to extend further the application of the Race Relations Act 1976 to the police and other public authorities'. It states that 'It is unlawful for a public authority in carrying out any functions of the authority to do any act which constitutes discrimination.' It covers the work of public bodies such as the police, NHS, local education authorities, and any private or voluntary agency carrying out a public function. There are, however, some authorities that are exempt from the Act, and they are listed. Those authorities that are required to comply with the Act 'shall in carrying out its functions, have due regard for the need:– (a) to eliminate unlawful racial discrimination; and (b) to promote equality of opportunity and good relations between persons of different racial groups'. As with the Race Relations Act 1976, the Commission for Racial Equality is responsible for administering the Race Relations (Amendment) Act 2000 and may issue codes of practice.

Special Educational Needs and Disability Act 2001

This Act states that it is an amendment to Part 4 of the Education Act 1996 to make further provision against discrimination on grounds of disability in schools and other educational establishments and for connected purposes. The Act makes it unlawful for schools to discriminate against disabled pupils and prospective pupils.

United Nations Convention on the Rights of the Child (1989)

The UN Convention on the Rights of the Child was ratified by the United Kingdom in 1991. It has no legal standing but is known internationally as an ethical code. The convention contains 54 articles. Many relate to anti-discriminatory practice. Article 2 says:

> State Parties shall respect and ensure the rights set forth in the present Convention to each child within their jurisdiction without discrimination of any kind, irrespective of the child's or his or her parent's or legal guardian's race, colour, sex, language, religion, political or other opinion, national, ethnic or social origin, property, disability, birth or other status.

Article 14 states: 'State Parties shall respect the right of the child to freedom of thought, conscience and religion.'

Approaches to work

We have seen that the law requires workers to be aware of many different things when they are working with children and parents. It is important that workers aim towards good practice that is constantly being evaluated, rather that just doing what is necessary or required by law. Different settings will have different ways of working, which may be influenced by the amount of time children are in the setting, the physical layout of the building or the support and direction from the management of the setting.

Some early years settings may have a particular philosophy of education that they follow, such as a Froebel, Montessori or High Scope approach. Whatever approach is taken, it is important that the welfare of the child is central to it and that the setting is meeting the religious, racial, cultural and linguistic needs of all the children in the setting. All children need to feel that they are respected as individuals and that their needs are being catered for.

Working within an anti-discriminatory framework is important for everyone. Children learn that we live in a diverse community, and they need to learn how to acknowledge and to respect that

---

A Chance to Think 9

Many pre-school settings have information leaflets that they hand out to people who are interested in the setting. Three different leaflets collected from settings in London described the approaches they had for working in the setting. Setting 1 described its approach as multicultural. Setting 2 said it took an anti-racist, anti-sexist approach. Setting 3 said it worked within an anti-discriminatory framework.

What is the difference in these three approaches?

Which one do you feel ensures that all the groups that go to make up the society in which we live are reflected in it?

Compare your answers with the sample answers in Appendix 1.

diversity. All groups are included in an anti-discriminatory framework because all are equally important, although not all groups are equally visible in society. Some groups are discriminated against, and it is important for workers to recognize this and work to help children, parents and colleagues to acknowledge it and try to develop strategies to prevent it. Our society comprises people of different races, religions, cultures, languages, disabilities, ages, gender, sexual orientation, ethnic origin, nationalities and colours. Some individuals may belong to more than one group and it is important for people to be recognized as individuals with their own needs, which may or may not be the same as those of another individual from the same group. Indeed, there may be as many differences within groups as there are between groups. Some workers feel uncomfortable addressing some of the issues that are raised by particular groups. For example, addressing the issue of sexual orientation is uncomfortable for some people, but it needs to be dealt with, as some of the children in the setting may be living and growing up in lesbian or gay homes. People working with young children may also be lesbian or gay. It is important for people to recognize that working within an anti-discriminatory framework might raise issues for them that need to be addressed. This will be discussed further in the sections, on parents and colleagues.

The whole environment needs to be taken into account when you are working with children and families. A child is an individual but also part of a family, whose members may belong to some of the different groups mentioned above. Children need to be helped to develop within this framework. An anti-discriminatory framework will help children to value and respect people from different groups. This is not something that can just be done on special occasions, but something that should be integrated and engrained into everyday practice. In Chapter 5 we shall look at how anti-discriminatory practice can be incorporated into children's play, but there is much more to it than that. It is about planning and about addressing the issues as they arise.

Sometimes it is not easy to work within an anti-discriminatory framework. It requires workers to think about their own attitudes and abilities. It can sometimes be uncomfortable, challenging

---

A Chance to Think 10

You are visiting the library with a group of 5-year-olds. When you get there, a father is choosing a book with his daughter, who has Down syndrome. Some of the children in your group start to make comments about the girl and ask you why she 'has a funny face'. Both the father and daughter have heard the comments.

How would you feel in this situation?

What would you do?

Compare your answers with the sample answers in Appendix 1.

---

or frustrating, as the environment around us continues to give out discriminatory messages to children and adults. It is important that workers try not to become disillusioned or so worried that they do nothing for fear of upsetting people, but continue to provide an anti-discriminatory environment for all who use the setting.

Parents and families

People who work with young children also work with parents and families, for children are not isolated units. Parents are generally the most important and influential people in a child's life and they usually have more information about their child than anyone else. Some children live with both birth parents, some with one parent; some children live with foster carers or in residential homes, and a number of children are adopted. This means that not all children will see their birth parents on a daily basis. A number of children may have parents who have died. Some children may have other adults in their lives who have 'parental responsibility' for them such as a court-appointed guardian or a step-parent. Whatever contact may be had with parents, be it daily, weekly or less regularly, it is still imperative to continue to recognize parents as important and influential people in their children's lives.

An anti-discriminatory framework is as necessary in work with parents as with children. Working with parents requires many different skills, and some workers may find this threatening, especially if they have not worked with parents before. Likewise, some parents may also feel threatened by what they see as professional childcare workers. Workers should be sensitive to the needs of all parents. Parents should be fully informed about the setting. Some settings have information books for parents that contain information about staffing, the setting's routine, equal opportunities policy and other important information.

The Children Act 1989 stresses the need to work in partnership with parents, as does the Care Standards Act 2000. The National Standards for full day care, out-of-school care, sessional care, crèches and childminding include Standard 12, 'working in partnership with parents and carers', which states, 'The registered person and staff work in partnership with parents to meet the needs of the children, both individually and as a group. Information is shared.' This is further amplified in the guidance document for sessional care, which says:

> The relationship between the child's parents and the registered person is crucial to the child's well-being, development and progress. Children benefit most where there is a trusting and mutually supportive partnership. The registered person and staff welcome parents into the setting and there is a two-way flow of information, knowledge and expertise.

The style of partnership can vary between settings as well as according to the differing needs of particular parents. For example, childminders and nannies will have more detailed daily contact with parents than will workers in a reception class of a school. It is important that parents are treated as equal partners. Treating all parents in exactly the same way is not working in partnership with them or valuing and respecting them as individuals. Workers need to be aware of the needs of parents, which may be influenced by many things. These may include hours or patterns of work; family composition, e.g. a single-parent family, lesbian or gay family or extended family; child-rearing practices; racial, religious, cultural or linguistic needs of parents; parental attitudes; and the special needs of parents. These are discussed in greater detail below.

A Chance to Think 11

Think about your own setting and the relationship you have with parents. Look at the entrance to the setting, and observe how parents are greeted on arrival and interaction during the time they are in the setting.

Is the entrance welcoming and, if it has posters and notices, are they accessible to all parents?

Are all parents made to feel welcome, valued and respected, and how does this happen?

Are all parents made to feel they can express their views about the setting and that they have a role to play in it?

Relationships with parents are formed at a home visit if carried out, or, if not, from the first time a parent steps through the door of the setting. It is important that this first contact is as positive as possible and that parents are made to feel welcome in the setting. Entrances should be kept clean and attractive. In settings with notice boards, boards providing information for parents, or display boards, these should be accessible and up to date (for example, notices could include photos of the staff and information about what is happening that day). A smile is one of the best ways of showing parents that they are welcome in the setting, as is allowing parents time to talk, or just to be with their children. This can sometimes feel threatening for workers and parents, as they may feel they are 'on show', but the more time parents spend in the setting, the less threatening their presence becomes for everyone. It also shows parents that their presence in the setting is welcome and that they are seen as having a valuable contribution to make to the setting and to the care of their children. Spending time with parents and getting to know them as individuals will, it is to be hoped, ensure that an equal partnership is being built, where parents feel able to voice their views and suggestions about the setting, and where workers can ask parents about issues on which they may need help or advice.

The parents' hours or patterns of work will influence the type of contact that may be developed between workers and parents.

Figure 1.1 A welcome notice.

Parents who work full time or during the night may be unable to come into the setting on a regular basis. They may only have time to drop off their children and then rush to work. It is important that parents are kept up to date on their children's progress and have a chance to communicate with workers. This may need to be done through day books, where what has happened during the day is written up (what the child has eaten, what and whom they have played with, etc.). Letters or telephone calls are another way of communicating, but it is still important for face-to-face contact to be established and maintained. Appointments may need to be made or a special time set aside that is convenient for both parent and worker. Some workplace nurseries or schools may have parents' evenings or open days, where parents can discuss issues regarding their child or the setting.

Family composition is another changing area in today's society. No longer are families necessarily made up of a mum, dad and two children. Families may consist of a mum and dad and three, four or more children. They may be single-parent families, with mother or father bringing up the children on their own with no, or limited, contact with the other parent. With more people getting remarried, step-parents and step-families are on the increase. Families may be made up of children from both previous marriages or partnerships, and children may spend time with both natural parents. Some children are brought up in lesbian or gay families, and other children are brought up in extended families, with brothers, sisters, aunts, uncles and grandparents being fully involved in the care of the children, including bringing them to and picking them up from the setting. This means that the setting might not see the parents on a daily, or even weekly, basis, but will be seeing members of the extended family. Whatever the composition of the family, workers need to be aware of it, as this will help them to understand the needs of the parents and the children. For example, many families of lesbians and gay men face discrimination and homophobia. Lesbian and gay parents may not find it easy to be involved in the childcare setting. They may be reluctant to share information with workers until they know and trust them. Another group of people who often face discrimination are lone male parents. In July 2001 *Nursery World* published an article titled 'Just Dad'. The article quoted Lynda Clarke of London University's Centre for Population Studies, who said that some 2 per cent of all children under 16 live only with their fathers. Colin Holt, a worker at the West Wiltshire Family Centre, said that single fathers do not fit into the existing support structures. Some feel they are looked upon with suspicion. Even if they are accepted, they still feel different. In a different article in the same month, Jimmy Donald of One Parent Families Scotland says, 'I do think that men try not to let on that they are finding it hard.'

It is therefore essential that workers do not make assumptions about parents and family structures. Workers need continually to evaluate their practice and work in a way that is welcoming and non-threatening to all parents and families. This can be done by showing a non-judgemental attitude towards parents and taking time to communicate with parents and build up relationships with them. The setting also needs to have explicit policies and procedures for working with parents that all staff are aware of and are working within. Workers need to discuss these policies and procedures as a team and support each other in this area of their work.

As well as differences in family composition there might be differences in child-rearing practices taking place in families attending the setting. These may be followed for social or cultural reasons. David White and Anne Woollett say in their book *Families: A Context for Development*, 'Different cultures have somewhat different ideas about children, how they want them to grow up and the activities in which it is considered that children should engage.' Practices followed can include picking up children every time they cry; letting children eat what and when they want; allowing children to fall asleep when they are tired and then putting them to bed; breast-feeding children up to the age of 5; babies sleeping in the parents' bed or in the same room as parents. In many cultures it is common practice for a mother and baby to share the same bed. Barry and Paxson, in a cross-cultural study of this issue, found that in 76 of 173 societies mother and baby shared the same bed, and in 42 societies they shared the same room (see Korner, 1991).

These may or may not be the same as the child-rearing practices used by workers in the setting but that does not mean they are bad or wrong. There is no one right way of bringing up children and there are many books published on how to bring up children, all giving different advice. People generally learn how to bring up children by remembering how they were brought up, observing how other parents are bringing up children and trying to do what they think is right. It is important for workers to recognize that there are a variety of ways of bringing up children and not to be judgemental about the ones that do not correspond with how they think a child should be brought up. Asking parents in a sensitive way is the best way of finding out about cultural variations in child-rearing practices. Workers may be asked to provide advice and guidance about bringing up children, and if this happens it should be made clear that it is their opinion being given and why they think it is valid. It must be remembered that for the majority of the time parents are able to bring up children appropriately

---

A Chance to Think 12

You have a new child called Claire starting in your setting and you are going to be Claire's key worker. Claire and her parents have been to visit the setting, but unfortunately you were away sick on the day of their visit. The manager has told you that the visit went well and that Claire appeared to be happy to be starting at the setting, as some of her friends are already there. The manager has given you all the background information you need, including the family composition. Claire's mother and her partner are both women. This is the first time you have worked with a lesbian family. How would you feel about this and how would you deal with these feelings?

How would you ensure that you work in partnership with Claire's parents?

The other children in the setting are aware that Claire is being brought up by two women and are beginning to ask about the family composition. What would you say to them?

Compare your answers with the sample answers in Appendix 1.

without help. Sometimes parents themselves do not have a good role model to follow for bringing up children, or they may be following cultural practices that are harmful to children and should not be condoned (e.g. female genital mutilation, which will be discussed in more depth in Chapter 6). Sometimes parents do not have the skills to bring up children appropriately. Some parents may be bringing up their children inappropriately, and if workers think this is the case, they need to be very clear as to why they think that, and what to do to help. Some children and parents may be attending settings so that parents can learn parenting skills. If this is so, parents need to be encouraged and respected for taking part in parenting skills classes.

Parents might have specific needs relating to their racial, religious, cultural or linguistic backgrounds. Some parents wish to keep their children at home for religious festivals and assume that workers realize that is what is happening, or phone in on the day their children are going to be away. If workers know when religious festivals take place they will be aware of when children might be absent. Parents will also not be able to attend the setting for events on particular days of religious significance (for example, Muslim parents may go to the mosque on Fridays). Workers need to be aware of parents' dietary restrictions, perhaps for religious reasons, if they are organizing an event with food or drink provided, or if parents are helping on an outing when

---

A Chance to Think 13

A new child, Fasil, is starting in your setting. Fasil's parents do not speak English. They are also not literate in their own language, which is Amharic.

How will you make these parents feel welcome in the setting?

How will you try to ensure that Fasil's parents receive the information they need and are able to feel valued and respected?

Compare your answers with the sample answers in Appendix 1.

lunch is being eaten. Religion is discussed in more depth in Chapter 3.

Britain is a multilingual society and some settings will be working with parents who do not speak English. It is important that workers develop ways of communicating with parents who do not speak English. A friendly smile of welcome and, if possible, knowledge of a few words, such as 'Hello', will make parents feel they are welcome in the setting. Interpreters may be needed on occasions, particularly when a child first starts in the setting, so that parents are clear as to what is happening and are able to ask any questions they have and express their points of view. Local authorities should be able to put workers in touch with interpreters and translators. If possible, notices and letters should be translated for parents. Settings should use interpreters whom parents trust. Often friends, relatives and older children are used as interpreters and trans-lators. Sometimes this will not be appropriate, because parents might not wish people close to them to be involved in interpreting for them as this raises issues of confidentiality.

Some parents might not be literate and may be embarrassed to tell workers this. Workers need to be aware of parents' feelings and needs concerning their illiteracy, and to make time to ensure that they talk to parents and tell them what is happening in the setting. Workers should not assume that parents can, or do, read notices on notice boards. They should be secondary to personal contact.

Workers also need to ensure that the setting is meeting the needs of, and working in partnership with, parents with disabilities. Some parents with disabilities may feel vulnerable coming into a setting. It is important that workers treat disabled parents as indi-viduals and do not make assumptions about them. Workers should try to find out what a disabled parent needs in order to help them to attend and feel comfortable and valued in the setting. For exam-ple, a visually impaired parent may or may not need help getting around the building, and if they have a guide dog workers need to be aware of this. A few parents may not be able to attend the setting and workers should develop channels of communication with them. It is possible to take photos of children in the setting, so that parents can visualize how they are spending their time. Some settings will have access to a camcorder and be able to make

---

A Chance to Think 14

You are in a room with a parents' group. One of the mothers is pregnant. The woman who is pregnant is white and the father of the child is black. The parents are talking together about pregnancy and childbirth. You are also involved in the conversation, when one of the mothers says to the woman who is pregnant, 'It's nice when anybody is having a baby, it's just such a shame that your child will be a mongrel.'

What do you think you would do in this situation?

Compare your answers with the sample answers in Appendix 1.

---

a video of how children are spending their time and their achievements in the setting. When taking photos it is essential that workers get permission from parents. The best way to find out about parents' needs is to ask them. It is important that parents are seen as parents first and as disabled parents second, and that workers are sensitive to their needs.

Some parents may feel very happy to come into the setting and voice their opinions and share information with workers. Other parents may feel shy about doing so, or may be lacking in confidence, either in themselves or in their parenting skills. Others may feel awkward about being in the setting depending on why their child is attending. For example, a parent who is having to attend the setting because he or she is required to may feel deskilled and resentful. Every parent is different and workers need to respond to them and work with them accordingly. Workers by their very existence in a setting are in an extremely powerful position. All parents are having to 'come into' the setting; they are the ones who are entering into what at first may be a new experience for them. This can create a situation where the worker is in a position of power and authority. Workers need to be aware of the power dynamics that arise and so work with parents sensitively.

One of the hardest things that workers may have to cope with is to work in partnership with parents who have very different attitudes to themselves, particularly if these attitudes are pre-judiced or stereotypical. Parents need to be aware of the ethos and aims of the setting. Some settings give parents copies of the equal opportunities policy and others have a statement of accept-able behaviour in the building, so that parents are aware from the very beginning of what is acceptable behaviour and what is not. Words on paper are not enough on their own. Settings need to develop ways of working with parents that allow parents to recog-nize and deal with their attitudes. This is not always an easy task, and workers need to be confident about tackling this issue with parents.

Colleagues

We have seen throughout this chapter that working within an anti-discriminatory framework can sometimes be difficult, chal-lenging, frustrating and, it is to be hoped, in the end rewarding. Workers need to examine their own attitudes, and the setting must develop ongoing ways of supporting and evaluating the practice of people working within it. People who work alongside others or in a team setting have each other as a valuable resource to do this. Staff meetings can be very supportive. They can be used to discuss how and why teams are going to approach issues, and how people feel about things. They can provide an opportunity to discuss situations workers have found difficult and to discover how colleagues might have dealt with them.

Sometimes working in a team can be difficult and challenging. It is not always possible to agree with every member of the team, and disagreements may occur in staff meetings. Sometimes we need to 'agree to disagree', while continuing to work to the same objectives and within an anti-discriminatory framework. Sometimes teams need to revisit policies and procedures to ensure that they are working within them or to evaluate and update them. All polices and procedures should reflect and state a commitment to anti-discriminatory practice and should be living and working documents. Effective communication between individuals and in teams allows all workers to be human and to recognize that no single person has the answer to every problem. It allows people to make mistakes and to learn from them. Some settings have supervision sessions, where individuals get the opportunity to discuss issues with their manager or colleague. Supervisory relationships, like any relationship have power dynamics in them, as seen, for example, in the case of a young worker supervising a person older than themself. Those taking part in supervision need to be aware of these dynamics and how they affect working relationships. Anti-discriminatory issues arising from supervision and day-to-day practice need to be addressed by those involved. It is possible, indeed highly likely, that colleagues will have differing opinions about attitudes and approaches to childcare. We have seen that everyone possesses attitudes and values. Individuals working in childcare are first of all people before they are workers, and so will have formative attitudes and values that they bring with them to their work. One hopes that some of these attitudes and values will be positive, allowing workers to be open to self-development and evaluation. On the other hand, some of the values held may be stereotypical and discriminatory – for example, it is possible for workers to be sexist. It is essential that workers are given support in dealing with the issues this raises for them as individuals and how it may affect the team. Isolated workers, or people who work on their own, such as childminders, nannies or foster carers also need support in dealing with issues raised for them in working within an anti-discriminatory framework. They might be able to get this from mutual support groups, where childminders or nannies working in the same area have a chance to get together. Childminders might also receive support from the National Childminding Association. For some individuals or groups of workers, a specific issue may arise for them on account of who they are, or because they are perceived to be part of a particular group.

For example, older members of the staff team may feel their experience is not being valued; gay and lesbian workers may feel isolated or unable to share their life experiences with the team. Workers who practise a particular religion may feel that this is not respected if they are being asked to undertake tasks that contradict their beliefs. For example, Jehovah's Witnesses do not celebrate birthdays.

One particular group of workers who have found issues raised for them in working with children and families are male workers, as the majority of workers in this field are women. Kevin Innes, a male worker, raised his concerns in a letter to *Nursery World* in 1999 in which he said:

> I am now 38 and love working with children. It is normal for women to work in childcare when they are in their fifties and sixties, but what about men? Will I be able to find childcare jobs when I reach my fifties and sixties, or will I have to stay in an office as the token male doing book work when all I want to do is work with children? Will parents want men of 50 or 60 looking after their children, or will men find themselves pushed out of the profession because of their age? I have children of my own and know the joy that comes from seeing them playing and enjoying themselves. But, as a parent, I also worry about the threat some men pose to children. As we male child carers get older, will those of us who have proved ourselves trustworthy be tarred with the same brush as men who abuse children?

Much research has been undertaken into issues faced by male workers, and researchers have found that it is difficult for male workers to find employment. Childcare is still seen as 'women's work' and male workers are constantly aware of the need to protect themselves and the children in their care in case there are child abuse allegations. Men in early years settings are not seen as 'real men', and parents view male workers with suspicion. Male workers are needed in this field, however, and there are many benefits to having male workers in a setting. They can help to balance the team, ensure children see male role models, give children a chance learn to communicate with both men and women, and provide a chance for children to develop healthy relationships with both men and women. In order to attract and keep male workers in childcare, employers have a responsibility to acknowledge that male workers face issues that their female colleagues do not. Employers need to address areas of concern not just for male workers but for all workers in order to recruit, retain and support them. This can be done by (a) providing ongoing support and supervision for all workers; (b) developing effective communication strategies and building a team so that everyone feels part of the team and is able to contribute to it; and (c) providing ongoing training and support for all staff around attitude development and anti-discriminatory practice.

Figure 1.2 Staff supervision.

Workers need to continue to receive relevant training and development that will be of practical help in the workplace. Everyone is continually learning and developing. Training and development does not have to be in the form of a course, but can include visiting other settings to see how they address a particular issue, such as working with children with special needs. It may include going to the library and getting some background information on a particular religion, or talking to a member of staff who has a particular skill or experience that may be useful. Nevertheless, it goes without saying that traditional courses are important. Workers get the chance to hear people considered to be experts in their field, and they have the added value of meeting workers from other settings and exchanging information and experiences. Sometimes it is possible to arrange for a trainer to attend the setting to address a particular issue with the whole team.

We have seen how new legislation is continually coming into force. Good practice issues also change, as do teams and the children and families people are working with. Workers themselves change. They learn new skills, gain fresh insights and acquire new knowledge, become more confident in themselves as workers and as members of teams. Through day-to-day work, meeting new people, encountering new and different situations and experiences, workers are having constantly to evaluate themselves and their practice. This may be a difficult and uncomfortable experience for some individuals. It can be hard to work with change and recognize the impact we have on situations, and that situations have on us, but if we are to grow and develop as individuals and workers in any setting, not just childcare settings, it is an essential part of life. Personal and professional reflection and evaluation are necessary in order that workers understand both their own role and impact, and the role and impact of others in their day-to-day work. Workers are constantly having to think about their own attitudes and the impact these have on others. New initiatives appear all the time and workers have to assimilate constant change. This requires the development of new skills or the refining of existing skills.

A Chance to Think 15

If you work alongside others, or in a team, think about the team and what you value and respect about your colleagues. Now think about what you would like your colleagues to value and respect about you. Now think about the needs of your colleagues and try to evaluate how sensitive you are to those needs.

Useful publications

Abbott, L. and Moylett, H. (1997) *Working with the Under-3's: Responding to Children's Needs.* Open University Press.

Alcott, M. (1997) *An Introduction to Children with Special Educational Needs.* Hodder and Stoughton.

All London Teachers against Racism (1984) *Challenging Racism.* Russell Press.

Ashmore, R. D. (1970) Prejudice: causes and cures, in B. E. Collins (ed.) *Social Psychology.* Addison Wesley.

BBC Education (1994) *Children without Prejudice: Equal Opportunities and the Children Act* (video). BBC.

Blackmore, J. E., Laure, A. A. and Olejuik, A. B. (1979) Sex appropriate toy preference and the ability to conceptualise toys as sex related. *Development Psychology* 15, 341–2.

Brown, B. (1993) *All Our Children, A Guide for Those Who Care*. BBC.

Brown, B. (1999) *Unlearning Discrimination in the Early Years*. Trentham Books.

Care Standards Act 2000. Explanatory Notes. HMSO.

Caruso, J. and Temple Fawcett, M. (1999) *Supervision in Early Childhood Education: A Developmental Perspective*. Teachers College Press.

Chakrabarti, M. and Hill, M. (2000) *Residential Child Care: International Perspectives on Links with Families and Peers*. Jessica Kingsley.

Cohen, R., Hughes, M., Ashworth, L. and Blair, M. (1994) *School's Out: The Family Perspective on School Exclusions*. Family Service Units/Barnardo's.

Commission for Racial Equality (1985) *Birmingham LEA and Schools: Referral and Suspension of Pupils*. CRE.

Commission for Racial Equality (2001) *Segregated Schools*. News release. CRE.

Dare, A. and O'Donovan, M. (1997) *Good Practice in Caring for Young Children with Special Needs*. Stanley Thornes.

Department of Health (1991) *The Children Act Guidance and Regulations*. Volume 1, *Court Orders*. Volume 2, *Family Support, Day Care and Educational Provision for Young Children*. Volume 3, *Family Placements*. Volume 4, *Residential Care*. Volume 5, *Independent Schools*. Volume 6, *Children with Disabilities*. Volume 7, *Guardians Ad Litem and Other Court Related Issues*. Volume 8, *Private Fostering and Miscellaneous*. Volume 9, *Adoption Issues*. Volume 10, *Index*.

Department for Education (1994) *Code of Practice for Identification and Assessment of Special Educational Needs* (being revised). DfE.

Department for Education and Employment (1999) *Recruiting Childcare Workers: A Guide for Providers*. DfEE.

Department for Education and Employment (2000a) *Childcare Start-up Guides: Good Practice in Childcare*. DfEE.

Department for Education and Employment (2000b) *Education of Young People in Public Care*. DfEE.

Department for Education and Employment (2000c) *Recruitment Strategies for Childcare Workers*. DfEE.

Department for Education and Employment (2000d) *Teamworking*. DfEE.

Department for Education and Employment (2001a) *National Standards for Under Eights Day Care and Childminding: Childminding*. DfES. Also Department for Education and Skills (2001) *Childminding: Guidance to the National Standards*. DfES.

Department for Education and Employment (2001b) *National Standards for Under Eights Day Care and Childminding: Crèches*. DfES. Also Department for Education and Skills (2001) *Crèches: Guidance to the National Standards*. DfES.

Department for Education and Employment (2001c) *National Standards for Under Eights Day Care and Childminding: Full Day Care.* DfES. Also Department for Education and Skills (2001) *Full Day Care: Guidance to the National Standards.* DfES.

Department for Education and Employment (2001d) *National Standards for Under Eights Day Care and Childminding: Out of School Care.* DfES. Also Department for Education and Skills (2001) *Out of School Care: Guidance to the National Standards.* DfES.

Department for Education and Employment (2001e) *National Standards for Under Eights Day Care and Childminding: Sessional Care.* DfES. Also Department for Education and Skills (2001) *Sessional Day Care: Guidance to the National Standards.* DfES.

Derman Sparks, L. (1989) *Anti-bias Curriculum: Tools for Empowering Young Children.* National Early Years Network.

Early Years Trainers Anti Racist Network (n.d.) *Equality and the Children Act: A Sources and Resources Pack.* EYTARN.

European Convention on Human Rights (2000) Council for Europe.

Gerbner, G. and Gross, L. (1976) The scary world of television's heavy viewer. *Psychology Today* 9, 41–5.

Goldschmied, E. and Jackson, S. (1997) *People under Three: Young Children in Day Care.* Routledge.

Hallam, S. (1996) *Grouping Pupils by Ability: Selection, Streaming, Banding and Setting.* Institute of Education.

Hallam, S. and Youtounji, I. (1996) *What Do We Know about the Grouping of Pupils by Ability?* Institute of Education.

Hyder, T. and Kenway, P. (1995) *An Equal Future: A Guide to Anti Sexist Practice in the Early Years.* National Early Years Network and SCF Equality Learning Centre.

In Safe Hands: A Training Pack for Working with Refugee Children (n.d.) Save the Children Publications.

Jeffcoate, R. (1984) *Ethnic Minorities and Education.* Harper & Row.

Lane, J. (1996) *From Cradle to School.* Commission for Racial Equality.

Maccoby, E. and Jacklin, C. (1974) *The Psychology of Sex Differences.* Stanford University Press.

Maclean, S. and Maclean, I. (2000) *Understanding the NVQ Value Base.* Kirwin Maclean Associates.

Maclean, S., Shiner, M. and Maclean, I. (2000) *From Birth to Eighteen Years: Children and the Law.* Kirwin Maclean Associates.

Miller, C. L. (1987) Qualitative differences among gender stereotyped toys: implications for cognitive and social development in girls and boys. *Sex Roles* 16, 473–87.

Millner, D. (1993) *Children and Race: Ten Years On.* Ward Lock.

National Early Years Network (1996) *Responsibility for Under-Eights: A Guide to the Law.* NEYN.

Newell, P. (1991) *The UN Convention and Children's Rights in the UK.* National Children's Bureau.

O'Hagan, M. (1997) *Geraghty's Caring for Children*. Baillière Tindall.

O'Hagan, M. and Smith, M. (1999) *Early Years Child Care and Education: Key Issues*. Baillière Tindall.

Owen, C., Cameron, C. and Moss, P. (1998) *Men as Workers in Services for Young Children: Issues of a Mixed Gender Workforce*. Institute of Education.

Parsons, C., Benns, L., Hailes, J. and Howlett, K. (1994) *Excluding Primary School Children*. Family Policy Studies Centre.

Pugh, G. and De'Ath, E. (1989) *Working towards Partnership in the Early Years*. National Children's Bureau.

Ramage, R. (1997) *Every Child Is a Gifted Child*. Kea Press.

Rosenkrantz, P. S., Vogel, S. R., Bee, H., Broverman, I. K. and Broverman, D. M. (1968) Sex role stereotypes and self concepts in college students. *Journal of Consulting and Clinical Psychology* 32, 287–95.

Rosenthal, R. and Jackson, L. (1968) *Pygmalion in the Classroom*. Holt, Rinehart and Winston.

Rotter, J. B. (1966) Generalised expectancies for internal versus external control of reinforcement. *Psychological Monographs* 80.

Rubovits, P. C. and Maehr, M. (1973) Pygmalion black and white. *Journal of Personality and Social Psychology* 25 (2).

Save the Children and EYTARN (n.d.) *Equality in Practice: A Conference Report*. Save the Children and EYTARN.

Siraj-Blatchford, I. (1994) *The Early Years: Laying the Foundations for Racial Equality*. Trentham Books.

Siraj-Blatchford, I. and Clarke, P. (2000) *Supporting Identity, Diversity and Language in the Early Years*. Open University Press.

Statham, J. (1986) *Daughters and Sons: Experiences of Non-sexist Childraising*. Blackwell.

Tattum, D. and Herbert, G. (1997) *Bullying: Home, School and Community*. David Fulton.

Tomlinson, S. (1984) *Home and School in Multicultural Britain*. Batsford.

Triandis, H. C. (1971) *Attitude and Attitude Change*. John Wiley.

Varma, V. (1993) *How and Why Children Hate. A Study of Conscious and Unconscious Sources*. Jessica Kingsley.

Vaughan, G. M. (1964) Ethical awareness in relation to minority group membership. *Journal of Genetic Psychology* 105, 119–30.

Wales Pre-School Playgroups Association and Mudiad Ysgolion Meithrin (n.d.) *Playing Together*. NES Arnold.

Wheal, A. (1999) *The RHP Companion to Foster Care*. Russell House Publishing.

White, D. and Woollett, A. (1992) *Families: A Context for Development*. Falmer Press.

Wilson, R. (1998) *Special Educational Needs in the Early Years*. Routledge.

Chapter 2

Race, religion and culture

A wide variety of races, religions and cultures are represented in, and go to make up, the society in which we live. This chapter will give an overview of what is meant by race, religion and culture. It will examine some of the issues involved and, I hope, allow workers to explore their feelings concerning these issues and how they may affect working practices. Individual religions and cultures will be examined in more depth in Chapter 3.

We saw in Chapter 1 that the Children Act 1989 requires workers to take into account a child's racial, religious, cultural and linguistic needs. The Education Reform Act 1988 says that schools must offer a curriculum that promotes the spiritual, moral, cultural, mental and physical development of pupils, the school and society. We also saw that from the Care Standards Act 2000 came the National Standards for under-eights and day care and childminding, which also require workers actively to promote equality of opportunity and anti-discriminatory practice, including working with parents to share information about cultures. In order to do this, workers must have an understanding of the meaning of each of these different terms. This chapter will use the definitions given by the *Concise Oxford Dictionary*.

- race: 'each of the major divisions of humankind, having distinct physical characteristics; a tribe, nation, etc., regarded as of a distinct ethnic stock';
- religion: 'the belief in a superhuman controlling power, especially in a personal God or Gods entitled to obedience and worship';
- culture: 'the customs, civilizations and achievements of a particular time or people';

- faith: 'firm belief, especially without logical proof; a system of religious belief; beliefs in religious doctrines';
- spiritual: 'of or concerning the spirit as opposed to matter; concerned with sacred or religious things; holy; divine; inspired'.

A Chance to Think 1
It is important that people working with young children are secure in their knowledge of themselves. Workers need to explore how they feel about various issues, including race, religion and culture. Think about yourself.

How would you define your racial background?

Would you say that you hold any religious views or that you are religious?

How would you define your cultural background?

Are these three things the same?

How does your background play a part in your work with young children?

Race

Race can be quite an emotive subject. Many people feel uncomfortable about it because they do not know what words to use, or they feel awkward, or worried, about saying the wrong thing. Some people express strong feelings when discussing the issue of race. Often these can be negative or discriminatory views. People working with young children and families need to acknowledge that racism and racial prejudice exist. Words like 'anti-racist' and 'multiracial' are often used in the childcare and education field. Workers need to work towards providing an anti-discriminatory environment so that all children can develop positive self-images and identities. This will be discussed in more detail in Chapter 6. As well as being good practice, it is also a legal obligation. The Children Act 1989 says that workers must take into account a child's racial origin when caring for children. The Race Relations Act 1976, the Race Relations (Amendment) Act 2000 and the Commission for Racial Equality all work towards the elimination of racism and discrimination on racial grounds.

We saw in Chapter 1 that research shows that young children recognize and put values on different skin colours, and that these values can be racist and discriminatory. Children have learnt that people with white skin are seen as having more powerful positions in society than people with black skin. These views are perpetuated through society at large, the media, language and literature.

A Chance to Think 2
Earlier in this chapter we saw a definition of the word 'race'. Some people think that classifying people according to racial grounds can be harmful, as it can lead to generalizations, prejudice and stereotyping. What is your opinion on this?

Racism exists, and is very damaging to everyone. Workers in childcare and education have a duty to recognize its existence and to work towards its elimination. Racism occurs when one race is perceived to be superior to another. At one time science and psychology tried to justify such perceptions. One view on IQ tests, supported by Jensen and Eysenck, tried to establish that white races had a higher intelligence than black races. This is not the case, and these theories are no longer considered justified. UNESCO pronounced in the 1950s that 'available scientific knowledge provides no basis for believing that groups of mankind differ in their innate capacity for intellectual or emotional development'.

Training is often needed by workers so that they can address the issue of race and how it can be fully implemented into the setting in a positive way for all children. All workers like to think that all children in the setting are being treated equally, but this, sadly, is often not the case. In many studies where workers' practice has been observed, workers have been found to be spending more time with white children, saying that Asian children are disadvantaged and criticizing black children more often than white children. It is important for workers to be aware that this is happening, either consciously or unconsciously, as it has implications for the way they work with children and families.

Figure 2.1 Children's pictures of themselves.

A Chance to Think 3

The Care Standards Act requires that all childcare and education settings that fall within its powers are inspected regularly. On visiting one setting in a rural enviroment, the inspector was told that 'We only have two children from [minority] ethnic backgrounds here so we don't need to address issues about race. Anyway, we treat all children here the same.'

What do you think about this statement?

Why does this setting need to address race?

How can it begin to address these issues?

Compare your answers with the sample answers in Appendix 2.

Children of mixed race (mixed parentage/dual heritage) have parents from two different races. For some children this is a very positive experience. Other children receive confusing messages about their identity. Some children feel torn between two races. This may mean that these children have difficulty in developing a sense of identity and high self-esteem. Children need to receive positive messages about their racial identity from both home and setting. The development of self-esteem is discussed further in Chapter 6.

A Chance to Think 4

Jason is a mixed-race child attending your setting. In the staff room you hear a colleague refer to Jason as a 'half-caste' and say, 'It's a shame because he is neither one thing nor the other.'

How would you react in this situation?

What can you do to try to change this worker's way of thinking?

What can you do to give Jason a positive sense of himself and his identity?

Compare your answers to the sample answers in Appendix 2.

Whatever setting workers are in, it is important to give all the children within the setting an understanding of, and respect for, the different races that make up society. Children and parents need to know that this is an integral part of the ethos of the setting; that their racial background will be not just acknowledged but respected and valued. In many settings that ethos is written down in the form of a mission statement that is available for all to see. Many settings also have policies and procedures on how to deal with issues on a day-to-day basis. It is important that these are not just pieces of paper for show, but that workers incorporate race issues into their daily work with children. The incorporation of race into the curriculum and daily activities is discussed in Chapter 5, and hair and skin care is discussed in Chapter 4.

Culture

Workers need to take into account children's cultural backgrounds. Cultural background is different from racial background, but, as with race, individuals have no control over the cultural background into which they are born.

Cultural background plays a very important role in child-rearing and has a large impact on the way a child develops. Each culture has its own set of values and ways of rearing children. These vary greatly. It is also important to remember that in every

A Chance to Think 5
We saw earlier in this chapter how culture can be defined, but there is much more to culture than simple definitions. A person's cultural background can have a profound effect on the way that person lives. Think about culture and write down all the things that may be included in this that influence a person's life.

Why will culture have an effect on the things that happen in childcare settings?

Compare your answers with the sample answers in Appendix 2.

culture there are subcultures and groups that have variations on such things as dress and language. Some of the things that vary between cultures are:

- size of family and family make-up;
- language;
- diet, food and ways of eating;
- dress;
- hair care;
- discipline;
- customs and traditions;
- religion;
- expectations of children;
- child-rearing practices;
- child development;
- music.

Sociologists and psychologists have long recognized the effect of culture on child-rearing practices and child development. In some cultures it is unacceptable to leave babies to cry; they will be picked up and comforted. In other cultures it is thought that children must learn that they will not be picked up every time they cry. In some cultures children sleep in their parents' room, or in their parents' bed, until they decide they want to sleep alone. In many cultures children may also be breast-fed until they are 4 or 5 years old. Some cultures hold quite different views from these. Young babies usually sleep in their own beds and often in their own rooms, and breast-feeding ceases early in a child's life. Research across cultures has found that children will wean themselves when they are ready. It is important to remember that there will be differences within cultures, and workers should not generalize about culture and practices.

Another aspect of child-rearing that varies across cultures is childcare. In some cultures mothers play very little part in caring for their child. Children may be cared for by childcare workers, extended family or their fathers. There is a difference across cultures in what is expected of children. Some cultures expect children to be quiet and obedient and to show respect for adults. Children may be expected to take responsibility and help in the home from a very young age, and to look after their brothers and sisters. In some cultures children are expected to work to help support the family. Children are seen as people, and childhood is not seen as a separate stage of development. In other cultures childhood is seen very much as a distinct stage of development, where children can have fun, grow, learn and develop without any of the responsibilities they will be expected to take on when they become adults.

The way children develop is guided by opportunities to practise their behaviour and their skills. These will all be influenced by the culture in which they are brought up, as can be seen from Piaget's theory of children's learning. He said that there are four stages to children's learning:

- sensori-motor stage (birth to 2 years);
- pre-operational stage (2 to 6 or 7 years);
- concrete operations stage (7 to 12 years);
- formal operations stage (12 years plus).

Psychologists have researched this theory across cultures to see whether all stages appear and in the same order. They found that in non-literate adults the formal operations stage was rare, leading them to conclude that this stage represented a culturally specific course of development in Western society.

Examination of child development across cultures allows us to see some of the similarities between cultures. These include a similarity in the sequence of sensori-motor development, smiling and the degree of distress at separation from parents. Also constant across a large variety of cultural groups is the development of language. This will be discussed at greater depth in Chapter 6.

Another important finding for childcare workers is that children learn more, can perform tasks better and find more meaning in activities using culturally appropriate material. This has implications for the type of equipment needed in settings, as well as the way activities are carried out. This was shown in a piece of research looking at children's memory. When asked to remember things of which they had no previous knowledge, children had a great deal of difficulty. In their own home, and using objects with which they were familiar, the same children could use their memory well.

Cognitive skills and behaviour patterns, and the development of personality, are related to the cultural context in which children are brought up. Workers must acknowledge that there are cultural differences in the way children are reared. It is not a case of one culture being right or wrong, and unless they are harmful to the child, workers should value and respect cultural variations in child-rearing practices.

There may also be different opinions about child-rearing practices between workers in a setting. It is important to remember that just as children's and families' values and practices will

---

A Chance to Think 6

Think about your own setting and the children, families and colleagues that make it up.

How many different cultures are represented in the setting, and what are they?

How much do you feel you know about the different cultures represented in your setting?

How can you show that you acknowledge, value and respect people's cultural backgrounds?

Compare your answers with the sample answers in Appendix 2.

be influenced by their cultural backgrounds, so will those of childcare workers. Different opinions about childcare issues should be discussed, with special emphasis on how they affect the setting.

Some children whose culture is not the same as that of the setting may feel torn between cultures. Children and parents need to know that as an integral part of the ethos of the setting, their cultural background will be acknowledged, respected and valued. How to incorporate such acknowledgement and respect into daily working practices will be discussed in Chapters 4, 5 and 6.

Religion

Individuals may be born into a religious family and brought up in the religion they hold. As people grow older, they will have to make their own personal decisions as to whether they continue to follow that religion. Some people choose not to enter formally or follow the religion in which they were brought up, though they may still follow some of its customs. Some individuals make a decision to follow a different religion from the one in which they were brought up. At present, Christianity is the dominant religion in British society. However, many other religions are represented in society and practised by many people. Workers need to acknowledge and be aware of this.

Religions have given the world many great things, including scriptures, literature, art, music, symbols and architecture. Some terrible things have also been done in the name of religion, with communities being torn apart by conflict.

Religions are treated by the media as news. Some headlines taken from different papers are as follows: 'Gypsies and their souls – Anna Moore hears that for Evangelical Gypsies, God holds the answer to the 1968 Caravan Act'; 'As with other religions, some Muslims believe in a strict enforcement of their faith. At times this has led to conflict'; and 'RE teaching that equates Jesus with Nelson Mandela hinders our children's understanding of history, art, music and literature'. The way religions are portrayed by the media influences the way people view them, especially if this is the only contact people have with the particular religion portrayed. Sometimes, stereotypical attitudes towards particular religious

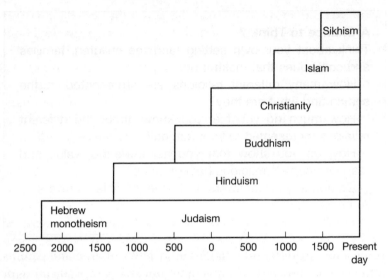

Figure 2.2 Ages of major religions.

groups are perpetuated by the media, and issues are often sensationalized in the interest of readership or viewing figures.

Religion has a long history. Some religions stretch back to the dawn of humankind and are recognized throughout the world as having firmly established beliefs and traditions. Other religions are newer and may not be as firmly established, or as widely recognized, as the major world religions.

Religions incorporate many things within them, including guiding principles on dress and dietary rules that an individual may follow. We have seen that everyone has a racial and cultural background. Some people also have religious beliefs that influence how they live their life. Children, families and colleagues can have a religious background of which workers need to be aware, and although workers cannot know every detail of every religion, they should have some knowledge of the many different religions practised in society today.

Some workers may not have many religions represented in their setting. Other workers' settings may have many different religions represented. Whatever setting workers are in, it is important to give all the children in the setting an understanding of, and

A Chance to Think 7

Think about your own setting, and the children, families and colleagues that make it up.

How many different religions are represented in the setting and what are they?

How much do you feel you know about the different religions represented in your setting?

How do you show that you acknowledge, value and respect people's religious backgrounds?

Compare your answers with the sample answers in Appendix 2.

respect for, the different religions in society. Children and parents also need to know that doing so is an integral part of the ethos of the setting.

Religions have very different beliefs, which may clash with each other. Workers need to develop policies and procedures concerning religion. These will address the issue of how the setting is going to meet the needs of the children, families and workers in the setting, including how to avoid their becoming involved in activities that may compromise their religious beliefs.

Just as children and families in our care come from different religious backgrounds, so do the individuals who work with children. Childcare workers are likely to disagree with some of the beliefs of the different religions, because there are so many different religions. Some have a core of beliefs that overlap, while others have differing and conflicting beliefs. Although workers may not agree with some aspects of people's beliefs, it is important to recognize that people have a right to those beliefs and to try to respect the way they feel about them.

Some workers will find that there is a conflict between their own personal beliefs and those of their colleagues or the families with whom they work. If this situation arises, it is important to deal with it, if possible through discussion with a senior colleague. For example, people who are Jehovah's Witnesses do not celebrate festivals such as birthdays or Christmas. A worker who is a Jehovah's

Witness may have a personal conflict over the celebration of festivals in the workplace. Discussion with a senior colleague should allow both worker and management to put forward their points of view. This will, it is to be hoped, lead to a solution that will be acceptable to both parties. Workers who work on their own (e.g. nannies or childminders) may be unable to do this. However, they may be able to talk to others in the same situation. Childminders might have the opportunity to discuss these issues with the National Childminding Association.

It is important to remember that everyone is an individual. People may observe all, some or none of the guidelines of their religion. It is important not to make assumptions about what families in our care or colleagues we work with believe or observe. One of the best ways of trying to make sure we have the right information is to ask parents or colleagues in a sensitive way about their religious backgrounds. By doing this, we are acknowledging the validity of people's religious background, and placing them in the position of being the most knowledgeable individual about their own beliefs. Parents and colleagues may also be able to help to gather more information and resources to help workers understand the religion.

It is important to recognize that some people may not have any religious beliefs or belong to a particular religion. These people may be either agnostics or atheists.

Agnostics

We need to remember that not everyone belongs to a recognized faith. There are people who have no religious beliefs. People who belong to a religion may acknowledge that a god, or several gods, exist. There are also some people who are not sure if they believe in a god or not. Some individuals are unable to acknowledge the existence of a god in any form. However, those with no religious beliefs, who do not worship a god, may follow guiding principles of daily living.

People who are not sure whether they believe in the existence of a god are called agnostics. People who are agnostics question the existence of a god. This is because no one can prove whether a god exists or not. The *Concise Oxford Dictionary* defines 'agnostic' as 'a person who believes that nothing is known, or can be known, of the existence or nature of God or of anything beyond material phenomena'.

Some families and colleagues in the setting may be agnostics. Workers should be sensitive to the feelings of people who feel they do not belong to any religion.

Atheists

Many people in the world have some sort of religious faith. However, there are also many people who have no religious faith. Some people believe that there is no god. Unlike agnostics, who are not sure whether a god exists, atheists are quite sure there is no such thing as a god in any shape or form. The word atheist comes from the Greek word *a-theos*, which means 'without god'. The *Concise Oxford Dictionary* defines the word 'atheism' as 'the theory or belief that God does not exist'. Many people call themselves 'humanists'. They try to live their life following a code of conduct for the good of humanity that they believe is right, and that helps both them and their fellow human beings.

It is important to remember that people have a right to these beliefs. Workers should not make judgements about people just because they do not believe in the existence of a god.

Useful publications

Albany Video (n.d.) *Coffee Coloured Children*. Video, for sale or hire from Albany Video, Film and Distribution, Battersea Studios TV Centre, Thackeray Road, London SW8 3TW.

All London Teachers Against Racism (1984) *Challenging Racism*. Russell Press.

BBC Education (1994) *Children without Prejudice: Equal Opportunities and the Children Act* (video). BBC Education.

Derman Sparks, L. (1989) *Anti-bias Curriculum: Tools for Empowering Young Children*. National Early Years Network.

Early Years Training Anti Racist Network (n.d.) *Combating Racial Prejudice against Jewish People: A Report*. EYTARN.

Early Years Training Anti Racist Network (n.d.) *Learning by Doing: The Anti Racist Way. A Conference Report*. EYTARN.

Isaacs, N. (1966) *The Growth of Understanding in the Young Child: A Brief Introduction to Piaget's Work.* Fletcher.

Jogee, M. and Lal, S. *Religions and Cultures: Guide to Beliefs and Customs for Health Staff and Social Care Services.* Religions and Cultures Publications.

Konner, M. (1991) *Childhood.* Little, Brown.

Millner, D. (1983) *Children and Race: Ten Years On.* Ward Lock.

O'Hagan, M. (1997) *Geraghty's Caring for Children.* Baillière Tindall.

O'Hagan, M. and Smith, M. (1999) *Early Years Child Care and Education: Key Issues.* Baillière Tindall.

Save the Children and Early Years Training Anti Racist Network (n.d.) *Equality in Practice. A Conference Report.* Save the Children and EYTARN.

Singh Ghuman, P. A. (1994) *Coping with Two Cultures.* Multilingual Matters.

Siraj-Blatchford, I. (1994) *The Early Years: Laying the Foundations for Racial Equality.* Trentham Books.

White, D. and Woollett, A. (1992) *Families: A Context for Development.* Falmer Press.

Chapter 3

Major religious beliefs

This chapter examines the major religions and cultures that make up the society we live in today. It gives an overview of each religion or culture, including a short history, the beliefs held by adherants of that religion or culture, the major festivals celebrated and the symbols that have meaning and are important. Dress and dietary requirements will be discussed in greater depth in the next chapter.

In this chapter it is only possible to provide an overview of the major religions and cultures. It is not possible to include every religion and culture or to go into great detail about them. The aim of the chapter is to provide readers with some information, so that they have a basic understanding of different religions and cultures. For readers wanting further information, useful addresses and a reading list are given. The order of the religions in this chapter does not imply any order of importance: they are listed in alphabetical order.

Buddhism

History and beliefs

Buddhism is based on the teachings of Siddhartha Gautama. People who follow his teachings are called Buddhists. They believe that Siddhartha Gautama was a Buddha. This means that he was an 'enlightened one'. Buddhists divide into two main types. The oldest form of Buddhism is practised by the Theravada Buddhists, who follow closely the teachings of the Buddha based on his doctrines. The Mahayana Buddhists follow a newer form of Buddhism and now number the majority. The Mahayana branch of Buddhism contains within it the Zen Buddhists.

Siddhartha Gautama was the son of a rich man. He was born in the Himalayas, in what is now Nepal, in 563 BC, and lived his life there. His father was worried about all the cruelty and suffering that happened in the world. He tried to protect Siddhartha from it by bringing him up inside a palace, so that he would not see what happened in the outside world.

When Siddhartha Gautama grew up he married a princess, and they had a baby son. When he was about 30 years old Siddhartha left the palace walls and saw four people. The first person was an old man, the second was a sick man, the third man was dead and the fourth man was a holy man. The holy man looked happy and peaceful. After seeing these four people, Gautama decided he had to do something. He thought there must be a way to ease people's suffering. In order to try to find some answers to these deep questions, which would not go away, Gautama left his life in the palace. He went to live with a group of wandering beggars and shared their life. Although he lived the life of a poor man for six years, he did not find any answers to his questions.

Gautama decided to leave the group of beggars and look elsewhere for answers to his questions. He lived on his own as an ascetic and meditated to focus his mind. Meditation is an important part of Buddhist life. After meditating and living alone for about six years, Gautama believed that he had found the answers to his questions. He believed that he had found how to help people live their lives in a way that would help them to avoid suffering. Gautama called this way of living *the middle way*. It is called this because it involves living between the extremes that are in life.

Gautama wanted to share his new knowledge and enlightenment with others. He wanted to tell them about his new beliefs and way of living. He did this by preaching a sermon to the people he had lived with. As a result of this, they became his disciples. In his sermon, Gautama explained the Four Noble Truths that he believed were in life.

1   The truth of suffering: all life contains suffering.
2   The cause of suffering: we cause our suffering.
3   The cessation of suffering: we can stop suffering.

4 The way that leads to the cessation of suffering: by avoiding the extremes in life.

Gautama said that suffering can be avoided by following the Eightfold Path in daily life.

1 right understanding;
2 right intention;
3 right speech;
4 right conduct;
5 right occupation;
6 right endeavour;
7 right contemplation;
8 right concentration.

Through understanding the Four Noble Truths and following the Eightfold Path, individuals may reach the goal of existence called Nirvana. Nirvana, or non-existence, is freedom and peace. Achieving it may take years, more than one lifetime. Buddhists believe that by transmigration, or being continually reincarnated, it is possible finally to achieve Nirvana.

Gautama taught for forty years and died when he was 80 years old. At first his teachings were not written down. Eventually they were written down in a holy book called the *Tripitaka*, or the Three Baskets. The language used to write the *Tripitaka* was Pali, an ancient language spoken by the Buddha. The *Tripitaka* is made up of 31 books in three different sections. The *Vinaya Pitaka* is about monastic discipline. The *Sutra* (or *Dharma*) *Pitaka* contains the Buddha story, the Precepts and other doctrines. The *Abhidarma Pitaka* contains advanced doctrines and philosophy. The Four Noble Truths and the Eightfold Path are contained in the *Dhammapada*. This is separate from the *Tripitaka*.

Siddhartha Gautama also gave Buddhists the Five Precepts. These are rules that should be followed every day. They are:

1 Do not kill or harm living things.
2 Do not steal, but give to others.
3 Do not misuse your senses.
4 Do not speak wrongly.
5 Do not use drink or drugs.

Buddhists do not worship a god, but the Buddha did not say there was not a god. He said that a god could not be defined, described or explored.

The place where Buddhists meet is called a temple or Vihara. No one day of the week is considered more holy than another, and Buddhists will go to the temple on any day.

Major festivals

The Buddhist calendar is based on the lunar calendar, which is determined by the movements of the moon. Each month has a full moon, which is celebrated in different ways according to the

Figure 3.1 A statue of the Buddha.

Table 3.1 Major Buddhist festivals

Month	Festival	Background information
May	Vaisakha Puja/ Wesak	A Theravada festival. Celebrates the birth, enlightenment and death of the Buddha. Mahayanists celebrate these events on separate days. Homes may be decorated with garlands of flowers and lanterns. Some people may release or free birds as a symbol of compassion and help.
June	Poson/Dhamma Vijaya	A Theravada festival. Celebrates the preaching and spread of Buddhism from India to other countries.
July	Asala	A Theravada festival. Celebrates the first sermon of the Buddha where he first talked about the Middle Way, the Four Noble truths and the Eightfold Path to enlightenment.
October	Kattika	A Theravada festival. Celebrates the monks leaving the Buddha to spread his word in India.
December	Bodhi Day	A Mahayana festival. Celebrates the Buddha's achieving enlightenment.
February	Parinirvana	A Mahayana festival. Commemorates the death of the Buddha.

branch of Buddhism followed and the country lived in. Different countries may have a festival to mark the full moon of each month, and not all are mentioned here. The major festivals are centred on the events in the Buddha's life and his teachings. The Buddhist calendar starts in the month of May with Vesakha (see Table 3.1).

Buddhist symbols

There are many different statues of the Buddha in the world. The ways in which the Buddha is represented in statues symbolize different meanings. If the Buddha is shown with his fingers near his heart and his palms touching, this symbolizes him preaching his first sermon. If the Buddha is shown with his right hand pointing down, this symbolizes him resisting temptation.

A Chance to Think 1
A child of a family who follow the Buddhist religion is starting in your setting and you are going to be her key worker. You do not know very much about the Buddhist religion.

How and where can you get information that may help you to become aware of the child's family's needs?

Compare your answers with the sample answers in Appendix 2.

Christianity

History and beliefs

Christians believe that there is one God. They believe that this God created the world and then sent his Son, Jesus, into the world to teach people about God and to be a saviour by sacrificing himself for the sins of humankind. The word 'Christian' comes from the name of Jesus Christ. The word 'Christ' is not the surname of Jesus but a title, which in Greek means 'anointed one' and is a translation of the Hebrew word for messiah or liberator. Christians believe that Jesus was sent by God to liberate people from their sins, to be the saviour of the world.

Christians believe that Jesus was born in Bethlehem to a Jewish couple, Mary and Joseph. When he was 30 years old he was baptized by a man called John the Baptist in the river Jordan. Jesus then called twelve people together to help him teach people about the Kingdom of God. These twelve men were called his disciples. For three years Jesus and the disciples travelled the country telling people about God. Christians also believe that Jesus performed miracles, such as turning water into wine, healing the sick and even raising the dead.

At the age of 33 Jesus was put to death by the Roman authorities in power at the time, at the insistence of the Jewish religious leaders, who accused him of blasphemy. He was crucified on a cross outside the city walls of Jerusalem. He was taken down from the cross by his followers and put in a tomb. After three days some of his followers went to anoint the body, but it was gone. They asked the gardener where the body was and suddenly realized that they were talking to Jesus. Christians believe that Jesus died on the cross, but after three days he rose again and appeared to his disciples on many occasions for a period of 40 days. He then ascended to heaven, having told his disciples to preach the gospels to people.

Because Christians believe that Jesus rose from the dead, they believe in a living Christ and that there is a resurrection to life after death. After his death, Jesus' disciples continued to teach people about God. Christianity spread throughout the Roman world and became accepted as a religion.

Christians were persecuted by Roman emperors. The Emperor Constantine was converted to Christianity and in AD 312 Christianity became the official religion of the Roman Empire. Because Rome was the capital of the empire, the Bishop of Rome (later called Pope) was the most important bishop in the church. When Emperor Constantine moved to Constantinople the power within Christianity shifted, and in AD 451 the Bishop of Constantinople was given the same powers as the Pope. In 1054 they had a struggle over the leadership of the church. This resulted in a split into two different branches of Christianity. These became known as the Eastern Church and the Western Church. Both branches of Christianity believe in the same basic things, but they have different ways of interpreting them and celebrating them.

The Eastern branch of the church now contains what is known as the Orthodox churches. Among these are the Russian Orthodox, Greek Orthodox, Eastern Orthodox, Ethiopian Orthodox and Egyptian Orthodox churches. These churches have their own rules and leaders or patriarchs. The person to whom all the Orthodox churches look for supreme leadership and guidance is the Patriarch of Constantinople. All the Orthodox churches follow what is known as the traditional Julian calendar, with Christmas (the celebration of the birth of Jesus) being celebrated on 6 January.

The Latin branch of the church was first made up of Christians who looked to the Pope in Rome as their head. In 1517 a German monk called Martin Luther split with Rome to form a branch of the church known as the Protestant church. A further split came in 1536, when in England Henry VIII also split from the Church of Rome. This branch of the church is known as the Anglican church. As with the Orthodox churches, there are several branches or denominations of Protestant churches, including Baptists, Methodists, Quakers, Presbyterians, Plymouth Brethren and Congregationalists. The Catholic (Roman) and Protestant churches follow the Western Christian calendar (Gregorian), with Christmas being celebrated on 25 December.

All Christians follow the teachings of Jesus, which are written down in the four Gospels, a part of the Christian holy book, called the Bible. The Bible is divided into two halves, the Old and New Testaments. Each testament is made up of books written by different authors. The Old Testament contains chapters on the creation of the world, guidelines on how to live life, prophecy and Jewish history, all written before the birth of Jesus. The New Testament contains writings that took place after the birth of Jesus, including writings by some of the disciples about the life of Jesus, together with letters, or epistles, by Paul, Peter, James and John. There is also a book on what Christians believe will happen at the end of the world.

The Christian holy day is Sunday. This is the day when Christians meet to pray, sing, think, read the Bible and worship God. Different branches of Christianity have different ways of worshipping together. The places where they meet are holy or special places. They have many different names, including cathedral, church, chapel and meeting hall.

All the branches of the church have special ceremonies where the sacraments are celebrated. These are services at which Christians can show others that they are practising their faith. The first is where individuals formally join the Christian church. This is called baptism, and may take place when individuals are adults or children. All branches of the church also celebrate the Eucharist, which is when people take part in a communion ceremony to celebrate the death and life of Jesus Christ. These two sacraments are called the Dominical sacraments, because Jesus (the Lord, or Latin *Dominus*) ordered that they should take place. The Roman Catholic and Orthodox churches have five other sacraments, which they feel show their devotion to the teachings of the church. These are confirmation, penance, extreme unction, holy orders and marriage.

Major festivals

All the major Christian festivals are centred on events that happened in the life of Jesus or the early church. They are celebrated at different times during the year. Advent is always on the four Sundays before Christmas, and both Christmas Day and Epiphany are celebrated on the same date each year. Ash Wednesday, the beginning of Lent, Easter, Ascension and Pentecost are celebrated on different dates each year, and can vary by as much as 28 days. They are dependent on the first day of the fasting season of Lent. The date of Lent is set by the date of Good Friday. This falls on the Friday of the first full moon of the spring equinox and Jewish Passover. It is usual for Christians to go to church to celebrate these festivals and observe these feasts. The Christian year begins in November with Advent Sunday. Table 3.2 shows the major festivals of the Christian year.

Christian symbols

The main symbol of the Christian church is based on the cross on which Jesus was crucified. This reminds Christians that Christ died on the cross to save humankind. Protestant and Orthodox churches generally (but not always) have an empty cross to show that Jesus rose from the dead. Different branches of Christianity have different designs of crosses. Churches of a Catholic or 'High Church' tradition may have a symbol called a crucifix. This is a cross with the body of Jesus Christ still crucified on it. This is to remind them of the agony that Jesus endured for them.

Table 3.2 Major Christian festivals

Month	Festival	Background information
November	Advent	Advent is the penitential season beginning four Sundays before Christmas. It is the time when Christians prepare for the coming of Jesus Christ on Christmas Day. It may be celebrated by the making of an Advent wreath. This has one candle for each of the four Sundays in Advent and one candle in the centre to represent Christmas Day. A candle is lit on each of the Sundays to show the coming of Christ at Christmas.
December and January	Christmas	The day on which Christians celebrate the birth of Jesus Christ. The Catholic and Protestant churches celebrate this day on 25 December. The Orthodox churches celebrate on 6 January. Christians may give each other presents to remind them that this is Jesus' birthday. They may have special food, such as Christmas cake and mince pies. They may also decorate their houses with Christmas trees.
	Epiphany	Marks the visit of the kings to the baby Jesus. The Western Catholic and Protestant churches celebrate this on 6 January.
February and March	Lent	The forty days leading up to Easter to remember Christ's fast in the desert. Many Christians fast at this time. Others may give up something that they enjoy. The date of Lent is set by the date of Good Friday. This falls on the Friday following the first full moon of the spring equinox.
	Clean Monday	The day Lent starts (Orthodox church).
	Ash Wednesday	The day Lent starts (Catholic and Protestant churches).
(or April)	Palm Sunday	Celebrates Jesus' entry into Jerusalem. Palm crosses are usually given out at church on this day.

Table 3.2 cont'd

Month	Festival	Background information
	Maundy Thursday	The day of Jesus' last supper with his disciples.
	Good Friday	The day Jesus was crucified. The end of Lent.
March or April	Easter and Easter Sunday	Begins on Easter Eve Sunday. The day when Christ rose from the dead. The most important day in the Christian calendar. Easter lasts for 40 days. Christians may give each other eggs to show that Easter is a sign of new life.
May	Ascension	Takes place 40 days after Easter Sunday. Celebrates the day Jesus rose to heaven. The last day of Easter.
June	Pentecost and Whit Sunday	Pentecost is the day when the Holy Spirit visited the followers of Jesus in order to give them strength to spread the word of God.
August	Assumption	Celebrated by the Orthodox and Catholic churches. A feast day to remember the day Mary the mother of Jesus was received into heaven.

Figure 3.2 Plain, Celtic and Ethiopian crosses.

Figure 3.3 A crucifix.

A Chance to Think 2

The setting you are working in wants to take a group of children aged 4 and 5 to visit local religious buildings, shops, houses, flats, fire stations and a hospital as part of a theme on buildings. One of the places the setting plans to visit is a church, where the vicar will show the children around.

What do you think about this idea?

What are some of the things you would need to take into account when organizing this trip?

What sort of things would you do with the children before the trip takes place?

How would you follow up the trip on your return?

Compare your answers with the sample answers in Appendix 3.

Hinduism

History and beliefs

Hindus believe in one supreme or high god called Brahman. The word 'Brahman' means 'all that is'. Brahman is the high god but he is represented in the form of many different gods. Hindus believe that God has many parts. Different images of him are needed to show the different parts that make him up, and these illustrate the different parts of life.

Brahman is the supreme god who made the world. He is then represented as the god Vishnu. The god Vishnu takes care of the world and has appeared in the world in ten different forms to fight evil. One of the forms he took is that of Rama, whose story is written in one of the Hindu holy books. Shiva is another important representation of God. He is the god who destroys old life in order to create new. Like Vishnu, Shiva has different forms. One of these is Kali, who is a goddess with great power.

Some of the other gods worshipped in the Hindu religion are Shakti, a mother goddess; Ganesh, who is the god of new beginnings and is represented as an elephant-headed god; Lakshmi, who is the god of wealth; and Saraswati, the goddess of learning and knowledge.

Hinduism is one of the oldest religions in the world, dating from about 1500 BC. Unlike some religions, which have a founder, Hinduism does not. It evolved over the course of many years and originated in India. The word 'Hindu' comes from a Persian word which means people who live by the river Indus. There are three main branches within Hinduism. Each of these worships a different representation of God: Vishnu, Shiva or Shakti. The three branches all believe in the same basic things, but may interpret and celebrate them in slightly different ways.

One of the things that is important in the Hindu religion is the principle of the three truths or three paths:

1   The law of identification: a person searching for his or her true self in relation to God. This can be found in the words written in the ancient language Sanskrit: *Tat twam asi*, which mean 'God and I are one'.
2   The law of Karma, which says that the way in which people behave will influence the form in which they are reincarnated in their next life.
3   The law of reincarnation: this is central to Hindu beliefs. All people are originally part of God, but they became separated from him. People are then caught up in the wheel of rebirth. They are born, live their lives, die and are reborn again. The aim of life is to become one with God again.

There are three paths to be followed that can lead to being reunited with God and so leaving the wheel of rebirth. The first path is to search for knowledge by reading and studying the Hindu religious books. The second path is to practise yoga and meditation, which will help both mind and body. The third path is to give devotion to God by worship, praying and serving him in daily life.

Knowledge can be gained by studying the Hindu religious scriptures. The most sacred and important of these is called the Rig Veda, which is a part of the *vedas* or holy books. The word *veda* means spiritual wisdom. There are four *vedas*, which were originally written in the ancient language of Sanskrit. They contain the duties of religious life and are called the Rig Veda, the Sama Veda, the Yajur Veda and the Atharva Veda.

The other holy books in the Hindu religion are the Brahmanas, the Upanishads, the Law Codes, the Puranas and the Great Epics. The two great epics are very important. The *Mahabharata* contains the story of the struggle of two families and the *Bhagavad Gita*, or the song of God, which describes the three paths to religious realization. The *Ramayana* contains the stories that explain Hindu beliefs. One story is about Rama and Sita, and is celebrated during the festival of Diwali.

The structure of Hinduism is made up of castes or social divisions that people are born into. Hindus believe that these are essential parts of the body. All are equally important and cannot work without the other parts that make up the whole. Table 3.3 shows the castes. There are also some people who are not born into a caste (Harijans).

Many Hindus worship God at home. There may be a shrine, a special place dedicated to God, in the home. There is no special day of the week that is considered to be more holy than the others when Hindus may join together to worship. The place where Hindus meet together in public to worship is called a temple or mandir. The mandir is usually dedicated to one main god, but will also have images of the other gods in it. These may be in the form of pictures or statues. The statues are treated in the same way as people. They are washed, put to bed and got up again to worship. A food offering, called a *prasada*, is given. There is a sacred flame

Table 3.3 Hindu castes

People represented	Hindu name	Part of body likened to
Priests	Brahmin	Head
Nobles or warriors	Kshatriyas	Arms
Merchants/tradesmen and general populance	Vaishyas	Stomach
Craftsmen/labourers and servants	Shudras	Legs

burning in the mandir. When people enter the mandir they will take off their shoes as a sign of reverence.

Hindus also believe that there are special holy places. One of these is the River Ganges, which people visit in the form of a pilgrimage.

Major festivals

The Hindu calendar is based on the lunar calendar, which is dictated by the moon's rotation. The Hindu new year begins in April. Table 3.4 shows the major festivals.

Table 3.4 Major Hindu festivals

Month	Festival	Background information
April	Chaitra/ Varsha-Pratipada	First day of the new year in the Hindu calendar.
	Rama Navami	The birthday of Rama (one of the forms of Vishnu). Celebrated by reading the *Ramayana*. Making candles and putting images of Rama in them, which are covered until midday, which is the time Rama was said to have been born.
June	Ratha Yatra	Celebrated mainly in Puri, but also in other places. Honours Lord Jagannath, the Lord of the Universe.
August	Raksha Bandhan	Celebrates Indra, the king of the heavens, and is a festival of protection. Sisters tie a *rakhi* (or amulet) around their brothers' wrists to protect them from evil. Brothers give sisters gifts.
	Janamashtami	Celebrates the birthday of Krishna, one of the forms of Vishnu. Some Hindus may fast until midnight, the time Krishna is said to be born. Many people go to the temple and sing, dance and give out sweets.
	Ganesh-Chaturthi	Celebrates the festival of Ganesh, the elephant-headed god of new beginnings. This celebration lasts for ten days.

Table 3.4 cont'd

Month	Festival	Background information
September and October	Navaratri/ Durga Puja/ Dusserah	This festival has many different names, but all celebrate the same thing: Rama beating the ten-headed king Ravana, and Durga's killing of the buffalo demon, good triumphing over evil. This festival lasts from four to nine days. Special dances and plays are performed.
October	Divali (Deepavali)	The word Deepavali means 'cluster of lights', and Divali is the festival of lights. It celebrates Rama's return to his kingdom after defeating Ravana. It is also associated with other gods, depending on the area in which it is celebrated. The festival lasts from two to five days. Special food is eaten. Lamps (divas) are made and cards and gifts are given.
January	Makar Sankranti/ Lohri	A time for making good neighbours.
February	Vasanta Panchami/ Saraswati Puja	Celebration to honour Saraswati, the goddess of knowledge. Also celebrates the start of spring.
	Mahashivratri	A festival dedicated to Shiva. Prayers may be said all night and celebrations held during the day.
March	Birthday of Sri Ramakrishna	Celebrates the birth of Sri Ramakrishna, a great Hindu teacher.
	Holi	A celebration of spring. This festival lasts between two and five days. People may throw coloured water and powder over each other. There may also be processions, dances and bonfires.

Symbols

When Hindus go to the temple they chant the word '*om*', a sound representing God in Hinduism. The symbol for '*om*' is shown in Figure 3.4.

Figure 3.4 The symbol for *om*.

A Chance to Think 3
You have been asked to organize some activities for the Hindu festival Divali, the festival of lights.
What do you need to take into account when doing this?
What sort of activities could you do with the children?
Compare your answers with the sample answers in Appendix 3.

Islam

History and beliefs

Islam is the name of the religion followed by Muslims. The word 'Islam' is an Arabic word meaning 'resignation' or 'surrender'. Muslims believe they have to surrender their lives to God. Muslims believe there is only one God, called Allah. Allah gave his words to the prophet Mohammed, who, Muslims believe, is the last and greatest prophet of God.

Prophet Mohammed was born in Mecca in about AD 570. His father died when he was very young and he was brought up by relatives. He married his wife, Khedijah, at the age of 25 and had three daughters. Mohammed had been concerned about religious matters for some time and when he reached the age of 40 he spent time in a cave on Mount Hira, outside Mecca, meditating. It was here that he was visited by the Angel Gabriel. Angel Gabriel told him of God's message, that there was only one God and he was to be God's prophet and tell people about him. Mohammed returned to Mecca to tell people what he had experienced. At that time people worshipped many different gods. Most did not listen to Mohammed, but a few did and became his companions. These were mainly his family, with his wife Khedijah becoming the first Muslim.

In 622 Mohammed decided to leave Mecca because of persecution, and travel led to Medina. This was a very important date as it is the date taken for the start of the Muslim calendar. While he was in Medina, Mohammed organized both political and religious activities. In 630 Mohammed returned to Mecca with an army of followers. He went to a place called the Ka'ba, which was a religious site where people worshipped many different gods. He tore down the statues of the different gods and dedicated the Ka'ba to Allah. The Ka'ba is now the most holy place in the Islamic religion.

At the age of 63, Mohammed died. No one was named to take over leadership of this new religion, so one of his companions became his successor. He was known as a caliph. At the time of his death, the words Mohammed had received from God were not written down, as Mohammed could not read or write; he memorized what he had been taught. It was only after his death that the third caliph, Uthman, wrote them down in a book. They were written in classical Arabic in a book called the Qur'an. The first authoritative version was compiled in Medina in about 650. The Qur'an provides Muslims with an almost complete guide on life. It contains statements on how to pray and keep the pillars of Islamic faith and practice. It is the body of teaching that instructs governments how to treat their subjects and other states. It also contains social teachings that are the basis of law and personal contact in Muslim societies. This is the most holy book in Islam and has 114 chapters.

The second most important book contains writings about the life and times of Mohammed. This is called the Hadith. It contains the example set by Mohammed, which all Muslims should try to follow. The words of the Qur'an and the Hadith put together form the Sunna, which is a guide for Muslims on how they should live their lives and conduct themselves. Eventually principles of interpretation evolved which hold true in modern times. The *sharia* or 'highway' of divine commands and guidance is clear, and no aspect of life falls outside it, for there are matters that the Qur'an and Hadith could not deal with, as they did not exist at the time.

After Mohammed's death Islam spread throughout the Middle East. It developed different ways of interpreting things and different traditions. There are now two main groups of Muslims in the world. The largest group are the Sunni Muslims, comprising orthodox Arabs and Turks. They follow closely the Sunna laid down by the prophet Mohammed. The second group comprises the Shi'ite Muslims, who have imams or teachers to interpret the word of the prophet Mohammed for them. The Shi'ites are mainly restricted to Iran.

Central to all Muslim beliefs are the Five Pillars of Islam. These are the five tenets that Muslims should hold to:

1   Belief in one god. This is called *shahadah*, and says, 'There is no God but Allah, Mohammed is the prophet of God.'
2   Prayer. This is called *salah*. Prayer is an important part of the Islamic religion. Muslims should pray five times a day and the prayers involve a set of movements. The first prayer takes place at daybreak, followed by further prayer at noon, mid-afternoon, sunset and at night. There are special rules laid down about how to pray. Before praying people should wash their hands, arms, face, head, legs and feet. When they pray they should use a special prayer mat and they should face Mecca. People can pray anywhere as long as they face Mecca.
3   Fasting. This is called *sawm*. Every year, during the month of Ramadan, Muslims fast. This means that between the hours of sunrise and sunset they do not eat, drink, smoke or have sex. Ramadan is a time of self-control and a chance to think and cleanse the body. It lasts for a complete lunar month. Young children and people who are ill or pregnant do not have to fast.

4   Compulsory charity. This is called *zakat*. Every year Muslims have to give part of their income to charity, usually around 2.5 per cent. The money can be given to the poor, or be used to build hospitals or schools, for example.

5   Pilgrimage. This is called *hajj*. During their life, Muslims should make a pilgrimage to Mecca, the holy city of Islam, if they are able to. During this time they will visit the Ka'ba. Men wear special clothes and women dress modestly.

Islam also contains the Articles of Faith. These are six things that Muslims believe in.

1   A belief in one God called Allah. Muslims have 99 names for God and they recite them all. Two of these names are God the Great and God the Merciful.

2   The Qur'an contains the words of God. The book was written by God and Mohammed was his messenger.

3   A belief in angels. Angels are God's messengers and it was the Angel Gabriel who spoke to Mohammed to give him the words of God. Angels are made of light. There are also *Jinn*, who can be good or bad.

4   God sent prophets into the world to tell people about him. There have been many prophets, including Moses, Abraham and Jesus. Muslims believe that Mohammed was the last and greatest prophet. When they say or write his name they also add the words 'peace be upon him'.

5   God has set a course for people's lives and controls them. People do still have free will that they can exercise but only within the course of life that God has set for them.

We have already seen that it is possible for Muslims to pray anywhere. There is also a special building called a mosque where Muslims meet together to pray and worship God publicly. Men and women will pray in separate areas of the mosque. All who enter the mosque must take off their shoes and wash before they pray. There are no statues or pictures of people or things in the mosque as this is forbidden by the Qur'an. The building will be decorated with patterns and Arabic writing from the Qur'an. Muslims consider Friday to be a special holy day. Families may go to the mosque, where a sermon will be preached.

Major festivals

Islam has only two officially recognized major festivals. These are Id-ul-Fitr and Id-ul-Adha. However, other events are celebrated. The Muslim calendar is based on the lunar calendar. This means that festivals will be celebrated on different days each year. The Islamic year has twelve months, but the months all have 29 or 30 days. This means that they will correspond with different Western months in different years. The Muslim calendar moves forward throughout the secular year. One year Ramadan may be in the winter, another year it may be in the summer. The Islamic year starts with new year celebrations at the beginning of the twelve months. Table 3.5 shows Islamic festivals.

Table 3.5 Major Islamic festivals

Month	Festival	Background information
Month 1 Muharram	Muharram/Al Hijra	New year's day. The life of Mohammed is remembered and greetings are exchanged.
	Ashura, tenth day of Muharram	This is remembered by Shi'ite Muslims as the day the grandson of Mohammed died. They may fast on this day. Sunni Muslims may fast as well.
Month 3 Rabi'al-Awwal	Milad-an-Nabi	Commemorates the birthday of Mohammed. There may be processions, and people may tell stories about Mohammed's life.
Month 7 Rajab	Lailat-ul-Isra	The night of ascension. Celebrates the journey Mohammed made to Jerusalem, when he spent a night in heaven. The Dome of the Rock is now built on the place where Mohammed ascended to heaven. This is considered to be a very holy site, after Mecca and Medina.
Month 8 Sha'abaan	Lailat-ul-Bara'ah	The night of forgiveness. Muslims see this as a preparation for Ramadan and the fast. They may stay up all night to pray. Special food and sweets are prepared and given out.
Month 9 Ramadan	Ramadan	The month of fasting from sunrise to sunset. The fast will be broken every evening with a meal.

Table 3.5 cont'd

Month	Festival	Background information
	Lailat-ul-Qadr	The night of power celebrated towards the end of Ramadan. Muslims may pray all night and read the Qur'an.
Month 10 Shawwal	Eid-ul-Fitr	A festival to mark the end of the fast. Families may go to the mosque. Special meals may be eaten and presents given.
Month 12 Dhul-Hijjah	The Hajj	The pilgrimage to Mecca.
	Eid-ul-Adha	Celebrates the end of the Hajj pilgrimage. A two- to four-day celebration. Muslims may sacrifice animals, with one-third of the sacrifice being given to the poor. This is the most important festival of the year.

Muslim symbols

The moon and the stars are important symbols in Islam. Muslims believe that Islam guides people through life just as the stars and the moon guide people over the desert. The crescent moon symbol is used by the Red Crescent, which is the Islamic equivalent of the Red Cross.

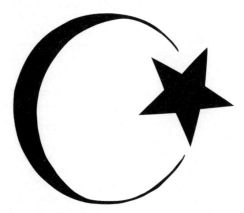

Figure 3.5 The crescent moon and star.

A Chance to Think 4

Your setting is short-staffed and is employing workers from an agency to cover for the week. The worker the agency sends is Fatma, who is a Muslim. Fatma prays five times a day, at daybreak, noon, mid-afternoon, sunset and night.

How do you think this will affect the setting?

How will the setting ensure that Fatma is able to pray at the times she is required to?

Compare your answers with the sample answers in Appendix 3.

Judaism

History and beliefs

Judaism is the oldest continuing faith in the world. Its most fundamental focus is the belief in one God. The Torah is the revelation of God's will, and contains every aspect of life. One of the most important things to strive for is the concept of loving one's neighbour and seeking justice and compassion.

Abraham is considered to be the first Jew. He was born and brought up in Chaldees (Iraq), in a society that worshipped idols. Abraham became aware that this was not right, left his birthplace and moved to a land that later became known as Israel. Abraham and his descendants were the first to worship the one God.

Many centuries later, Moses, the great prophet, led the children of Israel out of Egypt, where they had been slaves for many generations. He led them for 40 years through the desert until they arrived in the land of Israel. During this time Moses received the Ten Commandments from God on Mount Sinai. This code of laws later formed the basis of both Christianity and Islam:

1   You shall only have one God.
2   You shall not make false idols.
3   You shall not take the name of the Lord in vain.
4   You shall keep the Sabbath day holy.
5   Honour your father and your mother.

06 You shall not murder.
07 You shall not commit adultery.
08 You shall not steal.
09 You shall not give false testament.
10 You shall not covet your neighbour's house.

The Jewish Bible (called by Christians the Old Testament) is divided into three main sections. The first is called the Torah and consists of the first five books of the Bible. It contains the Ten Commandments and the 613 laws given by God dealing with every aspect of daily life: ethical, spiritual and practical. The Torah covers a time span from the creation of the world until the death of Moses.

The second part of the Jewish Bible is called Nevi'im (prophets), and consists of books of greater prophets, Isaiah, Jeremiah and Ezekiel, as well as twelve lesser prophets and the books of Joshua, Judges, Samuel and Kings. Nevi'im continues with the history of the Jews up to the Babylonian exile. Throughout the writings of the prophets is the fundamental belief that the Messiah will come and there will be a time of peace and tranquillity. The Jews do not believe that the Messiah has been, believing that the world needs first to be a worthwhile place. The third part of the Jewish Bible is called Ketuvim (writings).

There are different ways of observing Judaism. As in other faiths, people choose their own level of practice, which can extend from the very observant to the very liberal or progressive. Some Jews move from one strand to another.

Ultra-orthodox Jews believe that God personally wrote the Ten Commandments and the 613 commandments that followed. They believe that it is not up to any human to change any of these divine laws. The ultra-orthodox tend to live among themselves, have their own synagogues and schools and employ each other. Many adopt a style of dress that has not changed for centuries, and generally exclude the modern world from their midst. Ordination of women rabbis is not allowed.

Traditional orthodox Jews regard themselves as representing mainstream Judaism. They also believe that the laws were made by God, but at the same time they adopt a way of life that allows them to live as committed Jews in a changing modern world. In this group, too, ordination of women is not allowed.

The *reform* or *progressive* movement began in the nineteenth century in an attempt to recreate Judaism to allow its followers to conform more easily with life outside Judaism. Reform Jews believe that the Torah was inspired by God but written by human hand. Therefore the Law is open to interpretation to meet the changing needs of the community. The reform belief is that it is more important to observe the external parts of Judaism, like Shabbat, pursuit of justice and compassion, as against the laws that, for instance, disbar women from participating in certain rituals. The ordination of women is therefore accepted.

The *liberal* movement began as a splinter group of the reform movement and believes that sincerity in behaviour is more important than ritual. Women are ordained as rabbis.

The *conservative* movement began at the beginning of the twentieth century and is seen as lying between orthodox and reform Judaism, believing that the laws were inspired rather than written by God.

All the different sections within Judaism have rabbis. The rabbi is very learned in Jewish law and his or her role is as spiritual leader and teacher in the community. Rabbis do not act as an intermediary between the people and God and they do not necessarily lead the congregation in prayer.

The word 'synagogue' is Greek, meaning 'house of assembly'. This is the place were Jews meet to worship. It is also a focus for social events for people of all ages. In an orthodox synagogue men and women sit separately, with all the women in a gallery or on the same level behind a partition. Only men conduct services. In reform synagogues men and women can sit together and, religiously speaking, women can do anything men can do. Keeping the head covered is a sign of respect. Men wear some form of headgear, traditionally a small skullcap called in Hebrew a *kipah*. In an orthodox synagogue married women also wear a hat. Men in all synagogues wear a prayer shawl and in reform synagogues women are encouraged to do the same.

The most important part of the synagogue is the cupboard or alcove fronted by a decorative curtain and ornate doors. It contains the Torah scrolls and is usually on the eastern wall facing Jerusalem, the city holy to the Jews. The scrolls are sacred and must not be handled casually. A pointer is used to prevent people touching them when reading them.

Saturday is the Jewish Sabbath (Shabbat). Although it comes every week it is considered to be the Day of Atonement, the holiest day of the year. Shabbat begins just before sunset on Friday and finishes at nightfall on Saturday with a short ceremony in the home called *havdallah* (separation). During Shabbat it is forbidden for Jews to engage in activities that are considered to be work or creating: using electrical appliances or driving a car are considered work. The Shabbat laws are kept strictly by the orthodox but not so rigidly by progressive Jews. In all cases the Shabbat laws are set aside if there is a question of saving life.

Certain important events are marked in a person's life. For boys, the first of these is his Brit Milah, usually taking place eight days after birth, when he is circumcised. Circumcision takes place at home and is carried out by a qualified person, in the presence of family and friends. There is no equivalent ceremony for girls, but in orthodox synagogues prayers are said and in progressive synagogues a 'baby-naming' ceremony takes place.

At the age of 13 a boy becomes Bar Mitzvah. He marks the occasion by reading for the first time in public, and in Hebrew, the weekly portion from the Torah scroll, usually on Shabbat. He can now form part of the quorum of ten men needed to start a service and is expected to perform certain religious duties and be aware of his religious responsibilities. In orthodox synagogues there is now a ceremony called a Bat Chayil, which marks a girl's twelfth birthday. It is not a religious ceremony and usually takes place on Sunday. Progressive synagogues hold a service for girls in the same form as for boys.

Marriage takes place under a wedding canopy called a Cupah. Divorce has always been permitted but is regarded very seriously. The bill of divorce is called a Get.

A person's body is regarded as belonging to God and must be treated with respect. When someone dies the body is not left alone; a vigil is maintained until the burial. After the funeral, parents, spouses, siblings and children sit Shivah for seven days.

They sit on low stools in their homes and are visited by friends. Prayers are said every day.

Major festivals

The Jewish calendar starts counting from the creation of the world, and 2002 is the Jewish year 5762. The Jewish calendar is based on the lunar cycle. A year is usually 354 days. In a nineteen-year cycle an extra month is inserted seven times, each insertion forming a leap year. Because the solar and lunar years are different, no fixed dates can be given in the Gregorian calendar for Jewish festivals, although the dates in the Jewish calendar are fixed. Festivals are divided into three types: days of Awe, harvest festivals and minor festivals that are historical. Table 3.6 shows the major festivals.

Table 3.6 Major Jewish festivals

Month	Festival	Background information
Month 1 Tishri (September/ October)	Rosh Hashana	New year's day and the start of the Days of Repentance. The most serious time of the year. In the synagogue a ram's horn is blown to remind people of their sins and to think about how to get it right in the new year.
	Yom Kippur	This is the last of the ten days. It is the most solemn day in the Jewish calendar. People fast on this day and go to the synagogue to pray.
	Sukkot	This is a harvest festival. It commemorates the journey of the Jews from Egypt to Israel. Huts called sukkot are built and decorated with leaves, fruit and pictures. This is an eight-day festival. People may use the huts for eating in during this time.
	Simkhat Torah	Comes straight after Sukkot. It celebrates the fact that the Torah has finished being read and it is time to begin reading it over again. The Torah will be danced around the synagogue.

Table 3.6 cont'd

Month	Festival	Background information
Month 3 Kislev (November/ December)	Hanukah	Celebrates re-dedication of the second temple in Jerusalem. An eight-day festival. Every evening in the home one more candle is lit in the candelabrum known as a *chanukiah* until on the eighth day all the candles will be lit.
Month 5 Shevat (January/ February)	Tu B'Shevat	The new year for trees. The end of the winter season. Jewish communities all over the world plant trees.
Month 6 Adar (February/ March)	Purim	Celebrates the fact that Queen Esther saved the Jews of Persia from Haman, who tried to destroy them. Children wear fancy dress and go to the synagogue, where the book of Esther is read from the Bible. It is a happy carnival time.
Month 7 Nisan (March/April)	Pesach (Passover)	Pesach lasts for eight days. It commemorates the Jews fleeing slavery in Egypt and returning to the promised land. When they left Egypt there was no time to wait for the bread to rise and at Pesach no food containing yeast will be in the house. *Matzah* is eaten instead of bread. Pesach begins with a celebration meal called *seder*. The word *seder* means 'order'. A happy festival in which children are encouraged to participate.
Month 9 Sivan (May/June)	Shavuot	Also known as the Feast of Weeks, as it comes seven weeks after the start of Pesach. Celebrates the Jews receiving the Torah at Mount Sinai. The synagogue is decorated with flowers and the book of Ruth is read. Lasts for two days and is the harvest festival of olives, dates, grapes and figs. Dairy foods are eaten.

Jewish symbols

The origin of the six-pointed star is clouded, and it probably has no connection with King David. Although it has been found in the Ancient Synagogue of Capernaum, it was only officially adopted about 100 years ago. Today it is the central figure in the flag of Israel, and is often worn by men and women as a necklace.

The seven-branched candlestick, or *menorah*, has a longer association as an official Jewish symbol than the Star of David. The seven-branched candlestick was used in front of the altar in the temple and was never allowed to be put out. Today it is the official symbol of the state of Israel.

Figure 3.6 Star of David.

Figure 3.7 *Menorah*.

A Chance to Think 5

Elizabeth, a Jewish parent in your setting, has offered to come in and tell some stories to the children about Hanukah.

How would you react to this?

What value could this have to Elizabeth, the children and the staff in your setting?

Compare your answers with the sample answers in Appendix 3.

New religions

All religions have to have a beginning. Many groups that call themselves religions or faiths have begun to appear in society recently. Some of these new religions have been referred to as cults. The *Concise Oxford Dictionary* defines a 'cult' as 'a system of religious worship, especially expressed as ritual; a devotion of homage to a person or thing'. Workers may have heard of them through the media. Individuals may have met people on the street from different faiths wanting to share their faith with them. Many of these groups have strong, forceful leaders who will shape the group and its teachings. Some groups demand that their followers live in the way laid down by the leader. It is often young people who are interested in these new faiths. Some cause concern to people owing to their strong leadership of them and the way of life followed.

Not all new religions are cults: some have sprung out of existing religions but have different interpretations. Others are completely new with new beliefs and guidelines.

This section aims to try to give a short description of some faiths in a non-judgemental manner, so that if workers have families or colleagues in their settings who have been approached by or belong to these faiths they have some information about them.

Baha'i

The Baha'i faith was founded in Persia in about 1844 by Siyyid Ali-Muhammad, who was known to his followers as the Bab. The word *bab* means gate. The Bab was killed in 1850, and his work and teachings were taken forward by Mirza Husayn Ali, who had changed his name to Baha'u'llah. He lived for a time in Baghdad (Iraq) but spent the end of his life in Haifa (Palestine). Haifa is now a holy place for Baha'is.

Baha'is believe in one God and one religion. They believe that all religions come from God and are passed to people through messengers who live at different times. Jesus was one messenger, Baha'u'llah another, and Baha'is believe that God will send another messenger in the future to build on the work that has already been done. There are no leaders in the Baha'i faith; every Baha'i is thought of as a teacher. They are expected to live their life by a code of conduct that includes not drinking alcohol or taking drugs, and marriage is considered to be important. The Baha'is also believe that everyone is equal and is part of the world family.

The Baha'i calendar is made up of nineteen months, each containing nineteen days. The year starts in March. As well as having their own calendar they also have their own holy book and laws. Baha'is believe that people have souls and that heaven is being near to God and hell is being a long way away from God.

Christian Science

People who call themselves Christian Scientists belong to a church called the Church of Christ, Scientist. It was founded by Mary Baker Eddy, who was born in the USA. She married twice and spent her life looking for peace, by reading the Bible, and for healing, for which she looked to homeopathy for the answers. She found the answers to all her questions when in 1866 she believed she was healed from an injury by reading the Bible.

Mary Baker Eddy believed that prayer could heal people. She began to teach people about this, formed the Church of Christ, Scientist and wrote a book called *Science and Health with the Key to the Scriptures.*

Christian Scientists believe in one God. Bible study is an important part of their beliefs, as is reading and studying the *Christian Science Monitor.* This is a publication started by Mary Baker Eddy. They have their own churches and reading rooms.

Hare Krishna

The Hare Krishna movement was founded by Swami Prabhupada, who was a Hindu. He was born in India and spent most of his life there. He left India in 1965 to tell the world about his message.

Hare Krishnas follow the majority of the Hindu teachings. They study the Hindu scriptures, and believe that they are happy, have clear minds and know who they are. To achieve self-knowledge

Hare Krishnas chant a mantra. A mantra is made up of words or sounds that are repeated. The mantra used by the Hare Krishnas contains the names of God, such as Hare, Krishna and Rama. Hare means Lord, Krishna is the most important name for God and Rama is one of the other names used by Hindus to represent God. Like Hindus, Hare Krishnas believe in reincarnation.

Followers of the Hare Krishna movement live in temples. There are four stages to becoming a follower of the Hare Krishna movement:

1   Pre-initiation stage: a person is taught the movement, and may live in the temple.
2   Initiation: when people are ready they are given a hare name and formally join the movement by taking part in a fire ceremony.
3   Brahmin: this usually takes place about six months after the initiation ceremony and is when members are given their own mantra.
4   Sannyasa: this is the last stage, which only a few men get to. They have to promise celibacy, poverty, to preach and to do good things in their life.

Men are considered to be superior to women by the Hare Krishna movement. There are rules that should be followed in daily life. These include not eating fish, meat or eggs or drinking tea, coffee or alcohol. Sex is allowed only within marriage and then only to have children. Gambling and playing games are forbidden.

Jehovah's Witnesses

Jehovah's Witnesses are a worldwide Christian group who base their beliefs solely on the Bible. The group's origins can be traced to the 1870s, when a Bible study group was started by Charles Taze Russell, from Pittsburgh. The name of the group was changed to the Jehovah's Witnesses in 1931. Jehovah's Witnesses believe in the Bible as the word of God, and consider its books to be inspired and historically accurate. The New World translation is a translation of the scriptures from Hebrew, Aramaic and Greek into modern-day English.

There are two formal parts to worship. The first is baptism, which is an outward symbol by which individuals are welcomed into the faith and dedicate their lives to do God's will. The second, memorial, is a symbol of Christ's death, and is known as 'The Lord's Supper' or 'The Lord's Evening Meal'. Jehovah's Witnesses also meet together at five weekly meetings to study the Bible and other writings.

Jehovah's Witnesses believe that they are not allowed to receive blood in any form. This means that they are not allowed to have blood transfusions, although alternatives to transfusions (e.g. synthetic blood substitutes) are permitted. Jehovah's Witnesses do not celebrate any special festivals, as they do not appear to them to have any religious connections, although they respect the right of others to celebrate. Nor do Jehovah's Witnesses attend any kind of worship or religious education that is not held by the Jehovah's Witnesses themselves.

Mormons

Mormons belong to the Church of Jesus Christ of Latter Day Saints, founded by Joseph Smith, who was born in the USA in 1805. At the age of 14, Smith saw a vision of God, who told him not to join any of the churches but to be prepared for important work. When he was 18 he had another vision. This time it was of an angel called Moroni. The angel told him how to find a book written on gold in a language that was not English, which told the story of the history of the Americans. When he was 22, Smith translated the book he had found. The book was called *The Book of Mormon* and was published in 1830.

Joseph Smith and his church moved around America, often attracting trouble because of the views they held. Smith was eventually imprisoned and in 1844 he was killed in prison. The Mormons decided to move to Utah, where they built Salt Lake City, which is still the centre of the Mormon faith.

Mormons believe that Joseph Smith was a prophet and that all Mormons are saints. *The Book of Mormon* is their holy book. They may fast on the first Sunday of the month and they do not drink tea, coffee or alcohol. The most famous Mormon family is probably the Osmonds, several of whom formed a pop group in the 1970s.

Scientology

The Church of Scientology was founded by Lafayette Ron Hubbard in the 1950s. The church claims that it can improve people's lives and help with their problems. L. Ron Hubbard served in the US navy during the Second World War and was certified dead on two occasions. He said he got his health back using the principles of 'dianetics'. He wrote a book about it in 1950, called *Dianetics: The Science of Mental Health.* This was the beginning of Scientology. In 1967 there was some debate in the USA as to whether Scientology could be classed as a religion, but it is now seen as one.

Scientologists say that there are four parts to man:

1 the thetan: an immortal spirit, which is reincarnated;
2 the physical body: at conception a thetan enters the body;
3 the analytical mind: consciousness when a person acts normally;
4 the reactive mind: the subconscious.

Scientologists believe that man is good; Scientology can help man be closer to God; salvation can only be achieved through counselling, and Scientology can help people to solve their problems.

Many high-profile people are Scientologists, especially in the USA, including Tom Cruise, Nicole Kidman and Lisa Marie Presley.

Unification Church (Moonies)

The Unification Church was founded by Sun Myung Moon in 1954. Its followers are better known as Moonies. At the age of 16, Sun Myung Moon believed he saw a vision of Jesus. He then spent nine years studying the Bible and becoming an engineer. During this time he believed that he received further visions of Jesus, God and other prophets, who, he said, told him about the teachings of the Unification Church. These teachings were later written down by one of his followers in a book called *The Divine Principle.*

Moonies believe that they are to build a healthy and moral society by having God-centred families. They believe that because the first man created by God, Adam, sinned against God, this affected the rest of humanity. God then sent Jesus, who was killed before he could finish his work, so the world is still waiting to be saved by a new messiah.

Marriage is important in the Unification Church. It is the way in which God-centred families will be produced. Moonies also believe that people can only enter heaven in families. Marriages are arranged for people by the church. Moonies usually live together in large communities, spending their time involved in praying, working and recruiting new members. They worship on Sundays, with men and women sitting separately.

Rastafarianism

History and beliefs

Rastafarianism is a fairly new religion. As well as being a religion it is a way of life. It began in Jamaica in the 1920s, and has links with both Christianity and Judaism.

Marcus Garvey, who died in 1937, is the prophet of Rastafari. He was aware that the effects of slavery were still being suffered by black people. He is said to have prophesied, 'Look towards Africa where you will see a black king crowned, then you will see redemption.'

In 1930, in Ethiopia, a prince called Ras Tafari was crowned emperor of Ethiopia. Ras means prince and Tafari means he is to be feared. Ras Tafari took the name Haile Selassie when he became emperor. Haile Selassie traced his descent from King Solomon and the Queen of Sheba. At his coronation he was given the titles King of Kings, Lord of Lords, Conquering Lion of the Tribe of Judah. Rastafarians believe that Haile Selassie was the king that Marcus Garvey was talking about. They believe this is backed up by a passage in the Bible (Revelation 19:16), which says, 'And on his robe and on his thigh there was written the name: King of kings and Lord of lords.' Rastafarians believe that Haile Salassie was the living God, whom they call Jah. They believe that God became man as Haile Selassie, not as Jesus. They see Jesus as one of God's prophets, who came to live out the word of God, not as his son. Haile Selassie visited Jamaica in 1966, where he received a great welcome. Legend has it that he said to his followers, 'Warriors, priests, dreadlocks, I am he!'

Rastafarians base their beliefs on the Bible, both the Old and New Testaments. They do not cut their hair. It is left to grow into matted dreadlocks and covered with hats or scarves. This is based on the book in the Bible called Leviticus: 'They [priests] shall not make bald patches on their heads as a sign of mourning, nor cut the edges of their beards' (Leviticus 21:5). Haile Selassie is thought to have had dreadlocks when he was young.

Rastafarians do not have a place of worship. Some Rastafarians go to the Ethiopian Orthodox church to worship. Others meet in a hall or in each other's homes to discuss the Bible. Rastafarians also meet together on special occasions. Such a gathering is called a *nyahbinghi* or *'binghi*. Music, drumming, chanting and singing play an important part in these gatherings.

Reggae music is a popularized form of *nyahbinghi* drumming and chanting. A *'binghi* may last between three and seven days. Marijuana is smoked at these gatherings (and on a daily basis), as Rastafarians believe that it is a natural herb and given by God to be used to communicate with him.

Rastafarians also use their own version of English. They believe that God is within them. God spoke of himself as I and so the language is based on the letter I. This is to symbolize oneness with God. Vital food is Ital, holy is Ily, I and I means you and me or we.

Major festivals

Rastafarians follow the Ethiopian calendar. This is made up of thirteen months, twelve of thirty days and the thirteenth of five days or six in a leap year. The years follow a four-year cycle. Each year takes the name of an Apostle: Matthew, Mark, Luke or John. The year starts in September. Table 3.7 shows the major festivals.

Table 3.7 Major Rastafarian festivals

Month	Festival	Background information
September	Ethiopian new year's day	This takes place on 11 September. Each year is named after an apostle. It may be celebrated with praying, singing, dancing and drumming.
November	Anniversary of coronation of Haile Selassie as emperor (1930)	This takes place on 2 November. It is one of the holiest days of the Rastafarian year. It may be celebrated with praying, singing, dancing and drumming.
January	Ethiopian Christmas	This is celebrated on 7 January. It does not celebrate the birth of Jesus but recognizes his life and work.
July	Birthday of Haile Selassie (1892)	This is celebrated on 23 July. It is one of the holiest days of the Rastafarian year. Usually celebrated with *Nyahbingni* drumming, hymns and prayers.

Rastafarian symbols

Rastafarians may wear Ethiopian Orthodox crosses as a symbol of their Christian beliefs, and in acknowledgement of Ethiopia as their spiritual home. The lion is also an important symbol. It is considered to be a royal animal. It is mentioned in the title Conquering Lion of Judah, given to Haile Selassie at his coronation. Haile Selassie kept lions in his palace in Ethiopia. Rastafarians believe that Haile Selassie symbolized the bringing together of the power of animals, humans and all life in the last days.

A Chance to Think 6

Tafari, a Rastafarian boy in your setting, keeps his locks covered with a hat. You hear a new member of staff telling him to take off his hat indoors.

What would you do in this situation?

Compare your answers with the sample answers in Appendix 3.

Figure 3.8 Lion and Ethiopian cross.

Figure 3.9 Ethiopian Cross.

Sikhism

History and beliefs

People following the Sikh religion believe in one God. The founder of the religion was called Guru Nanak. Guru Nanak was born in 1469 in a small village called Talvandi, which is now in Pakistan. He married and had two sons. He gave up married life to try to find God's way. When he was 50 years old he built a town called Kartarpur. Many people came to see him and listen to his teachings. These people became his followers and were called Sikhs.

One of the teachings of Guru Nanak was about how to find salvation. He taught that salvation can only be reached by meditating on the name (*nam*) and the word (*sabad*) of God. In order to do this, people need teachers (*gurus*) to help them. When they think about the name and word of God they will have harmony (*haukam*).

When Guru Nanak died he chose another guru to carry on his work. All gurus chose the people who were to continue their work. Some chose their sons and others chose their followers as the next guru. There were ten gurus, who all made a contribution to the Sikh faith and helped it evolve to how it is today:

01 Guru Nanak, who founded the Sikh faith and wrote hymns;
02 Guru Anghad, who built temples and wrote down Guru Nanak's hymns;
03 Guru Amar Das, who introduced religious ceremonies and communal meals;
04 Guru Ram Das, who founded the town of Amritsar, a holy place;
05 Guru Arjan, who built the golden temple at Amritsar, put together all the hymns of the gurus in one book, called the Adi Granth, and was put to death as a martyr;
06 Guru Hargobind, who developed guidelines for living;
07 Guru Har Rai, who started hospitals;
08 Guru Har Krishna, the youngest guru, who died when he was 8 years old;
09 Guru Tegh Bahadur, who preached that everyone should be

able to worship whom he or she wants to, and was put to death because of this;

10 Guru Gobdin Singh, the last human guru.

Guru Gobdin Singh did not choose a human guru to follow him. He said that the scriptures were more important than the people who interpreted them. He felt that the Sikh faith had grown and developed, and did not need another person to take it forward. He made the Guru Granth Sahib the last guru. The Guru Granth Sahib is the writings of the Sikh faith. They are written in the script called Gurumukhi, a script started by Guru Anghad. The Guru Granth Sahib has 1430 pages and contains writings on how to live life.

Guru Gobdin Singh also formed the Khalsa. This is a form of Sikhism that follows the guidelines laid down by Guru Gobdin Singh. The word 'Khalsa' means 'God's own'. There are five symbols traditionally worn by the Khalsa, called the five Ks.

1   Kesh: uncut hair. Sikhs do not cut their hair.
2   Kanga: combs to hold the hair in place.
3   Kirpan: dagger. This is a sign of defending the faith, and is not used as a weapon.
4   Kara: steel bangle, a sign of eternity.
5   Kaccha: short trousers, a sign of action.

Men may also wear turbans like Guru Gobdin Singh. This is to keep their hair clean and in place. Some Sikhs may cut their hair and not wear a turban.

Sikhs believe that there are five prayers that should be said every day, three in the morning and two at night. They may be said at home or in the gurudwara, the place where Sikhs meet together. The word 'gurudwara' means place of the gurus. The gurudwara is an important place, used for worship and for community activities. There are no statues or pictures of God in it. When people enter the gurudwara they take off their shoes and cover their heads. The Guru Granth Sahib sits on a cushion with a canopy over it. It is treated like a person. It has a special resting place where it is taken each night, and it is returned to the cushion in the morning. Women and men sit separately during services. Music is an important part of the service. Everyone going to the gurud-wara will be given a special food to eat, called karah. After each service there will be a meal, to which everyone is invited. The meal will be prepared by women and men, who have equal status in Sikhism.

There are important events that take place during life. The first is the naming ceremony, where the new baby is taken to the gurudwara to be named. The second is the initiation ceremony. This marks the time when children become adults and join the Khalsa. This is where they will formally take the Sikh family name. This was the name chosen by Guru Gobdin Singh to show that all Sikhs belong to the same family. Boys are called Singh, which means lion, and girls are called Kaur, which means prin-cess. Marriage is the third important ceremony in a person's life. The last ceremony is cremation, which happens soon after the person's death. This is the ceremony where he or she goes to meet God.

The holiest place in the Sikh religion is the golden temple at Amritsar in the Punjab, which was built by Guru Arjan. Some Sikhs will visit the golden temple as a form of pilgrimage.

Major festivals

The Sikhs use the same lunar calendar as the Hindus. Because the calendar is dictated by the movements of the moon, the festivals fall on different dates each year. All the festivals centre on the events that happened in the life of the gurus. The Sikh calendar starts in the spring. The major festivals are shown in Table 3.8.

Sikh symbols

The five Ks are the main symbols of the Sikh faith. There is also a special emblem, called the Khanda. This emblem is made up of a circle, a double-edged sword and two scimitar swords. The circle symbolizes eternity: the universe has no beginning or end. The edges of the double-edged sword in the centre symbolize protec-tion and punishment.

Table 3.8 Major Sikh festivals

Month	Festival	Background information
April/May	Baisakhi	Celebrates the founding of the Khalsa by Guru Gobdin Singh, and the new year. People may go to the gurudwara. Verses from the holy book are recited for 48 hours before the festival starts. This is seen as the first day of the Sikh year.
May/June	Martyrdom of Guru Arjan	Guru Arjan was the Guru who put together the Sikh holy book, the Guru Granth Sahib. He built the golden temple at Amritsar. He was tortured and put to death by the Mogul emperor. This festival remembers him.
October/ November	Birthday of Guru Nanak	Guru Nanak founded the Sikh religion. This is the most important festival in the Sikh year. The Guru Granth Sahib is read from start to finish. This is called Akhand Path, and starts 48 hours before the festival, so that it finishes on the morning of the festival. People may spend the whole day at the gurud-wara singing and listening to sermons. Food will be provided during the day.
December/ January	Martyrdom of Guru Tegh Bahadur	This festival remembers Guru Tegh Bahadur, who was put to death by the Mogul emperor. This was because he preached that people should be able to choose the faith they wanted to follow, and he would not change his faith to Islam. Special hymns are sung in the gurudwara.
January/February	Birthday of Guru Gobdin Singh	Celebrates the birth of the last human guru and all his achievements. People go to the gurudwara, where verses are read from the holy book and hymns sung. Food is provided.

Figure 3.10 The Khanda.

A Chance to Think 7
Rajinder is a father of two children in your setting. He wears the five Ks. You hear some of the other parents talking about this and saying that he must be looking for violence because he wears a dagger.

What would you do in this situation?

Compare your answers with the sample answers in Appendix 3.

Useful publications

General

Allan, J., Butterworth, J. and Langley, M. (1987) *A Book of Beliefs: Religions, New Faiths, the Paranormal.* Lion Publishing.

Bach, M. (1977) *Major Religions of the World.* Abbingdon Publishers.

Bancroft, A. (1985) *The New Religious World.* Macdonald.

Bowker, J. (1997) *World Religions.* Dorling Kindersley.

Breuilly, E. and Palmer, M. (1993) *Religions of the World.* Sainsbury's/ HarperCollins.

Bury Business Centre (n.d.) *Articles of Faith.* Bury Business Centre, Kay Street, Bury BL9 6BU.

City of Westminster (n.d.) *Things of the Spirit: SACRE Guidelines for Collective Worship.* Broadgate.

Kindersley, A. (1997) *Celebration!.* Dorling Kindersley.

Buddhism

Publication for children

Samarasekara, D. and Samarasekara, U. (1986) *I Am a Buddhist.* Franklin Watts.

Christianity

Publication for adults

The Bible.

Publications for children

Killingray, M. and Killingray, J. (1986) *I Am an Anglican.* Franklin Watts.

Pettenuzzo, B. and Braham, M. (1985) *I Am a Roman Catholic.* Franklin Watts.

Roussou, M. and Papamichael, P. (1985) *I Am a Greek Orthodox.* Franklin Watts.

Williams, M. (1989) *The First Christmas.* J Sainsbury plc.

Hinduism

Publication for adults

The Vedas.

Publications for children

Anon (1988) *Hindu Festivals*. Wayland.
Aggarwal, M. and Goswami, G. D. (1986) *I Am a Hindu*. Franklin Watts.
Deshpande, C. (1985) *Diwali*. A & C Black.

Islam

Publication for adults

The Qur'an.

Publications for children

Ahsan, M. M. (1987) *Muslim Festivals*. Wayland.
Wood, J. (1988) *Our Culture: Muslim*. Franklin Watts.

Judaism

Publication for adults

The Hebrew Bible.

Publications for children

Lawton, C. and Goldman, I. (1986) *I Am a Jew*. Franklin Watts.
Turner, R. (1985) *Jewish Festivals*. Wayland.

New religions

Baha'i

World Order of Baha'u'llah (1938) *Shoghi Effendi*. Baha'i Publishing Trust.

Christian Science

Baker Eddy, M. (n.d.) *Science and Health with the Key to the Scriptures*. Christian
  Science Publishing Society.
The Christian Science Monitor.

Hare Krishna

Bhaktivedanta Book Trust (1983) *Chant and Be Happy: The Story of the Hare
  Krishna Mantra*.

Jehovah's Witnesses

Watch Tower Society (1984) *Awake!*
New World translation of the Bible.

Mormons

Church of Jesus Christ of Latter Day Saints (1981) *The Book of Mormon.*

Unification Church

Barker, E. (1984) *The Making of a Moonie.* Blackwell.
Unification Thought Institute (n.d.) *The Divine Principle.*

Rastafarianism

Publication for adults

Rastafarian Advisory Service (1988) *Focus on Rastafari: A Report.*

Publications for children

Gaynor, P. and Obadiah (1985) *I Am a Rastafarian.* Franklin Watts.
Yinka (n.d.) *Marcellus.* Akira Press.

Sikhism

Publication for adults

The Guru Granth Sahib.

Publication for children

Aggarwal, M. and Singh Lal, H. (1984) *I Am a Sikh.* Franklin Watts.

Chapter 4

Guidelines on personal care

We have seen in Chapters 2 and 3 that religions and cultures have guidelines on such things as how and when people should pray. In this chapter we will look in more depth at some of the other guidelines followed by different religions and cultures of which workers may need to be aware. We will look at the areas of diet, dress, hygiene, hair and skin care. This chapter will also examine these issues from a broader perspective, and will try to address the requirements for understanding and meeting the needs of all the individuals in our care.

Diet

The first area is diet. Here we define what we mean by the word 'diet', and look at what a balanced diet is and the influence food and drink can have in our life. This section also addresses some of the issues workers may need to consider when working with children, families and colleagues; for example, in menu planning, when cooking with children and at mealtimes.

A Chance to Think 1
There are often articles in magazines about diet. Some say, 'Follow this diet and lose 7 lb in a week.' Others say, 'New food discovered; try it in your diet.' Think about all the things you have heard about diets. When you think of the word 'diet', what do you think about?

Because we all have to eat and drink to stay alive, we all have a diet. The *Concise Oxford Dictionary* defines the word 'diet' as 'the kinds of food a person or animal habitually eats; a special course of food to which a person is restricted, especially for medical reasons or to control weight'.

It is important to understand that the diet a person follows may be influenced by a variety of things. People may choose a particular diet because of the guidelines laid down by the religion they follow. Other people may choose a diet because it fits in with their lifestyle or for moral reasons. Many people do not eat fish or meat because they disagree with the way animals are kept and killed. Some people do not eat it because they do not like the taste of it. People who do not eat meat, for whatever reason, are called vegetarians.

Some people may have little or no choice about the diet they follow. Some individuals may have special needs, which dictate what is eaten and how it is eaten. Their diets may be dictated by medical reasons, such as an allergy to a particular food. If a person is allergic to something it means that his or her body has

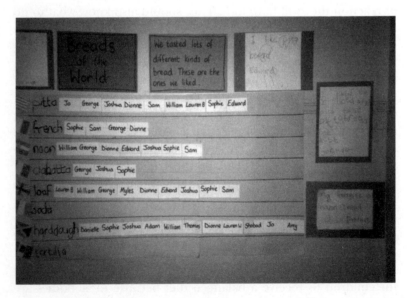

Figure 4.1 Breads that we like to eat.

A Chance to Think 2

Think about your own diet, the things you eat and drink. What do you enjoy eating and drinking? What do you dislike eating and drinking? Why is this?

Now talk to your family, friends or colleagues. Ask them if they will talk to you about their diets. Try to find out what sort of diet they follow and who or what has influenced their choice of diet. Some people may not want to tell you about their diet. Whatever happens, try to respect what people are telling you.

---

a hostile reaction to that thing. Some people are allergic to various ingredients contained in food or drink. This means that they must not eat or drink that ingredient. For example, some children are allergic to nuts. If they eat them their body may have a violent reaction, such as swelling up or an itchy rash, or they may be terribly sick. It is important for workers to be aware of children in the setting who are allergic to anything, and what sort of reaction they will have to it. They should also know what to do if a child does, by accident, ingest something to which he or she is allergic. Workers can obtain this information by asking parents or carers about a child's dietary or medical needs when the child first starts in the setting.

It is important, whatever diet a person follows, and whatever reason there is for following it, that it is a balanced diet containing all the different elements that are needed so that the body can receive all the nutrients it requires to grow and develop. The nutrients the body needs can be divided into six main groups. All six groups need to be present, and in the right amounts, to create a balanced diet. The groups are: proteins, fats and oils, carbohydrates, minerals, vitamins and water. For details of the food groups consult the works in the list of publications at the end of this chapter.

Everyone needs a balanced diet, but it is particularly important for children to receive a balanced diet because their bodies are still growing and developing. All childcare workers need to be aware of the dietary needs of the individual children that are in their care. This is especially true for those settings that provide meals for the children. Workers may be required to plan menus or cook food for the children in their care. In other settings, snacks may be given or cooking activities may take place.

There are other issues that need to be considered regarding food and diet, including the ingredients of different foods; for example, if a child is not allowed to eat pork, and the setting is having sausages for lunch, workers will need to check that beef or vegetarian sausages are provided as an alternative for that child. Food also needs to be presented attractively and appropriately for all children. Some children may need their food mashed or cut up depending on their individual needs.

One other important issue that needs to be thought through, for it plays a vital role in consideration of food and diet, is people's attitude to it. Everyone has an attitude to food and diet. Childcare workers are role models for children. The attitudes and behaviour workers display will be seen and heard by the children, and may be copied. This is especially true concerning food. Workers' reactions to food may influence how children feel about food and how their own attitudes to food are developed. There may be many different diets, or just one diet, followed in a childcare setting. There may be different ways of eating food (for example, with knives and forks, spoons or adapted cutlery, chopsticks or fingers). It is important that workers recognize, and try to respect, the different approaches people have to food and the way in which it is eaten.

People have different tastes when it comes to food and it is impossible for everyone to like or enjoy every type of food that is available. It is important, however, not to make negative or insulting remarks about food, people's diet or way of eating. Some children with special needs, for example, may need adapted cutlery, physical support or help when eating. It is important that children are treated as individuals and that their needs are catered for appropriately. Mealtimes are an important social activity, where adults and children interact together. They enable all children to learn about a variety of things, including food, diet, ways of eating and new vocabulary.

The Care Standards Act 2000 brought new guidance with it, including National Standards for Under Eights Day Care and Childminding. These were issued for full day care, sessional day care, crèches, out-of-school care and childminders. There are fourteen National Standards, which represent a baseline of quality below which no provider may fall. Standard 8, Food and Drink, states, 'Children are provided with regular drinks and food in adequate quantities for their needs. Food and drink is properly prepared, nutritious and complies with dietary and religious requirements.' The guidance for sessional day care amplifies this, pointing that adequate and nutritious food and drink are essential for children's well-being. The registered person and staff need to have a good understanding of children's dietary and religious requirements and meet these appropriately to promote children's healthy growth and development.

A Chance to Think 3

You are responsible for supervising Fred, a student in your setting. It is the first time he has helped you during lunchtime. All the children are sitting at the table waiting for lunch to arrive and talking about what they think it is going to be. Some children think it will be chips, others rice, and some think it will be spaghetti. When it does arrive it is spaghetti bolognaise. Fred says to the children, 'Oh, look. We have got worms for lunch and they are so long and slimy we will have to cut them up to kill them so we can eat them.'

What would you do in this situation?

Compare your answers with the sample answers in Appendix 4.

I mentioned at the beginning of this chapter some of the reasons why individuals may follow different diets. One of the reasons is the dietary guidelines or rules laid down by different religions. As outlined in Chapters 2 and 3, it is important to remember that individuals may follow all, some or none of the guidelines laid down by the various religions. The only way to be sure of what the children in our settings are able or allowed to eat is to ask parents when they start in the setting. It is important that workers do not make the assumption that groups of people who follow the same religion all have the same diet.

We now look at an overview of some of the guidelines laid down by different religions. This shows the main foods that may be eaten and those that may not. It does not show all the foods that may be eaten, as it is impossible to mention every type of food available. It also shows times of fasting followed by the particular religion. It is important to remember that this is an overview. For those people wanting more information, talking to colleagues and parents sensitively is a good way of finding out more information. An information list is given at the end of the chapter. As before, the guidelines are given in alphabetical order.

Buddhism

Some Buddhists are vegans. This means they will not eat any animal or animal product. Vegetarian and vegan food and non-vegetarian food should not come into contact with each other. Workers should use separate utensils in the setting to serve vegetarian and non-vegetarian food. If this is not possible, utensils should be washed between serving of the different foods.

May eat	May not eat	Fasting
Eggs (by some people)	Meat	Some Buddhists fast.
Cheese (vegetarian)	Fish	
Yogurt (vegetarian)	Shellfish	
Milk (soya)	Animal fat	
Fruit	Alcohol	
Vegetables		

Christianity

The different Christian denominations (see Chapter 3) may have different dietary guidelines. Generally no food is forbidden. Some Christians may abstain from meat and eat fish on Fridays.

May eat	May not eat	Fasting
All foods	No foods are forbidden Some Christians may not drink alcohol	Some Christians may fast on some holy days or during Lent. Some Christians may give up certain foods in Lent (see Chapter 3).

Hinduism

Some Hindus are vegetarians. In the Hindu religion the cow is considered to be a sacred or holy animal, so it is not eaten. Eggs are seen as a source of life and are generally not eaten. Workers should ensure that vegetarian and non-vegetarian foods do not come into contact with each other. Separate utensils should be used to serve the different foods. If this is not possible, utensils should be washed between serving of the different foods.

May eat	May not eat	Fasting
Cheese Milk Pork (unless vegetarian) Chicken (unless vegetarian) Lamb (unless vegetarian) Vegetables Fruit	Beef Eggs Alcohol	Some Hindus may fast on holy days, such as Janamashtami (see Chapter 3).

Islam

There are very strict dietary laws in Islam that are laid down in the Qur'an. Muslims do not eat any meat products from pigs, as this animal is considered unclean. Any other animals that are eaten must be slaughtered according to Islamic law. Correctly slaughtered meat is said to be *halal*. Workers should ensure that prohibited food is not in contact with non-prohibited food. Separate utensils should be used to serve the different foods. If this is not possible, utensils should be washed between serving of the different foods.

May eat	May not eat	Fasting
Chicken (halal)	Pork or any products	Muslims fast during the
Lamb (halal)	from a pig	month of Ramadan (see
Beef (halal)	Yogurt with rennet	Chapter 3).
Fish (halal)	Alcohol	
Shellfish (halal)		
Animal fat (halal)		
Fruit, vegetables		

Judaism

There are very strict dietary laws in Judaism. The law of *kashrut* means that meat and dairy products must be stored separately and must not be eaten together in the same meal. Some families have two sets of utensils for preparing meat and dairy products respectively. Families who do not use two sets of utensils will wash utensils thoroughly between using them with meat and dairy products. Workers should also ensure they use separate utensils. If this is not possible, utensils should be washed between serving of the different foods. All animals eaten must be slaughtered according to Jewish laws. Food that complies with all the Jewish law is called *kosher,* and forbidden food is called *trayf.* All fruit and vegetables are kosher but not all animals are. In order for an animal to be kosher it must have cloven hooves and chew the cud. Before meat is cooked it must be soaked and salted for one and one-half hours to remove as much of the blood as possible.

May eat	May not eat	Fasting
Eggs (with no blood spots)	Pork or pig products	Jews fast during Yom
Milk	Shellfish	Kippur (see Chapter 3).
Yogurt	Rabbit	
Cheese (not made	Horse	
with rennet)		
Chicken (kosher)		
Lamb (kosher)		
Beef (kosher)		
Fish (with scales,		
fins and backbone)		
Animal fats (kosher)		
Fruit, vegetables		

Mormons

Mormons do not eat or drink anything with caffeine in it, as this is a stimulant. This means that workers need to check lists of ingredients in food products to ensure they do not contain caffeine.

May eat	May not eat	Fasting
Anything that does not contain caffeine	Tea Coffee Alcohol Anything that contains caffeine	Mormons fast once a month.

Rastafarianism

Some Rastafarians are vegetarians. Most Rastafarians follow an Ital, a natural and clean diet. Workers should ensure that separate utensils are used to serve food that is forbidden and food that may be eaten.

May eat	May not eat	Fasting
Eggs Milk Yogurt Fruit Nuts Herbs Vegetables Chicken (unless vegetarian) Lamb (unless vegetarian) Fish (unless vegetarian)	Pork or pig products Alcohol Shellfish	There are generally no periods of fasting.

Sikhism

Many Sikhs are vegetarians. The cow is regarded as a holy animal and Sikhs do not eat beef or any meat products from the cow. Eggs are seen as a source of life and are generally not eaten. Workers should ensure that vegetarian and non-vegetarian foods do not come into contact with each other. Separate utensils should be used to serve the different foods. If this is not possible, utensils should be washed between serving of the different foods.

May eat	May not eat	Fasting
Milk	Beef or any meat	Some Sikhs may fast or
Yogurt	products from the cow	restrict themselves to
Cheese	Eggs	certain foods.
Chicken	Fish	
(unless vegetarian)	Animal fats	
Fruit	Coffee	
Vegetables	Tea	
	Alcohol	

Presentation and eating of food

We have seen that some religions have guidelines and some have strict rules about diet. It is important to remember that different individuals may interpret or follow the guidelines differently. So, for example, workers may have two children in the setting who are Rastafarians but they may follow different diets. Some individuals follow a diet because of the guidelines laid down by their religion but they might also have medical or other reasons for following a diet.

A Chance to Think 4

You have a new little girl, Yasmin, starting in your setting. You are aware that Yasmin's family are Muslims but you are not sure of what this means for Yasmin's diet. How can you gather the information you need to ensure that you plan appropriate menus, so that Yasmin's parents are happy with the diet provided in the setting?

Compare your answers with the sample answers in Appendix 4.

We have seen that food and diet play an important part in a person's life. We have seen some of the reasons why an individual follows a particular diet. There may also be differences in the way food is presented and how it is eaten. This will be influenced by a variety of factors, the main one being the way individuals were brought up and how they saw food presented and eaten. Some families eat their meals sitting round a table, with the meal being the focal point for a social occasion. Other families eat their

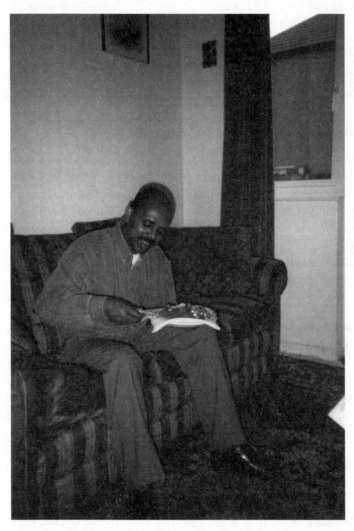

Figure 4.2 Eating Ethiopian *injera* (pancake).

A Chance to Think 5
We all eat different foods in different ways. Think back over all the meals you have eaten in the past week. Where were you when you ate and what did you use to eat them with? Did you eat with your fingers, with chopsticks, with a knife and fork?

What influences the way you eat your food?

meals sitting in front of the television. In some families people eat different meals at different times. Where food is eaten and what it is influence how it is eaten.

Most cultures have some food that is eaten with the fingers. Some children will eat all their food with their fingers if this is the way food is eaten at home. Children who then stay for lunch in the setting, where knives and forks are laid on the table, may be unsure of what to do with them. Workers need to value the experience and skill the children bring with them, whether it is eating

A Chance to Think 6
Mealtimes are a good time for workers to ensure that children experience a variety of foods from different countries and different ways of eating. Sarah works in a nursery where the children often have curry and naan bread for lunch. So that the children can fully experience how this can be eaten, Sarah has brought thali dishes for the children. This means that the meal can be served in the thali dish and the children are encouraged to use their fingers to eat the meal. This has been discussed with the parents and staff, who have all agreed that they would like it to take place.

What benefits do you feel that the children and adults in the setting are getting from this experience?

Compare your answers with the sample answers in Appendix 4.

with fingers or other implements, such as chopsticks, or a spoon and fork. The setting should try to be flexible and allow children to eat with their fingers or with the implements they are used to using at home. The other children in the setting can also learn the skill of eating with fingers or other implements. Children who are unfamiliar with knives and forks will soon learn the new skill with encouragement from the adults in the setting, and from observing the other children using them. It is important that children learning how to use new implements are not made fun of or ridiculed. This will make them feel that their experiences are not valued and will give the message to the other children in the setting that only one way of eating is right.

Mealtimes provide a valuable chance for children to interact together and learn from one another. They can learn about the way food is prepared and cooked. When you are doing this with children or talking about it with them, it is important to provide positive images and role models of both males and females preparing, cooking, serving and clearing up. Cooking with children is discussed in more depth in Chapter 5.

A Chance to Think 7

The setting you work in has a key worker system, with the children placed in family groups. One of the children in your group is Kevin, a 4-year-old with dyspraxia (difficulties with coordination and communication).

What do you think you need to be aware of when sitting down at mealtimes, for both Kevin and the other children in your group?

Compare your answers with the sample answers in Appendix 4.

Dress

The second area this chapter will cover is dress, including jewellery. We will examine what may influence a person's choice of dress, including religious, cultural, social and personal reasons for

---

A Chance to Think 8

Before going to bed at night, or when getting up in the morning, individuals may think or plan what they are going to wear. There are many different reasons for choosing to wear certain clothes or jewellery. Think about the clothes and jewellery you have worn over the past week.

What did you wear and why did you wear it?

---

that choice. This section also addresses some of the issues workers may need to consider when working with children, families and colleagues, for example when changing children, during play and when thinking about safety issues.

The *Concise Oxford Dictionary* defines the word 'dress' as follows: 'clothe, array (*dressed in rags; dressed her quickly*); wear clothes of a specified kind or in a specified way (*dresses well*); put on clothes; put on formal or evening clothes, especially for dinner; decorate or adorn'.

Childcare workers may spend at least part of their day carrying out activities that involve handling or talking about children's clothes or the way they are dressed. The most common example of this is helping children with toileting skills. At some stage during every day children go to the toilet. This will involve either the adult or the child rearranging the child's dress. In some cases it will mean removing part of a child's clothing. This is particularly true when individuals have wet or soiled themselves and may need changing.

Some of the children in the setting, or other individuals workers have contact with, might wear nappies or protective waterproof underwear. When you are thinking about who needs to wear nappies, it is important to remember it is not just babies. Older children and adults, as well as some children with special needs, may need to wear nappies and be changed. When they are changing someone, workers must be sensitive to the needs and feelings of the individual being changed. It should always take place in the bathroom or changing room away from others. Individuals should not be taunted or made to feel inferior or bad for needing to be changed.

There are several other issues that workers may need to consider regarding children's dress. One is the question of under what circumstances it is appropriate to alter or remove articles of children's clothing or jewellery. Reasons for doing this are when a child is too hot, for safety reasons (e.g. if a child wears clothes that constantly get caught up in equipment), making the child more comfortable or allowing the child to take part in an activity such as swimming. Before you alter a child's clothing or jewellery it is important to consider when it is not appropriate to do this. Workers need to be aware of, and to respect, the religious, cultural and social reasons that determine a child's or adult's dress. When they take children swimming, for example, workers need to consider that in some religions and cultures it is not considered appropriate for young girls to show parts of their bodies in public.

A Chance to Think 9

Lakshmidevi, a 4-year-old Hindu girl, attends your setting. She always wears lots of coloured bangles on both arms and sleeper earrings. These do not have any adverse affect on the way Lakshmidevi joins in the activities in the setting; nor do they have any safety implications. Some of the staff in the setting think that Lakshmidevi's jewellery should be taken off while she is in the setting as they are concerned about it getting lost or broken. They also think that this should be done after the parents have left, so as not to upset them. Lakshmidevi is not the only child in the setting who wears jewellery.

What do you think should be done in this situation?

What might be some of the consequences of removing Lakshmidevi's jewellery after her parents have left?

Compare your answers with the sample answers in Appendix 4.

The best way for workers to be aware of what is appropriate with regard to children's clothing and what is not is to ask their parents. Workers need to be aware of individuals' dress codes as they might have implications for the planning of outings, such as swimming, or during play activities, such as dressing up.

Some religions have guidelines about how a person should dress. Individuals follow these differently. Some people follow all, or some, of the guidelines, others do not follow any. The only way workers can be sure is not to make assumptions or judgements, but to ask individuals in a way that will not make them feel awkward or embarrassed.

There follows an overview of the guidelines laid down by some religions and cultures. It does not go into great detail as there is not enough space in this chapter to do this. Talking to parents and colleagues in a sensitive way about dress is a good way to obtain more information, or see the publications listed at the end of the chapter. Some of the guidelines apply to children and some apply to adults. It is important for workers to be aware of the guidelines for adults, as parents or colleagues may be following them.

Dress guidelines

Buddhism

Some Buddhists cover their hair. Jewellery may be worn from personal choice.

Christianity

There are no formal guidelines laid down on dress. Some Orthodox Christian women keep their hair covered. Generally, wedding rings are worn on the left hand by people who are married. Some individuals wear jewellery that has religious signifi-cance, such as a cross or crucifix (see Chapter 3). Other jewellery may be worn from personal choice.

Hinduism

Women should cover their legs, breasts and upper arms. Some Hindu women wear a sari. This is a long piece of material about five to six metres long, which is wound round the body in a special way. It is usually worn over a blouse and sometimes the midriff may be left bare. Some Hindu women wear a shalwar kameez. Shalwar are long loose trousers and a kameez is a long tunic with full- or half-length sleeves. Some women cover their hair with a long scarf called a chuni or dupatta. Married women may wear colourful clothes, wedding bangles and other jewellery which is generally not removed. Widows generally remove jewellery and wear white. Young girls may also wear bangles and jewellery, which should not be removed. Married women may also have a dot on their fore-head, called a bindi or chandlo. Some women who have been to a religious ceremony have a dot called a tilak put on their forehead by the priest.

Men should cover themselves between the waist and knees. Some Hindu men wear a kameez and pyjama or dhoti, which is a type of trouser.

Islam

Women should keep their bodies covered from head to foot. Any clothes worn should conceal the shape of their body. Some Muslim women wear a shalwar kameez, some a sari, some other clothing depending on cultural background. Muslim women should cover their hair. This may be done with a long scarf called a chuni or dupatta. Married women may wear wedding bangles, which are generally not removed. Other jewellery may be worn that has religious significance or from personal choice. Young girls may also wear bangles and jewellery.

Men should be covered from waist to knees. Some Muslim men wear a shalwar kameez and others may wear a gallibaya, again depending on cultural background.

Judaism

The different groups in Judaism have different guidelines on dress. Women should dress modestly. Some Jewish women cover their hair. This may be done by wearing a hat or headscarf. Some jewellery worn has religious significance; other jewellery may be worn from personal choice.

Men may cover their head with a hat or they may wear a kippa. This is a small round skullcap worn at all times by some men and by all men in the synagogue.

Rastafarianism

Rastafarian women, men and children may wear clothes in red, yellow and green. These are the colours in the Ethiopian flag. Some Rastafarians think of Ethiopia as their spiritual home. Some Rastafarian men and women have dreadlocks and keep their hair covered. Some jewellery is worn for religious significance, such as an Ethiopian cross; other jewellery may be worn from personal choice.

Sikhism

Women should cover their legs, breasts and upper arms. Some women wear a shalwar kameez, and some cover their hair with a chuni or dupatta. Some Sikh women wear a sari, usually over a

---

A Chance to Think 10

Shelan works in a day nursery. The manager of the nursery has decided that the children should go swimming once a week. It has also been decided that all the staff should take it in turns to supervise the sessions and go swimming with the children. The staff and parents have not been consulted about this.

Shelan is a Muslim, and observes the guideline that she should cover her hair and body in public. Shelan feels that she is unable to get into the swimming pool with the children, but she is happy to accompany the group to the pool and help with the session.

If you worked with Shelan, how would you feel about this?

How could you support Shelan during this time?

Compare your answers with the sample answers in Appendix 4.

blouse and underskirt. Married women may wear wedding bangles, which are generally not removed. Young girls may also wear bangles and other jewellery. Women may also have a bindi, a dot on their forehead which is considered fashionable. Other jewellery may be worn from personal choice.

Men should be covered from the waist to the knees. Some men may wear kameez and pyjama. Many Sikhs wear a turban. Young boys will wear a hair covering, which should not be removed. Some men also wear the five Ks (see Chapter 3).

We have seen that there are many different things for workers to take into consideration concerning children's dress. It is important that workers do not assume that all individuals have the same needs. Some individuals may dress in one way because of the guidelines laid down by their religion. Some individuals may have

---

A Chance to Think 11

James is a worker in your setting. Throughout his career James has been aware that some people think it is strange for a man to be working in a childcare setting. He is also aware that a few parents may have concerns about a man looking after their children, particularly when it comes to the area of supervising children in the bathroom and changing children. Because he is aware of these feelings and concerns, James has always ensured that he tries to deal with them and reassure parents. Lalita is an 18-month-old Hindu girl who is in the process of learning to use the potty. James is in the bathroom helping Lalita when her father arrives to collect her. Lalita's father says to James that he does not want him changing Lalita, as it is not right; he says he wants only female workers to supervise his daughter in the bathroom.

How would you feel if you were James in this situation?

How do you think this situation should be handled?

Compare your answers with the sample answers in Appendix 4.

lots of clothes and always come to the setting in what appear to be new clothes. Other individuals may not have many clothes, or may wear second-hand clothes. It is important that workers do not make judgements about colleagues, parents and children based on the way they dress or the number of clothes they have.

Workers also need to consider the needs, wishes and rights of adults they come into contact with through work. These include parents, carers, students, other professionals and colleagues. It is important that we do not assume that all adults will have the same reasons for choosing to dress in a particular way. Indeed, adults may alter their style of dress to suit the situation in which they are placed. Colleagues may wear one style of dress when working with children, and another when going to, for example, a child protection conference.

A Chance to Think 12

George is a student in your setting. On his first visit to the setting the manager explained that although the setting did not have a uniform, it did have certain expectations about the way individuals dressed. Workers and students were expected to dress in a way that would allow freedom of movement when they were with the children, and not to wear anything dangerous to themselves or the children, such as long dangly earrings or large belt buckles. Workers were also asked to dress in a way that would not be considered offensive to other staff or parents. After George had been in the setting for about a month he told his supervisor he was a transvestite, and asked if it would be OK for him to wear a dress to the setting.

What would you say if you were George's supervisor?

How do you think this situation should be handled?

Compare your answers to the sample answers in Appendix 4.

Often it is not easy for workers to hold in balance every consideration. Sometimes it might feel like walking along a tightrope when you try to keep everyone happy, not really succeeding. Sometimes workers disagree with what another person thinks, says or does, and occasionally mistakes may be made. It is important to realize that everyone is human, and no one individual can know everything and be right all of the time. The knowledge that mistakes may be made and that not everyone can always be satisfied should not stop people from trying to do what they think is right.

Some settings have a dress code that they expect staff to follow. In some settings workers may not be allowed to wear jeans to work. In other settings uniforms may be provided, such as a sweatshirt with the setting's name on it, or work clothes may be provided to keep workers' own clothes protected. In some settings workers may be expected to wear a particular colour. There can be several reasons for this, including presenting a particular image to the people who use the setting. Settings that have a dress code need to consider the needs of both the setting and those who work there.

The issues of settings providing dressing-up clothes and protective clothing for play will be addressed in Chapter 5.

Hygiene routines

The third area this chapter addresses is hygiene. Here, we examine what we mean by hygiene, how individuals' hygiene routines may vary and the things that may influence these routines. The section also addresses some of the issues workers may need to consider when working with children, families and colleagues – for example, hygiene routines, toilet training, hair and skin care. The *Concise Oxford Dictionary* defines the word 'hygiene' as 'a study, or set of principles, of maintaining health; conditions or practices conducive to maintaining health; sanitary science'.

Everyone's hygiene routine is based on, or influenced by, a variety of things. Children's routines will be influenced by the adults they have contact with, as well as their own independence skills. Adults' hygiene routines may be influenced by religious or cultural guidelines as well as personal preference and access to the equipment needed to facilitate hygiene routines. A family living in bed-and-breakfast accommodation, and having to share a

> **A Chance to Think 13**
> Everyone has a personal hygiene routine. Things this may include are keeping teeth clean, flossing teeth, keeping hair clean and tidy, shaving, using the toilet, having a shower, wash or bath, washing clothes and keeping them clean and tidy. Think about your own hygiene routine.
>   What does it consist of?
>   How often do you do these activities?
>   How would you feel if you could not carry out any of these activities?

bathroom with several other families, may have a different hygiene routine from a family with its own bathroom and washing machine. Sometimes individuals may have what workers consider different or inappropriate standards of hygiene (e.g. some families wear clean clothes every day, others wear the same clothes for more than one day). Some people brush their teeth three times a day, and other individuals brush theirs once a day. Some people wash their hair daily, others weekly and some less often. It is important that workers do not make judgements about individuals solely because they do not follow the same personal hygiene routine as themselves. Workers must be aware of the needs of the children in the setting regarding hygiene routines. All children should have a hygiene routine appropriate to their individual needs that allows them to remain healthy. If, and when, it is apparent that a child's health or welfare is suffering owing to a poor hygiene routine, then workers may need to discuss hygiene routines with parents and carers and support them in a non-judgemental manner. For example, if a child in the setting is coming in in the same clothes all week, has not been washed and smells, the other children or parents may make negative comments about the child. This is not a situation that anyone would ask to be in but it is important for workers to approach it in a sensitive manner by talking to the parents and trying to help them as appropriate. The child may, or may not, be aware of the situation, and some parents may not realize that this is an inappropriate hygiene routine. It may be that the family does not have access to a washing machine or many changes of clothes. Workers may be able to suggest ways of helping the parents to be aware of their children's needs and hygiene routines.

Some hygiene routines are influenced by religious or cultural traditions. For example, some Sikhs, Muslims and Hindus consider having a bath as not being clean, because of sitting in water that contains the dirt that has just been washed off. For this reason, many individuals prefer having a shower. Settings, particularly residential settings, that are involved in this part of a child's hygiene routine need to ensure that children are able to take showers. If this is not possible, then a bowl should be provided so that water can be poured over the body. Some Sikhs, Muslims and Hindus traditionally use the left hand for washing and the right hand for eating.

A Chance to Think 14

Jane and Tom are children who attend your setting. They are living on the fourth floor in a bed-and-breakfast hotel as the family are homeless. They have to share a bathroom with four other families on the same floor. They do have access to a washing machine, but it is in the basement and is often being used by other families. Jane and Tom's parents are on income support. Jane is 4 years old and very independent. She is always clean and well dressed. Tom is 15 months old and wears nappies. Sometimes when he comes to the setting he smells of stale urine and he is wearing the same nappy that he went home in.

What would you do in this situation?

Compare your answers with the sample answers in Appendix 4.

We have seen that hygiene routines can be influenced by many things. One that we have not yet discussed is a child's independence. Babies need to have everything done for them, and as children develop and become steadily more independent they are able to do more for themselves. It is important to remember that all children are individuals developing at different rates. How much children do for themselves will depend on their skills as well as what they are allowed to experience and do for themselves. A child with special needs, for example, may be able to gain total independence in his or her hygiene routines given time and encouragement, or may not. Some individuals never gain total control of their bowels, for example. Others are unable to wash themselves or clean their teeth owing to lack of physical coordination. Children with special needs should be allowed to participate as fully in their hygiene routine as they are able to. Children will only develop control over their hygiene routine if they are shown what to do and allowed to do things for themselves, while making mistakes and learning from them. For example, when children first start to go to the toilet on their own there are always accidents, until they learn to recognize when they need to go and know they need to allow time to get to the potty or the toilet. This will happen with different children at different ages, and may be affected by the external environment. If a family lives in bed-and-breakfast accommodation and the toilet is on a different floor, a child may take longer to develop independent skills in toileting. If a setting is involved in toilet training, this should be done in partnership with parents. Parents may have a different view from that of the setting and it is important that attitudes towards this are discussed, so that a coordinated approach can be taken. People belonging to some cultures do not use toilet paper and individuals will wash themselves after using the toilet. Workers need to provide a bowl of water so that this can happen.

Hair and skin care

We have seen that people have different general hygiene routines. They will also have different routines and needs with regard to skin and hair care. Some of these are because of religious or cultural tradition and some because of the type of hair and skin people have and individual ways of caring for it.

We saw earlier in this chapter that some religions have guidelines that hair should be covered. They are Orthodox Christianity,

A Chance to Think 15
Think about your own hair and skin care. What is your daily routine for caring for your hair and skin? Why do you do this? What would happen if you did not do this?

Now think about the children in your setting. What do you need to do about hair and skin care for the children in your setting?

Islam, Judaism, Rastafarianism and Sikhism. Some individuals follow these guidelines and others do not, but workers may have children in their settings, both boys and girls, who will keep their hair covered. Rastafarian men and women may grow their hair into dreadlocks. This happens when the hair is left uncombed and allowed to matt into locks. Although hair is not combed it is still cared for and groomed, and covered to ensure that dirt does not come into contact with the hair. Many Sikh men and women grow their hair long and do not cut it for religious reasons.

It is important for workers to be aware of the needs of the children in the setting regarding hair and skin care. All workers are involved in hair and skin care in some way or another, even if it is just because children wash their hands in the setting, or get sand in their hair. Workers in residential establishments will have much more involvement than workers in settings where children and parents attend together, or children attend for part of the day. The best way to get information about the needs of the children in the setting is to ask parents. Parents should also be informed about the types of activities that take place in the setting that may have an effect on a child's hair or skin, so that they can provide whatever is necessary or advise workers on how they would like them to deal with hair and skin care matters (e.g. nappy rash or children wearing sand hats to prevent getting sand in their hair).

There are many things to consider about hair and skin care. Some children have an allergy to soap. Some children have eczema, which requires the use of special creams. Some children need to use a moisturizer on their skin. Some children need their hair combed at the setting while other children do not.

Workers need to be especially careful about activities that might damage a child's hair or skin. Too much exposure to water in the water tray, the bathroom or when swimming can dry the skin and it may be necessary to have some hand cream or body lotion or cream for children to use. Black skin can get very dry after swimming or water play and may start to turn an ashy colour if not moisturized regularly. Parents should be fully informed of any type of lotions that the setting is using, as they may not want their child to use hand cream at all or they may want them to use a particular one that they use at home. Children's skins are all different; they are different colours and of different types, and it is important that they are respected as such and that settings do not have just one routine that is used by all children.

Outside play can also damage skin, especially in the summer, with the risks associated with exposure to the sun. All children, whatever their skin colour, can and do burn, and it is important that their skin is protected when they are outside by a sun tan lotion and by keeping them covered up as much as possible.

When children are swimming it is important to protect their hair. Some children who have to keep their hair covered for religious reasons will still need to do this when they are swimming. Some parents may want their children to wear swimming caps; others may want to style their child's hair in a particular way to keep it tidy. Children with long, straight hair may need their hair combed after swimming, whereas children with Afro hair, plaits or weaving may not.

It is traditional in some cultures to put oil, grease or fragrant oils in the hair for religious or cosmetic reasons. In others, people may put oil or grease in their hair to keep it in good condition. Workers need to acknowledge and respect this. If individuals do put oil or grease on their hair it means that some things may stick to it, such as sand. Getting sand out of Afro hair can be difficult as it can take a long time to comb through. It is a good idea for settings to provide sand hats, so that all children can play in the sand and not worry about getting it in their hair. This should be done in a positive way, with all children being able to wear hats if they want to, and not as a way of making children feel awkward or singled out.

Workers should, with parents' permission, check children's hair if there is an outbreak of head lice. All children, with whatever type of hair, can get head lice, but they may be slightly more difficult to detect in Afro hair. If children have head lice, parents should be advised on how to treat them. Some parents may be upset that their child has head lice, as they see it as being dirty and unclean. Workers need to reassure parents that having head lice is not due to dirty hair, and is not something to be ashamed of. Because head lice become resistant to treatments after a time, it is important for workers to keep up to date with what the current treatment is in their area. This information can be obtained from health visitors or pharmacists.

A Chance to Think 16

Amarjit is a four-year-old Sikh boy who attends your setting. He wears his hair uncut and plaited in a *jura* (bun) on the top of his head. This is covered with a white cloth. One day, by accident, the cloth comes off and Amarjit's hair comes down. Some of the other children notice this and start teasing Amarjit, saying that because he has long hair he is a girl. Amarjit is very upset by both the teasing and the fact that his hair has been uncovered.

What would you do in this situation?

Compare your answers with the sample answers in Appendix 4.

Useful publications

Anon (1988) *Food and Your Child.* Time Life Books.

Department for Education and Employment (2001a) *National Standards for Under Eights Day Care and Childminding: Childminding.* DfES. Also Department for Education and Skills (2001) *Childminding: Guidance to the National Standards.* DfES.

Department for Education and Employment (2001b) *National Standards for Under Eights Day Care and Childminding: Crèches.* DfES. Also Department for Education and Skills (2001) *Crèches: Guidance to the National Standards.* DfES.

Department for Education and Employment (2001c) *National Standards for Under Eights Day Care and Childminding: Full Day Care*. DfES. Also Department for Education and Skills (2001) *Full Day Care: Guidance to the National Standards*. DfES.

Department for Education and Employment (2001d) *National Standards for Under Eights Day Care and Childminding: Out of School Care*. DfES. Also Department for Education and Skills (2001) *Out of School Care: Guidance to the National Standards*. DfES.

Department for Education and Employment (2001e) *National Standards for Under Eights Day Care and Childminding: Sessional Care*. DfES. Also Department for Education and Skills (2001) *Sessional Day Care: Guidance to the National Standards*. DfES.

Henley, A. (1982) *Caring for Muslims and Their Families: Religious Aspects of Care*. National Extension College.

Henley, A. (1983) *Caring for Hindus and Their Families: Religious Aspects of Care*. National Extension College.

Henley, A. (1983) *Caring for Sikhs and Their Families: Religious Aspects of Care*. National Extension College.

Hill, S. (1990) *More than Rice and Peas: Guidelines to Improve Provision for Black and Ethnic Minority Families in Britain*. The Food Commission.

Macauley, D., Mores, P. and Douglas, J. (1987) *Food and Diet in a Multiracial Society: Caribbean Pack*. National Extension College.

Chapter 5

The role of play

We have seen in previous chapters that there are many things that need to be considered when we are looking at how young children grow and develop, in both body and mind. One of the most important influences on a child's development is the play and activities that they are involved with. Play is something children take part in every day, whether it is on their own or with other children or adults. Understanding the importance of play has a major impact on how and what play experiences workers should provide for young children.

Play is considered so important that is it included in the UN Convention on the Rights of the Child. Article 31 says, 'Every child is entitled to rest and play and have an opportunity to have the chance to join in a wide range of activities.' The Care Standards Act 2000 brought new guidance with it, including the National Standards for Under Eights Day Care and Childminding. These were issued for full day care, sessional day care, crèches; out-of-school care and childminders. There are fourteen National Standards, which represent a baseline of quality below which no provider may fall. Standard 3 is 'Care, learning and play', which states, 'the registered person meets children's individual needs and promotes their welfare. They plan and provide activities and play opportunities to develop children's emotional, physical, social and intellectual capabilities.' This is further qualified in the guidance documents to the National Standards. The guidance for full day care says about Standard 3:

> Children's care, learning and play are supported best where the registered person and staff are clear about the main purpose of the provision.

The development of children's emotional, physical, social and intellectual capabilities is promoted effectively when they take part in a wide range of activities. Staff meet children's needs through sensitive and appropriate interactions that promote children's self esteem. Staff plan first hand experiences that enable children to make choices as they develop their knowledge, skills and understanding. Children's care, learning and play are supported well by staff who monitor children's progress regularly and use this information to provide for their individual needs.

This chapter examines the role of play in more detail. It looks at how and why children play, and what they learn from it. It also examines the role of the adult in children's play, including how to plan, provide and evaluate children's play and activities within an anti-discriminatory framework. This chapter does not examine the different theories of play, owing to lack of space, but a list of publications is given at the end of the chapter for people who want further information.

In Chapter 1 we saw how research shows us that children as young as 2 can tell the difference between skin colours. We also saw that by the age of 3 children are playing with what adults consider to be gender-appropriate toys. This puts paid to the idea that young children do not notice things such as colour or gender differences, and are not taking in the images they see around them. These research findings are useful information for workers, as they show that what we do and say in front of children, and the activities provided to facilitate play, need to be thought about and provided within an anti-discriminatory framework. The Charter for Children's Play says:

> many children lack adequate or appropriate play opportunities because they are: single children at home; children in high rise blocks/flats; children living by busy roads; children in hospital; children with disabilities and special needs; children living in temporary accommodation; children living in areas with inadequate play provision; children in rural areas; children who are denied access to play opportunities because of racism, sexism and cultural constraints; children living in institutions; travellers' children; children who are not allowed out because of fears for their safety; children visiting relatives in prison. (National Voluntary Council for Children's Play, 1992, p. 3)

As long as there have been children in the world there have been things for them to play with. The importance of children's play has not always been as strongly recognized as it is today. Children's play is now regarded as an important part of a child's life, and in order to facilitate children's play, parents and workers need to provide children with toys and activities to enable their play to be rich and varied. Mia Kellner-Pringel said in her book *The Needs of Children*, 'Play is an intensely absorbing experience and even more important to children than work is to an adult' (p. 43).

Play is a child's work. It is by playing that children learn about the world around them. Children need to be provided with a variety of play experiences that they can take part in on their own, with other children and with adults. They also need to be given the opportunity to play in different environments, both indoors and outdoors, with and without equipment.

A Chance to Think 1
Try to remember some of the play experiences you have observed the children in your setting taking part in over the past few days. Pick two different play experiences and try to describe them. The following things may help you.
When did this play take place?
Where did it take place?
How many children were involved?
What were they doing?
Why were they doing it?

It can be seen by looking at just two different play experiences that play can take place in a variety of ways and can be very different depending on who is playing, what they are playing with, why they are playing and how they are playing. The word 'play' is used by many people in many different contexts. Some adults may say to children, 'You can play when you have finished your tea.' Some adults may even say to people who work with young children, 'There's nothing to your job; all you do is play with children all day.' Workers can be quite frustrated that some people still think like this, and that is why a good understanding of the role of play, the role of the adult in play and the importance of play is necessary for workers. This enables workers to be confident in providing play experiences for children within an anti-discriminatory framework, so that both children and adults benefit from it. Awareness of and confidence about providing play in an anti-discriminatory way will also mean that workers can explain these principles to parents and students in the setting. Information is passed on so that everyone involved with children is trying to work in the same way, bringing harmony, not discord.

The *Concise Oxford Dictionary* defines 'play' as follows: 'occupy or amuse oneself pleasantly with some recreation, game, exercise etc'. Childcare workers know there is more to play than this. It can be difficult to define play in a concise way. One definition that endeavours to cover all the aspects of play comes from the Charter for Children's Play. Part of it says:

> Play is a generic term for a variety of activities which are satisfying to the child, creative for the child and freely chosen by the child. The activities may involve equipment or they may not, be boisterous and energetic or quiet and contemplative, be done with other people or on one's own, have an end product or not, be light-hearted or very serious. (p. 9)

Children can learn many things from their play experiences, including learning about themselves and other people, as well as extending their skills in all the areas of development. The role of the adult includes being aware that all children are individuals, and that play needs to be planned to meet the needs of all children. The Charter for Children's Play says, 'service providers should work to ensure that no children are denied play opportunities because of discrimination, racism, sexism or cultural constraints; the effects of disability and special needs; through poverty or because of social, environmental or other restrictions' (p. 8).

Physical skills

Children learn physical skills, such as moving about and manipulating objects. Children learn to crawl, walk, run and jump, and have almost total control over their physical skills. Some children may not have as much control over their physical skills as others (e.g. some children with cerebral palsy may be floppy, have poor balance or not be able to control all their movements). This does not mean that a child with cerebral palsy is unable to participate in play. Indeed, it is vitally important that he or she is able to partici- pate fully, along with the other children in the setting, in the whole range of play activities. Looking at individual children's physical skills and providing appropriate play may have implications for adults, such as providing physical help or support for children so that they are able to be fully involved in play activities. The role of the adult in play is important. All children are individuals and have different needs and experiences with regard to physical play, be it large or small physical play. Workers should be able to plan and provide play and activities that meet the needs of all the children in the setting, extending their experiences and physical skills.

A Chance to Think 2
A new child called Magdy is starting in your setting and you are going to be his key worker. Magdy has cerebral palsy.
How would you feel about this?
What might you need to be aware of with regard to Magdy's physical skills?
How would you ensure that Magdy was included in play activities as fully as possible?
Compare your answers with the sample answers in Appendix 5.

Social skills

Children also learn social skills through their play experiences. They learn who they are and how they fit into the world. Children learn very quickly that the world can be an unfair place for some groups of people. When you are providing play within an anti- discriminatory framework it is important to provide positive images of all groups in everyday situations, not just groups who are represented in the setting. We live in a world made up of many different groups of people, interacting together to make up the social environment. Children gather images from television, comics and the things people say to them. Some of these images may be discriminatory, and workers must address these issues in the setting, as otherwise they are colluding with these images. Moreover, no setting will have all groups represented in it. A setting that has no Chinese children, for example, should still work towards providing positive images of and attitudes towards Chinese people, culture and language, so that the children in the setting will recognize, value and respect them.

A Chance to Think 3

You have been asked for your advice by a setting whose staff have just received their inspection report. In it, the inspection officer says that the setting is presenting a very Eurocentric view of the world to the children.

What do you understand by this?

Do you feel that the setting needs to do anything about this?

Why is it necessary to address this issue?

How would you advise them to start addressing these issues?

Compare your answers with the sample answers in Appendix 5.

Intellectual skills

Through play, children learn intellectual or cognitive skills. They learn how to reason, solve problems, think and concentrate. Workers should provide play experiences that will enhance all children's intellectual abilities. Caroline Harvey wrote an article in *Nursery World,* a childcare magazine, reporting on a piece of research she had carried out. She discovered that during free-choice play boys dominated particular toys that encouraged intellectual development. She wrote, 'Girls are therefore missing out on the opportunities to develop their concentration and attention span.' Workers must recognize that sometimes free play is not equal play, and ensure that opportunities are provided for all children to take part in all areas of play.

A Chance to Think 4

You are covering for a colleague in a room you do not usually work in. All the toys are put out in the afternoon for free play. There is a selection of toys, including the home corner, book corner, cars and the garage, pencils, paper and stencils, water play with sinking and floating toys, wooden construction, threading, jigsaws and a lotto game. During this time you notice that only the boys are playing in the water tray. They are playing quite constructively. On several occasions two girls try to join in but are unable to. A member of staff tells them not to disturb the boys, as they are playing nicely and learning about science, and that they can have a turn later. By the end of free play the two girls have still not had a turn. You notice that the same thing happens the next day.

Do you think that all the children have equal access to the water tray?

What can you do to ensure that this situation does not happen for a third day running?

Compare your answers with the sample answers in Appendix 5.

Emotional skills

Play provides one of the safest ways for children to learn about their emotions. Workers need to provide play experiences to stimulate this, and a safe and secure environment for them in which to do it. Children can role-play different situations, such as being different people, and experience the emotions generated by the situation. If children are feeling angry or frustrated they can release their emotions in a secure way by pounding at malleable activities, such as clay or dough, or by kicking a ball outside. All children feel emotions and workers should aim to provide an environment where all children are able to express their feelings and emotions in a safe, secure and non-judgemental way. For example, if one child is upset by the way he has been treated, he should be allowed to vocalize or express it. This, it is hoped, will mean that all those involved in the situation can try to examine why that child is upset, what, or who, has upset him, and how it can be put right. Sometimes the play in which children are involved, or people's response to it, may trigger an emotional reaction. Workers should respond to this in a way that will help the child to deal with it in a constructive way. For example, if a boy falls off a bike and is hurt he may cry. This is a natural reaction, and if every time this happens he is told, 'boys don't cry', he may come to think that the reaction he has when hurting himself is wrong and unacceptable. There are times when it is all right for people to cry, no matter who they are.

A Chance to Think 5

Sabrina is a little girl in your setting. She goes into the home corner to play with two other girls who are already in there. One of the girls says to Sabrina, 'I'm not playing with you, my mummy said I'm not allowed to play with black children.'

How do you think this would make Sabrina feel?

What would you do in this situation?

Compare your answers with the sample answers in Appendix 5.

Language skills

The other main area of development learnt through play is language. Play helps children to learn language skills and new vocabulary, and to express themselves through language, including languages that may not be spoken at home. This is true of all children, whatever language they speak, be it Urdu, English, Arabic, sign or symbol language. Children can be introduced to and taught to value and respect a variety of languages through play (e.g. through books and music). It is important for workers to recognize that all languages are equally important and to ensure that children, parents or workers who do not have English as a first language are not made to feel inadequate, but are respected for the skills they have in communicating in the language they use. This includes sign language or symbol languages, such as Bliss symbols. Language development will be discussed further in Chapter 6.

> **A Chance to Think 6**
> Most of the workers in your setting have English as a first language. You feel that more needs to be done by the setting to provide positive models of languages other than English, including sign and symbol languages such as Makaton and Bliss symbols.
>
> Where can you find out about sign and symbol languages if you don't already know about them?
>
> What is your setting doing already? Try to evaluate how effective this is.
>
> Now try to provide suggestions as to how the setting can improve its provision in this area.
>
> Compare your answers with the sample answers in Appendix 5.

Planning play

Children under 3

Children under 3 have their own particular needs and requirements as a group. They also have their own individual needs and requirements, which will need to be planned and catered for. We have seen how quickly young children develop attitudes, and workers need to remember this in their planning. Children under 3, like all children, need to feel valued and respected. They need to have a planned routine that makes them feel secure in themselves and in those caring for them.

As with all age groups, workers need to plan routines, the environment and children's play so that they meet individual and group needs and positively provide anti-discriminatory practice. All the activities discussed later in this chapter can be adapted so that children under 3 may take part in them. This may be done by planning effectively for this age range: doing activities on the floor; using larger equipment so that children are able to hold or see it; using different equipment as needed – for example, board books instead of paper books; having a larger adult : child ratio;

allowing for different time scales for activities when required; providing protective covering for the floor so that it does not matter about the mess; ensuring it is the process and not the end product that is important; making sure workers are aware of children's individual needs and likes and dislikes; allowing and supporting children to explore and discover; and giving children time and space.

There are of course particular resources that this age group need – for example, pull/push toys, posting boxes, a ball pool, mirrors, rattles, mobiles, soft toys and shape sorters. The choosing and using of resources will be discussed later in this chapter. Two activities that have not been mentioned so far that are particularly good for this age are Treasure Baskets for babies between 6 and 9 months and Heuristic Play for children aged 10–20 months. Both of these involve children exploring and discovering and using objects that are not commercially manufactured toys.

Three- to five-year-olds

Careful planning is vital if anti-discriminatory practice is to become a reality in settings. Planning needs to take place on various levels, beginning with long-term planning. This may take the form of a business or development plan and needs to take into account the philosophy of the setting; the development of policies and procedures; the implementation of anti-discriminatory practice; patterns of attendance; links with inspection reports; working with parents; curriculum development and learning objectives; staffing; resources; and any other issues that are indicated in the particular setting. Long-term planning should be followed by medium-term planning. This may include planning around themes or objectives; activity planning; and planning of staff deployment and resources. Finally there needs to be short-term planning, in the form of a more detailed working document. This may cover specific learning intentions/objectives, activities, resources, adults' role, children and their needs, teaching and learning strategies, and any other information that is helpful to workers. When planning, workers need to be aware of the requirements to plan for all elements of learning, including knowledge and understanding, skills and attitudes. Throughout this book we have seen how important attitudes are, and how quickly they develop. Workers need to be aware of this and incorporate this knowledge in their planning. Planning needs to be based on a thorough understanding of child development and individual children's needs. All planning documents should be written in a way that makes them accessible and easily understood by others. Although we have just seen that planning is a necessary part of working with children and young people, workers should remember that not everything can be planned, and not all learning can be planned. Children also learn through unplanned experiences and from the hidden curriculum.

We have seen that there are many things that children learn from play and that adults have a vital role in this. Adults plan play and provide resources, time and space for it to take place. Adults should also evaluate play experiences so that they can see what the children have gained from it, and plan for the new play session so that children's development continues to take place. This is often called a planning cycle:

Plan

Implement

Evaluate

A Chance to Think 7

Think back to the two play experiences you examined earlier in this chapter.

What did all the children involved in them learn from the play experience?

What was your role as an adult?

If you were involved in that situation again, would you behave in the same way?

It is important that anti-discriminatory practices are incorporated into play in an everyday way. They are not something that should be tagged on at the end, or something that should be seen as exotic. Each setting needs to discuss how good practice can be incorporated into play, so that all workers in the setting have a common understanding of the reasons why it is necessary. Workers also need to look at their own attitudes towards anti-discriminatory play. Once a setting has decided to work in this way, it should begin to become familiar to workers and will eventually be integrated into the everyday life of the setting. Providing anti-discriminatory play only for special occasions, such as festivals, is what Louise Derman Sparkes, in her book *Anti-bias Curriculum*, calls a 'tourist approach'. It is about visiting different cultures, or groups, but not including or integrating them into the mainstream of the setting. It keeps them to one side and makes them exotic or different.

In some settings there are lots of posters of children from different races and cultures, as a very visible sign that the setting is aware of differences, but this is all that is done. This is often called 'tokenism', because only a token gesture is being made to include different ways of life. Like the tourist approach, it does not include all groups equally on a day-to-day basis.

Having appropriate resources in a setting is only a small part of working within an anti-discriminatory framework. Indeed, just having resources that reflect positive images is in itself not enough. Resources may be used in a negative or stereotypical way that can be damaging to children if workers have been told they must use them but are not clear why. Resources can also be used in a discriminatory way. For example, if workers make negative comments when putting out or when using the resources, these attitudes will be picked up by the children.

We have seen throughout this book that adults' attitudes to anti-discriminatory practices are important. This is particularly true in the area of children's play, as play can have a major impact on a child's development. The attitude a worker has towards play can have a positive, or negative, effect on children. Indeed, as we have just seen, play, and play equipment, can be used in a discriminatory way to exclude or to give them negative messages about groups or individuals. For example, if all the images of

---

A Chance to Think 8

You have been asked to evaluate the play taking place in your setting and to make some recommendations for the way forward. Think about the approach to play that may be taken by different members of staff in the setting. Now try to evaluate it using the information contained in this chapter.

How would you describe the play that takes place in your setting?

Do you think this approach is acceptable?

Does it provide a positive experience of play for all children?

What recommendations would you make for the way forward?

---

elderly people show them to be ill or infirm, children may begin to think that when they become elderly they will also be ill. It is important that children see positive images of elderly people doing ordinary everyday things, such as shopping and going out and enjoying themselves.

The role of the adult is sometimes not easy, as it means that individuals have to examine their own attitude to the groups that make up society. Sometimes it can be hard for workers to know what to do or say. It can also be quite frightening. Sometimes workers may feel that it is easier not to do anything than to do something and possibly upset someone. However, it is important to pick up on, and in a sensitive way challenge or question, what has been seen or said – for example, other workers talking about the 'difficulties' of having a child with a hearing impairment in the setting, or children talking about girls who cannot be doctors; they have to be nurses. But it is important for workers to recognize and acknowledge that no one knows everything, and sometimes mistakes are made. It is also important that the fear of making mistakes does not stop people trying to do the right thing as they see it. Not everyone has experience of working with all the different groups in society. One way of trying to ensure that mistakes are not made in the provision of play or play equipment is to talk to other people. This may include talking to parents, colleagues, students, going to visit other settings that are working towards providing anti-discriminatory play or contacting organizations that research anti-discriminatory play such as the Early Years Trainers Anti Racist Network.

Once all workers in the setting have an understanding of what it means to provide anti-discriminatory play, part of the adult's role is to think about and plan children's play. Planning is important and will take place at different stages. One stage of planning is thinking about what resources are needed and how to use them. Planning should start with the child and take into account the individual needs of children as well as the needs of the group. Children should be able to experience play at first hand. They should be fully involved in play and the planning of it. Spontaneous play is important, but in order for spontaneous play to take place, the adult will have to have set the scene or provide resources for it most of the time. Play needs to be planned, provided and evaluated.

There are many different approaches that can be used for planning children's play and the activities to be provided. One way is to plan around a theme to take into account the early years curriculum – or areas of learning and experience. This ensures that all the areas of a child's development are catered for. Most people have heard of the National Curriculum, which is taught in schools and was introduced by the Education Reform Act 1988. Workers in schools need to be aware of the requirements of the National Curriculum and how to fulfil them.

In September 2000 the 'Foundation Stage' was introduced for children aged 3 to the end of the reception year. This brought with it the 'Early Learning Goals', which the majority of children should reach by the end of the Foundation stage. The Curriculum Guidance for the Foundation stage says:

> All settings that receive grant funding for the education of children aged three to five are required to plan activities that help children make progress in their development and learning. Young children will have had a wide range of different experiences and will have a wide range of skills and interests when they join a setting or school at the age of three, four

or five. They need a well planned and resourced curriculum to take their learning forward and to provide opportunities for all children to succeed in an atmosphere of care and of feeling valued.

There are six Early Learning Goals and all are equally important. They are:

- Personal, Social and Emotional Development;
- Communication, Language and Literacy;
- Mathematical Development;
- Knowledge and Understanding of the World;
- Physical Development;
- Creative Development.

The Early Learning Goals are not a curriculum in themselves but goals for children to work towards. How workers plan for these will depend on the philosophy of the setting they work within and the age of the children in the setting – for example, a Montessori setting may plan and work in a different way from a reception class. The Training Support Framework for the Foundation stage describes a high-quality curriculum as having the following characteristics:

1 It is in the hands of the practitioners.
2 It is dependent on practitioners and parents working together.
3 It ensures that children are secure and confident.
4 It respects the cultural differences and abilities of all children.
5 It builds on what children already know and extends their interests.
6 It uses various approaches and teaching methods.
7 It recognizes feelings and involves other people.
8 It encourages children to learn for themselves.
9 It is dynamic.

It is important for workers to be familiar with the Early Learning Goals if they are working in settings that follow them.

When planning around the goals, workers need to take into account both the needs of the children as a group and the needs of individual children within the group. It is also important to remember that although the goals are written relating to whole areas, children's learning is not compartmentalized. The goals do not specifically mention an anti-discriminatory approach, but the curriculum guidance for the Foundation stage, as part of the principles for early education, says, 'Practitioners should ensure that all children feel included, secure and valued.' It also says, 'No child should be excluded or disadvantaged because of ethnicity, culture, or religion, home language, family background, special educational needs, disability, gender or ability.'

It can be useful to plan around a theme. This allows the whole room or setting to concentrate on one theme, ensuring continuity between workers. It should be flexible enough to take into account the needs of individual children in the setting. It ensures that anti-discriminatory practices are incorporated into the theme right from the start, and extends all children's learning in a planned and positive way.

A Chance to Think 9

We have seen the different areas that are incorporated in the Early Learning Goals. Using these areas, plan two play activities for each area on the theme of food. You may wish to look at the transport theme in Figure 5.1 for guidance.

Compare your answers with the answers in Appendix 5.

This is only one way of planning. There are other ways with which workers may be familiar. Try to think about different ways of planning, what their good and bad points are and which one would be most suitable for your setting.

Planning is good practice and helps workers to provide balanced high-quality play. This is essential for all children. It is also a requirement of the Care Standards Act 2000, Children Act 1989 and the Education Reform Act 1988.

Children aged 5–16

We have already discussed the National Curriculum and the Key Stages through it. It is easy to think that as children grow older they do not need to play, or that they 'grow out of' play. As

Planning web

Communication, language and literacy

1. Introduce new vocabulary around transport and talk about the role of transport.

2. Story tapes, stories, rhymes, e.g. Mr. Gumpy's Outing, Fire Engines, five astronauts in a flying saucer.

Creative development

1. Drawing transport for wall picture labelled in a variety of languages.

2. Music relating to transport and moving like trains, buses, boats, etc.

Physical development

1. Using body to move from place to place, e.g. running, walking, stopping.

2. Using wheeled transport to move from place to place.

Mathematical development

1. How we came to the setting discussion, counting and graph.

2. Transport jigsaws.

Knowledge and understanding of the world

1. How transport works – fuel, engines, wheels, people; visit to transport museum.

2. Water transport using the water tray with world people.

3. Making transport with construction toys – large and small.

Personal, social and emotional development

1. How do people in wheelchairs use transport – discussion and visit from blind parent to talk about using transport.

2. Safety rules and transport, e.g. behaviour on the bus, safety belts, road safety.

3. Role-play different jobs with transport (gender issues, girls can drive trains).

Figure 5.1 Planning for the theme of transport.

children grow older, the nature and how they play will change, but play is still a vitally important part of a child's life at any age. Older children need to be able to play for all the same reasons that younger children play, and play needs to take place both indoors and outside. Anti-discriminatory practice needs to be incorporated into this, as with any other stage of a child's life.

We have seen what play is, why children play, what children learn from play and the role of the adult in play. We will now look at some very practical examples of anti-discriminatory play ideas for children up to the age of 7 years. It is not possible to mention every single idea, but the following sections give some ideas for different areas. Some of the suggestions may need to be adapted, depending on the age and abilities of the children involved in them.

The role of the adult

The adult has many things to do and to be aware of when working with children. Workers need to provide a choice of planned play activities in a safe, stimulating and secure environment. Workers should check equipment and resources for safety and evaluate them before the children use them to ensure that they are not discriminatory.

Equipment and activities should be displayed attractively so that they look inviting to play with. Children like to choose and put out toys, and workers should encourage them to do this, as it helps a child's independence and self-esteem. There needs to be a choice of activities laid out in an environment that enables all children to have access to them. Some may be on tables and some may be on the floor. Whatever the layout, workers should ensure that all children are able to move around the environment easily. Sometimes the environment or the equipment will need to be adapted or used on a one-to-one basis with children, depending on their individual needs and abilities. Workers also need to be aware of the requirements of children's dress, when to provide protective clothing, and how and when it may not be appropriate to adjust or remove children's clothing because of religious or cultural requirements.

Figure 5.2 A worker checking resources.

One of the most important aspects of the adult's role in children's play is his or her attitude towards it. Workers should encourage children in their play and be positive about their achievements. Children should be provided with both familiar and new experiences in play that stimulate them, so that they learn through play and have fun at the same time. If workers have a negative or discriminatory attitude towards play, this will rub off on the children in their care. We saw in Chapter 1 that young children pick up behaviour and attitudes from the environment in which they live. The same applies to play. If children are told that certain toys are boys' toys or girls' toys they will accept this and it will influence the attitude they have towards them. It is therefore important for workers to try to present a positive attitude. Workers should provide children with experiences that help them to counteract stereotypes both in the resources they provide and in the way they help children to become individuals who feel valued.

The other important role adults have in children's play is supervision, direction and involvement. The level of supervision that is required will vary according to the type of play and the children involved in it. Workers will need to make continual judgements about what is appropriate for different situations. Some activities require one-to-one supervision or adult involvement. Other activities require workers to 'keep an eye on them' from a short distance away, with no direct involvement. Because of the different levels of supervision or involvement needed it is important for workers to know the needs of all children in their care. This will guide them as to when, how and what is appropriate and necessary on each occasion. One day it may be appropriate to sit on the floor and be involved in the children's play. Another day it may not be appropriate. Sometimes it is necessary to intervene carefully and sensitively in children's play. This may be at a child's request; in order to extend play, or introduce a new concept; if play or language is becoming discriminatory and children are being upset; or if play is becoming dangerous. Adults should not interfere in children's play but intervene appropriately.

Workers need to have a thorough knowledge and understanding of child development and how children grow and develop at their own individual rate within this framework. They need to know and respect every individual child they care for and provide for their needs. This includes knowing the children's likes and dislikes, as well as being aware of and providing the resources they need to enable them to grow and develop as secure individuals possessing a strong sense of identity and self-esteem. Resources will be discussed later in this chapter, and the development of identity and self-esteem in Chapter 6. In order to provide for individuals and groups of children, workers need to develop observational skills, which are then used to observe and evaluate practice. By observing children, workers can gain a greater understanding of them. They can find out a great deal about the skills, knowledge and attitudes the children possess as well as the strengths and needs any particular child may have. This information can then be used to help workers plan their provision and also to share information with parents about their child. In addition, it can be used to help in the development of the team and the setting.

Before undertaking observations, workers need to ensure they have thought about, and planned for, confidentiality, permission, resources needed, the context of the observation and its aims and objectives, the rights of the children and parents, and their own role in observing. Workers need to be aware of the role they play in observation and the bias they bring to it. As we have seen, all workers bring part of themselves to their practice. The same is true for observational skills. Just by observing a child, workers are choosing what to, and what not to, observe. They may be a non-participant observer or a participant observer. Just by being present, a worker may alter a child's behaviour, and they need to be aware of that. We have seen how children's behaviour and attitudes may be influenced by, for example, culture, gender and the environment in which they live. All children are different, and workers need to be aware of a child's background and take this into account when observing. Workers may subconsciously 'set children up to fail' by their own lack of understanding about observation and how to undertake it. Observation styles and recording can take many different forms, including free description, structured description, pre-coded categories, longitudinal, target child, sociograms and tracking. Workers need to ensure that they are clear about making observations and their role in them before undertaking them.

Workers need to keep records in their settings. This is a requirement of legislation, including the Children Act 1989 and the Care Standards Act 2000. Workers also need to be aware of the requirements of the Data Protection Act 1998 when keeping records. The National Standards for Under Eights Day Care and Childminding arising from the Care Standards Act 2000 cover full day care, sessional day care, crèches, out-of-school care and childminders. Standard 14 relates to documentation. It says, 'Records, policies and procedures which are required for the efficient and safe management of the provision and to promote the welfare, care and learning of children, are maintained. Records about individual children are shared with the child's parent.' The Out of School Care Guidance to the National Standards says the focus for Standard 14 is as follows:

> The registered person and staff maintain useful records that underpin
> the successful management of the setting. Staff observe children's devel-
> opment and keep records that help them meet each child's needs.
> Children's records are openly shared with parents and their contributions
> are valued.

Chapter 1 illustrates some of the issues workers need to be
aware of when working with parents within an anti-discriminatory
framework. When keeping records, workers need to be aware
of the difference between fact and opinion, and how they are
recorded. As with all area of work, record-keeping needs to be
discussed and understood by the whole team. Teamwork and its
importance was discussed in Chapter 1.

One of the most important things that workers need to
be aware of all the time, and in all areas of their work, is that
they are seen as role models and representatives of the setting
they work in. Everyone they come into contact with – children,
parents, other professionals and individuals who visit the setting
– will see them in that light. They will either consciously or subconsciously make judgements about the way the worker presents
themselves and what they do, or do not do. We saw earlier in this
chapter that individuals develop attitudes and opinions from
everything they see, or do not see, in their environment. Workers
are part of that environment and so need constantly to be aware
of the role and impact they have in people's lives.

Resources

The resources and equipment used in the setting are very
important. They can have a powerful effect on children. They
provide a starting point for play, as well as extending it. How
equipment is presented to children will influence how it is used.
The images in it will be absorbed by the children and, because
they are presented by adults whom children trust, children will
take these images on board. This is why it is extremely important
for workers to evaluate all resources before children have access
to them, including resources and equipment that have been
bought, borrowed or made. All children should have access to the
equipment and resources that are available in the setting.

All equipment and resources in the setting need to be evaluated to see what kind of messages they give to people who use them. Resources should contain visual images, such as books, jigsaws and posters, containing positive images of the groups that make up society. Images should be realistic, and not exotic or caricatured. They should not marginalize people (e.g. jigsaws containing pictures of people in wheelchairs but in the background). The images should not stereotype individuals (e.g. women always doing the cleaning). Pictures of families should show the different types of families that are represented in society. Not all families are made up of a mother, father and two children. Some families have one parent, some have step-parents or extended families. Some children are brought up in a family with two parents of the same sex and some live with foster parents, or are in care. It is important that whatever background children come from, or whatever individual characteristics children have, they see positive images of themselves in the equipment and resources used in the setting. Parents, carers or television might give children negative messages about some groups in society, and workers with young children need to address this. We live in a diverse world. The equipment and resources that are used with children should reflect this. They should help both parents and children to value and respect diversity.

Sometimes it is difficult or expensive to get good-quality resources that have positive images of the different groups in society. This should not be seen as an excuse for not having any resources. There are many ways to get equipment and resources. Parents can be a good source of resources, and asking them promotes good practice. By working together, children and parents can see that they have a valuable contribution to make to the setting. Parents may be able to write captions for displays in languages other than English. They may be able to lend the setting equipment from their home or provide suggestions for cooking or menus. Local markets can often be a good place to buy resources that are cheaper and more authentic than those in catalogues. Going there also makes a good outing for the children, who get to see the variety of goods for sale, and can also help to choose what to buy (e.g. fruit and vegetables such as yams, mangoes and lychees; hair extensions for a hairdressing corner;

People crayons

Books

Chinese meal setting

Instruments

Puzzles

Dolls

Figure 5.3 Resources available from shops and catalogues.

or material for the table or displays). It is possible for workers and children to make resources. Photos of children, or that children have taken, are useful. They are specific to the children and the setting, and can be used to create, for example, a photo book about an outing. Children can then see images of themselves involved in something positive. Remember that it is essential to get permission from parents to take and use photos of children.

While having a variety of resources in settings that promote positive images is important, it is important too for workers continually to evaluate these resources. Teams need to consider how they choose and use resources. Having anti-discriminatory resources does not make a setting, or workers in it, work in an anti-discriminatory way. Indeed, as stated earlier, it is possible to use resources in a negative, discriminatory or stereotypical way – for example, by using resources only at a particular time of year to celebrate festivals, or if workers make discriminatory comments when putting out resources or do not sit down and use them actively with the children. All these actions give children messages that the resources and those individuals reflected in them are not valued and respected by the individuals using them. As we have seen all the way through this book, it is the attitudes that workers have and the way they act that are important. Workers need to be constantly evaluating their own attitudes and ways of working, as well as providing resources and using them effectively.

A Chance to Think 10

Look at some of the equipment and resources that are used regularly with the children in your setting. Think about the images they contain, how they are used, who uses them and the messages they are giving to the children.

Is there any equipment, or way in which equipment is being used, of which you feel particularly proud? Why is this?

Is there any equipment, or way in which equipment is being used, about which you feel uneasy? Why is this?

Can you think of anything you can do that would stop you feeling like this?

The Working Group against Racism in Children's Resources produces a set of guidelines for evaluating resources, as does the Pre-School Learning Alliance. Their addresses are included in the information list at the end of the book.

Art

Art in one form or another takes place in most settings on most days. The *Concise Oxford Dictionary* defines 'art' as 'creative activity, especially painting and drawing resulting in visual representation'. What is art to one adult is not art to another. The same is true of children.

How can anti-discriminatory practices be incorporated into art? When thinking about painting we need to acknowledge that there are many different forms of painting. Most settings have an easel that is set up for the children to use. It is important that the children can reach the easel and use it. Some children may need physical help to stand at an easel. Some children may not be able to use an easel at all. If this is so, they should still have access to painting. It may be easier for them to paint on a table, on the floor or on an adapted easel.

Thought needs to be given to the colours of the paint, pencils and crayons provided. It is important to provide flesh-coloured paints, crayons and pencils of all the different skin tones, so that children can produce a representation of themselves or others. These should be available at all times, not just on special occasions. Most catalogues now sell skin-tone crayons, pencils and ready-mixed skin-tone-coloured paints, but if settings cannot afford these they should mix up their own paints. This is a good activity to do with children, as it gives them a chance to talk in a positive way about their skin colour and that of their friends. Children like drawing themselves and other people. They are aware of differences in skin colour and it is the responsibility of workers to ensure that an environment is created where children value and respect both themselves and others. It is only by talking about skin colour differences and addressing the issue that this can be done.

Painting does not have to take place with brushes. There are many other methods, including bubble painting, string painting, finger painting, foot painting, fruit and vegetable printing and bike painting. These various forms develop different skills. All children can have a go at them and they can all produce beautiful results. When you are printing with fruit and vegetables, try to use things like pineapples, plantains and kiwi fruit, as well as apples and potatoes. Bike painting takes place outdoors, which may be a new experience for some children. The floor is covered with paper, paint is put down and the children ride through it, creating an abstract design. Children in wheelchairs can also do this. Children's efforts should be noticed. Not all children will be producing the same thing. Ten children producing ten identical ducks is not art. Art is an individual experience. If a child thinks something is beautiful, then it is beautiful to him or her. As discussed earlier in this chapter, the adult is vitally important in ensuring that all children have access to art activities.

Art is also about appreciating the creations of others. Children should be given the opportunity to see art created by others, perhaps by a visit to an art gallery, or by watching a parent or student actually doing an art activity. It is also important to display both the children's and other people's art attractively. Posters of original paintings can now be bought quite cheaply. Again, there should be a variety of these by different artists from different cultures and backgrounds (e.g. African art, Indian art, modern art). Children should be encouraged to talk about these. How do they make them feel? Which ones do they like? Do they have pictures at home? If so, what sort?

Construction

Construction toys are available in most settings, from traditional wooden blocks to new construction kits, such as Construct-O-Straws and Duplo. There are many wonderful things that can be done with construction kits, and it is important that all children have access to them. Some people still think of them as boys' toys. This is not true: girls have as much fun and learn a great deal from construction toys.

As already discussed, the role of the adult in setting out construction toys, whether on a table or on the floor, and supervision is important in ensuring that all children have access to this type of play. Some children may need help in manipulating, or putting together, some construction toys. In addition it might help if workers describe the equipment, as all children learn from hearing about things. This can be particularly true for children with a visual impairment, who might also need time to explore the equipment. It is now possible to get construction toys with large pieces, which may be more appropriate for some children. They are fun, as all children can see progress being made very quickly and almost life-size models can be created.

There are many exciting things that can be put out with construction toys. Farm animals, wild animals, sand and water can make landscapes, countries, seas and boats. Pens and paper can be put out with construction toys so that children can plan and design what they are going to make. Pictures can also be put out to give children inspiration – for example, pictures of different styles of homes: caravans, houseboats, houses, high-rise flats. Play people, dolls or Duplo world people can be put in the homes that the children build.

Cooking

The only chance some children get to experience cookery activities is in the setting. When cooking activities take place it is important to ensure that both boys and girls participate in all aspects of them, including the preparation of ingredients, the actual cooking and the clearing away. The ingredients used must be appropriate for the children taking part in the activity. For example, a Hindu child may not be allowed to use ingredients that have beef products in them, because the Hindu religion considers the cow to be a holy animal and it is not eaten.

Children can be introduced to ingredients and food that they have not experienced before. For example, fresh fruit salad could use mangoes, pineapples and lychees as well as oranges, bananas and apples. Sandwiches could use French bread, pitta bread and houmus as well as sliced bread. Shopping in the market or in supermarkets can be an activity, so that children can be involved in choosing ingredients. Parents might like to come into the setting and be involved in cooking activities, or might be able to provide recipes that are new to the setting.

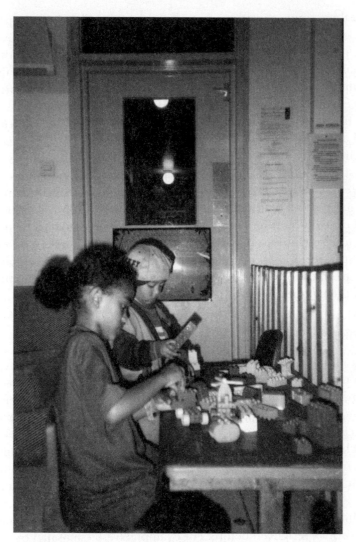

Figure 5.4 Playing with construction toys.

Craft

There are many different craft activities that can be done with children. As in art, it is the process of being involved in craft activities that is more important than the finished product. Craft activities include cutting, sticking and collage, papier maché, junk modelling, modelling, making mobiles and many more.

Often, old Christmas and birthday cards or pages from catalogues and travel brochures are cut out with scissors. These may provide children with images that are mainly Christian and white European (e.g. a white Father Christmas, models in smart clothes, exotic holiday locations). It is important, when you are providing children with these types of cutting experiences, to think about the type of messages that children are receiving from these images (for example, a child who is a Jehovah's Witness does not celebrate Christmas or birthdays, but may be cutting out cards from these celebrations). Asking parents of different religious or cultural backgrounds to bring in cards for their religious celebrations is one way of trying to ensure that children have different images to cut out. This needs to be done sensitively, as some parents may find it offensive for children to cut up cards that have religious significance; this is something the setting may need to address. Instead of cards, pictures from magazines could be used, and they should be pictures of diverse things, such as animals, landscapes, homes, buildings, elderly people and different people's faces. Different styles of materials are also good for cutting, as they provide a different experience from cutting paper. Some children, particularly children who have never used scissors before, may need some help in learning how to cut. Dual-handled scissors can now be bought to make this easier. It is important to provide left-handed as well as right-handed scissors, as it is very difficult for left-handed children to cut with right-handed scissors.

In sticking activities the same holds true as in the cutting activities about the images used. One sticking activity that extends children's awareness of themselves and others is to make a collage of faces. This could include the faces in the setting, both children and adults. All the children in the setting could be involved in this by drawing pictures of their faces, or they could cut out photos. The activity could be extended by the cutting out of as many different faces from magazines as the children can find. The finished picture could be mounted and displayed. Another activity that extends children's awareness of the world is making smell or touch pictures. This can be done by using spices, such as coriander or nutmeg, fresh or dried herbs and anything else that can be stuck down to make a picture that smells. Touch pictures can be made with any materials or resources that have different feels to them (carpet, different styles and types of materials, dried herbs, rice, different-shaped pasta, etc.). Children can be introduced to new smells and textures, and much discussion will come out of this. What does it smell or feel like? What do you think it is? What do you think it is used for? Where do you think it comes from? This activity is good for all children, and especially those who need their senses developed.

Work with papier maché is a very good craft activity that can be used to make all sorts of exciting things (moonscapes, landscapes, balloon mobiles, hands, models and much more). When you are making papier maché, try to use papers in languages other than English, so that children can see different scripts and styles of writing. Newspapers and magazines can now be bought in newsagents in many different languages, or perhaps parents or colleagues could bring some in.

Another way of introducing children to different scripts and languages is through junk modelling. Try to use boxes and cartons that have different languages and scripts on them. This

---

A Chance to Think 11

You have been asked to prepare and carry out a craft activity for a group of children aged 6 and 7. One of the children, Veronique, is partially sighted. The things she sees are fuzzy and she has difficulty seeing things that are close up. This is the first time you have done an activity with this group of children.

What do you need to consider when planning this activity?

What sort of activity will you do?

How will you ensure that all the children are able to participate in the activity?

What is your role when doing this activity with the children?

Compare your answers with the answers in Appendix 5.

is now fairly easy, as most packets have more than one language on them (for example, some sweets have Arabic writing on the packet, some raisin packets have French and German writing on them). If necessary, ingredients for cooking can be bought from shops that stock packets in different languages. They can first be used for cooking and then saved for junk modelling. The table can also be covered in newspaper that is in a language other than English.

Dance and music

Most adults enjoy some sort of music and dance, and so do children. There are many different styles of dance and music: ballet, jazz, tap, modern, country and western, classical, reggae, soul, rap, calypso, garage and pop music, to name but a few. It is important that all children have the opportunity to listen to, and appreciate, different kinds of music and to dance or move in different styles.

Children can be introduced to dance and movement by being allowed to move in the way the music makes them feel, as well as being shown and introduced to new and unfamiliar movements. If dance or movement sessions become too formal, children may feel inhibited. Dancing and movement sessions should be an enjoyable occasion for children. Movement is one way for children to express themselves through the music. For some children, music and movement sessions can be very therapeutic. It is important during dance or movement sessions for different types of music from around the world to be played for the children to dance to. Pictures of a variety of people from around the world dancing in different styles can be displayed, and used as a starting point for discussion.

Music can also be played while children are resting. Tapes of all types of music from around the world can be put out with head-phones so that children can choose and listen to them on their own. Tapes of different styles of world music can be bought at most music stores these days. One way to gather a large and changing tape collection is to ask colleagues and parents to lend tapes from time to time.

Another way of making music is with voices or instruments. All settings sing songs. It is important to introduce children to a variety of songs in different styles and languages. These need to be introduced with a positive attitude, with workers showing that they are valued and enjoyed. Children may not understand the words of the song (for example, 'Frère Jacques' is commonly sung, but some adults, as well as children, do not understand what they are singing). Parents may be able to teach workers short songs in their own language. This makes parents feel valued and gives the children the opportunity to experience and value a variety of languages. Some parents in the setting may want to know why children are singing songs in a variety of languages. Workers should feel confident in using different languages and explain to parents why it is a positive experience for the children.

Music sessions with instruments are also a good way of expanding children's musical experience. It is now fairly easy to buy instruments from around the world, such as small steel drums, tablas, pan pipes and maracas. These introduce children to different sounds and ways of making music. It is not necessary for settings to have lots of expensive instruments, and children enjoy making instruments, and making music from everyday things, such as rulers, spoons and empty yogurt pots. Making and using instruments introduces children to concepts such as pitch, tone and volume, and stimulates the use of the senses.

Displays and interest tables

When displays or interest tables are used with children, one of the most important things is to ensure that they can see and be involved with them. Displays can include large wall pictures done by the children, posters, photos or displays of children's work. It is important that, whatever the display, workers check the images that are in it, to ensure that they contain positive images of the groups that make up society. Images should be realistic, and not exotic or caricatured. They should not marginalize people, or stereotype individuals. Displays should be labelled to introduce children to written language. Displays can be labelled in a variety

A Chance to Think 12

You are working in the toddler room in your setting with children aged from 15 months to 2 years. You are organizing a music session involving all the children, which includes instruments and songs. James, one of the children in the room, has a hearing impairment, with moderate hearing loss.

How will you prepare this session?

What sort of things will you do in it?

How will you ensure that James is able to participate in the session?

Compare your answers with the sample answers in Appendix 5.

of languages, including symbol languages such as Bliss symbols, and parents might be able to help with this.

Children should be involved as much as possible in putting together displays. Some children will be involved in getting the picture or display ready; other children can help workers to assemble it. Displays of children's work, of something they have made or a piece of art work, show that workers value what children do. Children's work should be displayed attractively where they can see it and show it to parents, carers or friends. All children should have the opportunity to display their work. It does not matter that it may be unrecognizable to an adult; it is what it represents to the child that is important.

Many things can be used as backing, including sugar paper, newspaper (in a variety of languages) and textured backing such as corrugated card and material. Local markets often have different styles of material for sale, or parents may be able to lend material occasionally. Children's work should be labelled with their name and, if appropriate, a label explaining what it is (e.g. a title on a painting). Displays should be changed regularly to keep everyone interested in them.

Interest tables can be on a variety of subjects. They may be part of a theme, such as time, taste, fruit or the weather. They may be nature tables, or colour or number tables. Interest tables should be at child height, so that the children can be involved in them. Children can provide ideas for an interest table, bring in things from home for it or find things for it in the setting. Like all displays, interest tables should be labelled and laid out attractively. They should contain both new and familiar things. A taste table could have tastes that are familiar in the setting, but also introduce children to new tastes. A fruit table should have both familiar and new fruits. Children should be able to experience an interest table with all their senses: looking at it, lifting up things and feeling them, tasting them where appropriate. This will both stimulate the senses and encourage discussion.

A Chance to Think 13

Your setting is looking at a theme on homes and you have been asked to set up an interest table and display with the children. The children involved are 2 to 5 years old. Some children in the setting live in bed-and-breakfast accommodation; others live in a variety of accommodation, including flats, houseboats and houses.

How would you involve the children?

What sort of things would you include in it?

Compare your answers with the sample answers in Appendix 5.

Drama and imaginative play

Imaginative play is a great way for children to explore direct roles within a safe and secure environment. They may be a bus driver, a parent or even a childcare worker. All children should have access to imaginative play, and boys and girls should have equal access. It is perfectly natural for a boy to want to dress up in all kinds of clothes and act out roles, and this will not impede any area of his development.

Drama can be provided in a variety of ways. It does not have to be a big production, for anyone in particular or for a special occasion. Children love to act out their favourite stories. Workers should try to ensure that children have a wide choice of stories to choose from, including stories from a variety of cultures as well as stories depicting people in non-stereotypical roles (for example, 'Princess Smartypants' by Babette Cole is a funny story about a princess who does not want to get married). Children should be encouraged to act out the role they feel happy with, so that if a girl wants to act out a role that in the story is actually a boy, thatis quite acceptable. All children should be able to take part in drama or role-play. It is important for children to interpret stories without adults making the activity too formal, so that children are not frightened of making mistakes. Workers should provide children with the props, imagination and time to explore the world of drama.

Most settings provide some sort of imaginative play daily, from farm animals to the home corner. How can anti-discriminatory practices be incorporated in this area of children's play?

The home corner

Home corners can be very versatile places and can be turned into many different things. The props or equipment should be as accurate as possible and reflect the variety of cultures that make up society (for example, as well as plates and knives and forks, the home corner could also have in it thali dishes, woks, Chinese bowls and chopsticks). If these have not been used by the children before, it is important that they do not suddenly appear overnight. Children should be introduced to them so that they know what they are called, what they are for and how to use them. As emphasized all through this book, they should not be put in a home corner just for special occasions, but should always be available to the children. Calendars and newspapers in a variety of languages and styles, and pictures and photos of families or people in the setting, can make the home corner very specific to the setting.

Other props in the home corner could include dressing-up clothes that reflect the different styles of clothes and materials available worldwide (e.g. saris, shalwar kameez or kimonos). Some people may feel that using these types of dressing-up clothes, which are in fact children's versions of clothes worn daily by adults, is not appropriate, as people's cultural background and traditions are being trivialized by being used as playthings. The only way for workers to discover whether this is so is to ask parents and colleagues for their opinions. Both boys and girls should be encouraged to dress up. Some parents worry if they see their son dressing up, and workers need to think about their response if parents say that they do not want their son to use the dressing-up clothes.

Dolls are a popular prop in the home corner. There should be a variety of dolls available for the children to play with (e.g. black dolls, mixed parentage dolls, dolls with special needs, baby dolls, elderly dolls, boy dolls as well as white girl dolls). There should also be a variety of clothes available for them.

Workers need to think about access to the home corner, who is playing in it and the type of play that is taking place. For example, are the younger children, or children with special needs, playing the role of the baby or someone who needs caring for? If so, workers need to intervene to ensure they are not always seen in this role, but are also playing the role of the carer. Sometimes it is appropriate for workers to join in the play taking place, or to encourage children who do not generally play in the home corner to use it.

The hospital or dentist corner

If settings do not have much space, the home corner can be turned into a hospital or dentist corner. In settings that do have space, the hospital corner may be out at the same time as the home corner. This allows children to act out any fears and enables them to ask questions they may have about these scenarios in a safe and secure environment. Both boys and girls should be encouraged to take the role of doctors, dentists, oral hygienists and nurses, and not to see the roles as gender stereotyped.

Dolls or teddies can often take the role of patients and there should be several dolls provided that reflect different cultural backgrounds. Children with special needs or younger children should not always take the role of the patient but in turn be the dentist, nurse and doctor.

Children might like to make get-well cards to use in the hospital. These can be made in languages other than English. Books about hospitals and dentists may also be used to expand the activity, and these should be checked to ensure that they are not depicting stereotypical roles.

Sometimes it is possible to visit hospitals or dentists with small groups of children. This is particularly good if a child is due to go into hospital or to the dentist, and is not sure what is going to happen. It is also possible to ask dentists to visit the setting and check the children's teeth.

A Chance to Think 14

Some settings feel that children should not be playing with props that represent doctors' instruments. For example, some workers in an environment where children are exposed to illegal drugs feel that giving children a replica of a syringe might encourage children to see its use as acceptable.

What is your opinion about this?

The hairdressing corner

In settings that do not have much space, it is possible to turn the home corner into a hairdresser's or to make use of it as a separate activity. A variety of equipment should be provided, including aprons, plastic scissors, mirrors, curlers, Afro combs, brushes and old hairdryers with the flex cut off. Empty shampoo bottles or empty boxes of hair colour can also be used. These should be washed carefully first, and should show pictures of people with different types and styles of hair. It is also possible to get both black and white flat toy heads as well as 3D heads with hair on, which children can style. Hair extensions can be used in the hairdressing corner. Both boys and girls should be encouraged to use the hairdressing corner.

Table and floor toys

There are many toys that promote drama and imaginative play, including animals, cars, trains, dolls and doll's houses, shops, puppets, telephones and many more. Whatever is put out for the children to play with, or if they can choose activities themselves, all children should have access to all activities. Workers should be aware of who is playing with what, and it may be necessary to intervene appropriately if some children are being denied access to some activities.

Sometimes it will be appropriate to set out an activity on the floor, and on other days it will be appropriate to put the same activity out on a table. It is also exciting for children when activities are mixed and matched (e.g. putting bricks and play people out with the train track, or cars and animals out with junk in the sand tray). This ensures that activities are kept fresh and different, and means that it is acceptable for children to play with toys in a context different from that for which they may have been intended.

Language and literacy

Language and literacy can often be difficult to separate from other activities, as language particularly is often a central part in them. It is important, though, to think about them separately, so as to ensure that workers are meeting the needs of children and families in the setting, as well as providing positive examples of languages and literacy styles. Language development is discussed in greater detail in Chapter 6.

One of the first areas to spring to mind when one is thinking about language and literacy is probably the book corner. Workers should provide a variety of books for children: story books, theme or interest books, picture books in a variety of illustrative styles, books in a variety of languages, including dual-language books, and books with sign or symbol languages. Workers must check books before using them with children, to evaluate whether they are suitable. The sort of things they should be looking for are the suitability for the age range of the children, the images the book contains, and whether images are or are not stereotypical, tokenistic or caricatured. Children need to see positive images of individuals and groups of people. Books should not present people or situations as exotic. Children need images to which they can relate and that are part of their everyday experiences, as well as books that will introduce them to new ideas in a way that values the diversity of the world. All children need to see themselves reflected in the books in the setting, so that they feel valued as individuals. There are a variety of places to get books from, including book clubs, shops and libraries. Children often like to bring their own books to read in the setting but it is still important for workers to check these before reading them with children. If it is impossible to find books containing positive images of all the children in the setting, one option is to make books using illustrations provided by the children or photos of the children (with parental permission). Parents might also be able to provide illustrations of writing in languages other than English, and this makes the books very specific to the setting. It is now possible to get story tapes to put in the book corner, so that children can listen to stories on their own, learning to turn over pages when the tape tells them to.

Another way of using cassettes to develop language skills is to play sound lotto games. The soundtracks lotto from UNICEF has many positive sounds and images from a variety of countries and cultures. Music cassettes are also a good way of introducing children to a variety of languages.

Discussion cards can be used to promote language skills. These are cards with a picture and sometimes a caption saying what the picture is. There may be several cards in a series, which need to be put in the right order to tell a story. These can be bought from most catalogues but it is very easy to make them with photos or pictures cut from magazines. This has several advantages: it is cheaper than buying them, workers can ensure that the images are not stereotypical or discriminatory, they are specific to the setting and parents can also be involved in providing images and writing.

All labelling in the setting should be clear and in a variety of languages: on children's paintings, on notice boards for parents and on displays. If children's coat pegs are labelled with their names, then for those children whose home language does not use the Latin alphabet, it is possible to write their names in both English and their home script, thus encouraging children to recognize their names in both scripts and showing that they are both valued. This can also be done on any work they produce, such as paintings.

Malleable play

The *Concise Oxford Dictionary* defines 'malleable' as '(of metal etc.) able to be hammered or pressed permanently out of shape without breaking or cracking; adaptable, pliable, flexible'.

The malleable activities that take place in settings usually involve clay, Plasticine and dough. There are many ways to ensure that anti-discriminatory practices are incorporated into malleable play activities. These include putting out thali dishes, chappati pans or Chinese bowls and chopsticks with the activity, instead of rolling pins, saucepans and cutters. Dough can be made warm or cold, or with different textures, using porridge oats, for example. This gives children different experiences when they touch it and try to mould it.

Other types of malleable play include setting things in jelly and then letting children try to get them out. This is particularly good for younger children. You can mix porridge oats or wallpaper paste with warm water and food colouring to make a sticky, pliable mixture. Cooked pasta is good for this too. If cannelloni is cooked with some oil and food colouring until it is just soft, and then left to cool, the children can use it like a construction toy, as it sticks together. Spaghetti cooked with food colouring, cooled and put out will eventually form a dough that can be cut with scissors. Some people may feel that playing with food is not acceptable, and workers need to ensure that if settings are using food, this is acceptable to parents and workers.

Some children like malleable play activities: they may find them soothing, relaxing or a way of releasing frustrations or emotions. Other children are not quite so keen on them: they may feel inhibited, not like the look or feel of the activity or be afraid of getting dirty. Protective clothing should be available for children so that their clothes do not get dirty. Workers also need to be aware of skin care needs. A child who has sensitive skin, or eczema, may be reluctant to play with malleable material. It is possible to buy gloves for children to wear, or to make malleable material that will not aggravate the skin. Workers should talk to parents to find out what it is that their child cannot play with, and what action needs to be taken in the event that they accidentally have contact with it.

Manipulative play

Manipulative play involves such things as jigsaws, threading, pegs and pegboards, stacking toys, activity centres, sorting games, postboxes and many more. Like all toys, they should be checked to ensure that they are suitable for the children in the setting. Jigsaws should contain positive images of individuals and groups of people. Touch jigsaws, which are good for all children but particularly those who are visually impaired, can be bought or made. It is possible to make jigsaws out of photos backed on card and covered, to ensure that puzzles have personal relevance to the setting. Puzzles can be made of festivals, 'people who help us' and outings. It is not enough to put out jigsaws; workers need to talk to children about the images in them in a positive way.

A variety of manipulative activities can be made, which ensures that at least some are suitable for every child in the setting. This may be particularly necessary when you are working with children with special needs, as some commercially available equipment may be expensive or too complex for some children. Threading activities can be made using pictures of buildings, such as a synagogue, or pictures of food. Their size will depend on the abilities of the children for whom they are being made. Postboxes can also be made using boxes with one or two shapes to put in them.

Mathematics

Mathematics does not just involve numbers and counting. Jigsaws provide a good early mathematical experience, as they introduce children to space, size, number and pattern. We have already seen how jigsaws need to be evaluated.

Figure 5.5 Jigsaws help children to develop language and communication skills.

Children can be introduced to patterns in the world around them: Arabic patterns, Indian patterns and many more. They can make patterns using equipment in the setting, both indoors and outdoors. The water tray or water activities are good places for learning about mathematical concepts: sinking and floating, volume and capacity, and numbers. All children should have access to the water tray, and again it can be used indoors or outdoors (e.g. measuring the rainfall). Sorting and classifying can be done using thali dishes, Chinese bowls, wooden bowls or wicker baskets as containers. Baskets from a variety of cultures can be bought from Oxfam and UNICEF shops or local markets.

Counting and number work can be done in writing or orally in a variety of languages. Some children may be able to count and do complex number work in their home language but not in English, and their ability should be recognized and valued.

Likewise, some children may be able to do quite complex number work orally, but not in writing. Some cultures have traditional games that help children learn their numbers. For example, in Tigray in Ethiopia a game called 'negash' is played, which involves moving shells or stones around a board. This game can now be bought from Oxfam and used with children.

We saw in Chapter 1 that girls and boys develop different skills and that boys tend to have better mathematical and spatial skills than girls. It is therefore very important that girls are encouraged to play with activities that develop mathematical skills.

A Chance to Think 15

You are supervising Anna, a student in your setting. The college has set Anna a project called 'Mathematics and the under twos', and she has come to you for advice. How would you define maths and the under twos?

What practical activities can you suggest to Anna that can be done to encourage mathematical development in the under twos?

Compare your answers with the sample answers in Appendix 5.

Outdoor play

Not all settings have an outside space in which children can play, but it is important that all children are able to go outside and play. Some children experience outdoor play only at the setting. This is particularly true of children who live in high-rise flats or alongside busy roads. Some of the things children play with indoors should be available outside as well (e.g. sand, water and construction toys).

Outside play has exciting experiences of its own, such as mud, digging in soil, plants and worms. These may be new experiences for some children, and may need explanation of what they are and encouragement to play with them. All children should be encouraged to explore the outside environment, which adults need to ensure is as safe as possible. Some children dislike getting dirty and, if necessary, protective clothing should be provided.

Climbing frames, bikes, wheeled toys and urban junk, such as milk crates, old tyres and planks, are great fun outside and can be turned into many exciting games. All children should have access to this type of play. Children with special needs, such as those with impaired mobility, may need to have some outside equipment adapted so that they can join in. Outdoor play does not just have to take place when the weather is fine. It is possible to go out in the wind, rain and snow if children and workers have appropriate outdoor clothing. As with all activities, workers need to supervise children effectively and comply with the adult: child ratios required by legislation.

Outings

Outings into the environment are a good way for children to learn about the world in which we live and a good way of involving parents in the setting. There are many places to go to, and outings do not just have to be for special occasions. Children on a trip to the shops or market may see things they do not possess or use at home. Indeed, they may not get the chance to go shopping other than when at the setting. Swimming can be a regular outing. Workers need to be aware of religious and cultural issues concerning removing children's clothing and of individual needs regarding hair and skin care.

Outings can be organized to extend the theme the setting is pursuing. A theme on 'buildings' could include a visit to a mosque, church, synagogue or other religious building. A theme on 'people who help us' can include a visit to a hospital, dentist or fire station.

It is possible to visit other childcare settings where children may have friends, or to play with a special piece of equipment, such as a ball pool. Art galleries or museums, particularly museums with moving parts that have special areas for children, are good places to visit.

Parents may like to join in outings if they are able to. Working parents may not be able to join in as much as they would like, and workers need to ensure that parents are given as much notice as possible if the outing is going to affect them (for example, if it is an outing that involves the whole setting, if children need special clothes or if children are going to return late).

Science and technology

Science is about exploration and problem-solving, ourselves and living things, forces and energy, materials. Technology is about identifying needs and opportunities, designing, planning and making things, using computers and tools. Girls and boys should have equal access to science and technology activities. Science and technology are often split, either consciously or unconsciously, along gender lines, with girls doing science activities such as cooking or gardening, and boys doing woodwork. Workers need to be aware that this may happen and to develop strategies to ensure equality of access for all children.

Science and technology does not have to be 'high tech' and expensive, with computers and suchlike. It should be as everyday and accessible as possible: exploring nature outside, making ice cubes and watching them melt in the water tray, mixing things so that they change (for example, in cooking, mixing paints or making dough).

A Chance to Think 16

In your setting you have observed that a student is doing science and technology activities only with boys.

What would you do in this situation?

What would you do if the student said that this was done deliberately, as he felt that it was wrong to do science and technology activities with girls?

What signals is this sending to all the children in the nursery?

Compare your answers with the sample answers in Appendix 5.

Videos, television and computers

Many children and settings have computers, televisions and videos. As with any other resource, workers need to plan and evaluate how these are used. Some children get a great deal of pleasure from these and can learn new skills – for example, how to operate technology and acquire keyboard skills. Often, however, using these media can be a very solitary activity, and we have seen how television and video can portray discriminatory images of both groups and individuals, so workers need to choose and use the resources carefully. In these days of rapid technological advances, children benefit from having access to computers with adult supervision. Computers can provide, for some children, a way of communicating. For others, computers may need to be adapted so that children can use them – for example, providing a larger keyboard than standard, using brighter graphics, making the facilities wheelchair accessible. For all children, use of televisions, videos and computers should be monitored and evaluated by workers.

Useful publications

Abbott, L. and Moylett, H. (1997) *Working with the Under-3's: Responding to Children's Needs.* Open University Press.

Anning, A. and Edwards, A. (2000) *Promoting Children's Learning from Birth to Five: Developing the New Early Years Professional.* Open University Press.

Bararash, L. (1997) *Multicultural Games.* Champaign, Ill.: Human Kinetics.

Basic Skills Agency. *Mathematics at Home and at School: Making a Difference Together* (video). Department for Education and Employment.

Basic Skills Agency. *Reading and Writing Together: Learning at Home and at School* (video). Department for Education and Employment.

BBC Education (1994) *Children without Prejudice: Equal Opportunities and the Children Act* (video). BBC.

Bilton, H. (1998) *Outdoor Play in the Early Years.* David Fulton.

Browne, N. and France, P. (1986) *Untying the Apron Strings: Anti-sexist Provision for the Under-Fives.* Open University Press.

Bruce, T. (1987) *Early Childhood Education.* Hodder & Stoughton.

Bruce, T. (1991) *A Time to Play in Early Childhood Education.* Hodder & Stoughton.

Bruce, T. (1996) *Helping Children to Play.* Hodder & Stoughton.

Bury Business Centre (n.d.) *Articles of Faith.* Bury Business Centre, Kay Street, Bury BU9 6BU.

Campbell, R. (1996) *Literacy in Nursery Education.* Trentham Books.

Department for Education and Employment (1998) *National Literacy Strategy.* DfEE.

Department for Education and Employment (1999) *National Numeracy Strategy.* DfEE.

Department for Education and Employment (2000) *National Literacy Strategy: Supporting Pupils with Special Educational Needs in the Literacy Hour.* DfEE.

Department for Education and Employment and Qualifications and Curriculum Authority (2000) *Curriculum Guidance for the Foundation Stage.* DfEE and QCA.

Department of Education and Science (1978) *The Warnock Report on Special Educational Needs.* HMSO.

Derman Sparks, L. (1989) *Anti-bias Curriculum: Tools for Empowering Young Children.* National Early Years Network.

Dowling, M. (2000) *Young Children's Personal, Social and Emotional Development.* Paul Chapman.

Drummond, M., Lally, M. and Pugh, G. (1989) *Working with Children: Developing a Curriculum for the Early Years.* National Children's Bureau.

Early Childhood Education Forum and National Children's Bureau (1998) *Quality in Diversity.* National Children's Bureau.

Edgington, M. (1998) *The Nursery Teacher in Action.* Sage.

Goldschmied, E. and Hughes, A. (n.d.) *Heuristic Play* (video). National Children's Bureau.

Goldschmied, E. and Jackson, S. (1997) *People under Three: Young Children in Day Care.* Routledge.

Hurst, V. (1997) *Planning for Early Learning.* Paul Chapman.

Hyder, T. and Kenway, P. (1995) *An Equal Future: A Guide to Anti-sexist Practice in the Early Years.* National Early Years Network and SCF Equality Learning Centre.

Kellner-Pringel, M. (1980) *The Needs of Children,* 2nd edition. Hutchinson.

Konner, M. (1991) *Childhood.* Little, Brown.

Lindon, J. and Lindon, L. (1993) *Caring for the Under Eights.* Macmillan.

Lindon, J. and Lindon, L. (1994) *Caring for Young Children.* Macmillan.

Matterson, E. M. (1975) *Play with a Purpose for Under Sevens.* Penguin.

Minet, P. (1989) *Child Care and Development.* John Murray.

Montague-Smith, A. (2000) *Mathematics in Nursery Education.* David Fulton.

Mortimer, H. (2001) *Special Needs and Early Years Provision.* Continuum.

National Children's Bureau. *Infants at Work* (video). NCB.

National Voluntary Council for Children's Play (1992) *A Charter for Children's Play.* NVCCP.

Newson, J. and Newson, E. (1979) *Toys and Playthings.* Allen & Unwin.

Nutbrown, C. (1999) *Threads of Thinking.* Paul Chapman.

O'Hagan, M. (1997) *Geraghty's Caring for Children.* Baillière Tindall.

O'Hagan, M. and Smith, M. (1999) *Early Years Child Care and Education: Key Issues*. Baillière Tindall.

Riddick, B. (1982) *Toys and Play for the Handicapped Child*. Croom Helm.

Siraj-Blatchford, I. (1994) *The Early Years: Laying the Foundations for Racial Equality*. Trentham Books.

Siraj-Blatchford, I. (ed.) (1998) *A Curriculum Development Handbook for Early Years Educators*. Trentham Books.

Siraj-Blatchford, I. and Clarke, P. (2000) *Supporting Identity, Diversity and Language in the Early Years*. Open University Press.

Sylva, K. and Lunt, I. (1992) *Child Development: A First Course*. Blackwell.

Wales Pre-School Playgroups Association and Mudiad Ysgolion Meithrin (n.d.) *Playing Together*. NES Arnold.

Westminster City Council (n.d.) *Great Expectations*. Westminster City Council.

Whitehead, M. R. (1990) *Language and Literacy in the Early Years*. Paul Chapman.

Young, S. and Glover, J. (1998) *Music in the Early Years*. Falmer Press.

Chapter 6

Communication and identity

This chapter examines three main areas in childcare and education. They are very different but are areas of which workers need to be aware. They are: language development and communication; child protection; the development of identity and self-esteem. We examine anti-discriminatory practices within each of these areas.

Language development and communication

Workers are continually communicating with children and other adults. This communication may be either conscious or subconscious, may be planned and thought about, or may be an immediate response to another person. Workers never cease communicating. Children and adults pick up messages from workers even when they may think they are not communicating. Workers give out constant messages with the body language they use, as well as by using language or other communication media. It is through language and communication skills that individuals are able to make themselves understood and also understand others. Language and communication skills form a vital part of social interaction. It is therefore important that workers are aware of how they communicate and how children learn language and communication skills.

All children develop ways of communicating. This is an important skill, as it enables us to interact with one another and not be isolated as individuals. Sometimes communication will be through a spoken language or languages. At other times it may be through a sign or symbol language, such as British Sign Language, Makaton or Bliss symbols. Other ways of communicating include gestures and body language. Workers must be aware of the communication systems and needs of children in the setting, and provide the necessary support and encouragement for its use and development.

In this section of the chapter we examine the development of language and communication skills. The terms used with regard to language and communication are defined. Theories of speech and language development are examined. This section also discusses how workers can support language and communication skills. A list of publications is given at the end of the chapter for workers wanting more information on language development and communication.

We can see that children use many different ways to communicate, both with one another and with adults. The systems children use to communicate will be influenced by their individual development, any special needs they may have, such as a hearing impairment, the communications skills they possess and the situation they are in. Not all children will develop the use of a spoken language and some children will develop and be able to use more than one spoken language.

The *Concise Oxford Dictionary* defines the word 'language' as 'the method of human communication, either spoken or written, consisting of the use of words in an agreed way; the language of a particular community or country, etc.'. 'Communicate' is defined as meaning 'transmit or pass on by speaking or writing'.

A Chance to Think 1
Think about children in your own setting. Think about different times of the day: when children arrive in the setting, at sleep and getting-up time, outside play and quiet time.

How do children communicate with one another at these times?

Do children use different communication skills with one another and with adults?

How many different languages are used in your setting?

Theories of language development

Not all children will develop spoken language skills. This may be because of special circumstances, such as a hearing or speech impairment. Later in this chapter we look at communication skills other than spoken language, but this section focuses on the development of spoken languages.

The majority of children will develop some form of spoken language. It is amazing to think that when children are born they are able to communicate only through crying and movement, but by the time they are 4 or 5 years old they can communicate through one or more spoken languages. Language development takes place in stages, or a sequence, with one stage being followed by another. The age at which children reach these stages varies because all children are individuals and develop at different rates. Psychologists have discovered that language development is consistent across a large variety of cultural groups and that the sequence of language development is the same across cultures.

There are many theories of language development. One theory is that the environment children are in will influence how they learn a language, together with accent and dialect. So as well as learning language, children will also develop and use dialect and accent. The *Concise Oxford Dictionary* defines a 'dialect' as 'a form of speech peculiar to a particular region', and 'accent' as 'a particular mode of pronunciation'. A child brought up hearing English spoken will learn to speak English, and a child brought up hearing Arabic spoken will learn to speak Arabic. Children's communication and vocabulary also vary depending on whether they are talking to an adult or friend, and whether they are at home or school. Distinct vocabularies are used for the classroom (formal), the playground (slang) and the home (informal or familiar).

Another theory put forward by psychologists is that children learn language through imitation (Ervin-Tripp) and conditioning (Skinner). Imitation is where children imitate the language they hear around them. Conditioning takes place when adults reward or praise children for something they have said that is funny or right, or tell them if it is rude or wrong. If children are encouraged or praised, they will want to say what they said again, or say something new in order to be praised. They will also not want to be told off, so they will learn to change their language in order to stop this happening.

Some psychologists (e.g. Chomsky, Lenneberg) believe that language development is innate, or that children are pre-programmed to learn language. This means that they are born with the ability to learn language. Chomsky believes that there are many common features of all languages – that is, whatever language children are learning, they use the same system of rules to do it. He called these rules 'universal grammar'. He said that this is done because humans possess a 'language acquisition device' that enables them to learn language. Piaget believed that there is a relationship between language and a child's intellectual activities. Vygotsky believed that interaction in the social environment is important for language development and that adults need to 'scaffold' a child in order to help him or her develop.

The development of one spoken language

People who speak one language are called monolingual. We will now spend some time looking at how children with no special needs develop one language. This is done in stages, and although for the purpose of this section ages are put against these stages, it is important to remember that all children are individuals and develop these skills at different rates. People working with young children need to be aware of the stages of language development and the needs of children in order to be able to provide appropriate help, support and encouragement for children.

Birth to one month

A newborn baby's use of her voice will consist of crying. The cry may sound different depending on whether she is hungry, uncomfortable or in pain. As she gets older she will make other sounds with her voice including gurgling, cooing and noises made in her throat.

One month to three months

A baby may stop crying when she hears familiar soothing voices. She will gurgle and coo. She is beginning to smile when spoken to and is developing more control over her lips and voice.

Three to six months

A baby will now turn her head in the direction a voice is coming from. She will make many more sounds with her voice, including 'ka' and 'ba' sounds, and she will practise making sounds, including laughing and shouting.

Six to nine months

Between 6 and 9 months the baby makes more sounds, including 'adad', 'der' and 'amem', and will be trying to copy sounds. She will now begin to use her voice deliberately to gain people's attention.

Nine to twelve months

By now a baby is beginning to 'talk' to people in her own language or jargon. She is showing enjoyment in familiar words and can carry out a simple instruction, such as 'wave to granny'. Babies are also beginning to recognize their own names. They may say two or three words, such as 'dad dad' or 'mum mum'.

Twelve to fifteen months

Children practise talking a lot, much of it still in their own language or jargon. They may use four or five recognizable words, but understand much more than they can say. By this age children are learning to recognize the word 'no' and its meaning.

Fifteen to eighteen months

At this age children show a great deal of interest in words and vocalizing. They particularly enjoy trying to join in singing, have a vocabulary of around six to twenty words, and may often use the word 'no'. They understand much more than they can say. They may also echo words that they like the sound of, or those that come last in a sentence. This is called echolalia.

Eighteen months to two years

Children can understand what people are saying to them. Their vocabulary has grown to fifty or more words that they can use in short sentences. They are beginning to ask 'what's that?' as well as joining in songs. They use their names to talk about themselves (e.g. 'Jamie want').

Two to two and a half years

Children will start to use the pronouns 'I', 'me' and 'you' instead of names to talk about themselves and others. They also ask a great many questions, especially 'what' questions.

Two and a half to three

Children hold simple conversations with people and may talk to themselves. They enjoy talking and will still be asking many questions at this age, including 'who' and 'where' questions. They enjoy words in any form, including rhymes, stories and conversations.

Three to four years

By now children are talking quite fluently and they possess a very large vocabulary. They may be beginning to recognize swear words and use them to see the effect this has. At this age children have learnt how to use grammar accurately, although they still make mistakes. They may know their own name, age and address. Their speech sounds much more adult and they use tone and pitch to vary it.

Four to five years

Children's vocabulary is now very extensive, up to about 300 words. They still ask many questions, particularly about the meaning of words they do not understand. Their speech is now much more adultlike and they generally use grammar accurately. Children may be able to recognize words in writing, particularly their own name.

Five to six years

Children's vocabulary continues to expand and they are interested in new words. They may be able to write words and will be beginning to read.

Six to eight years

Children's speech and language is now very sophisticated. They have a very large vocabulary and are generally capable of reading and writing.

The development of more than one language

A great many people in the world are bilingual or multilingual. Much of the vocabulary used when one is talking about more than one language is confusing and may be used in the wrong context. A short definition of the most commonly used words is given to try to ease some of the confusion.

- bilingual: able to speak two languages;
- multilingual: able to speak more than two languages;
- first language: the first language learnt;
- mother tongue: the language spoken in the family;
- majority language: the major language spoken in a country.

Many people worry that a child learning to speak two or more languages will be confused or unable to communicate effectively in either language. This is not the case. We saw earlier in this section that the same system is used when learning all languages. Research has shown that bilingual children learn their first words at the same time as monolingual children, and that bilingual and monolingual children often have a similar range of vocabulary.

Research also shows that there are no negative effects regarding development when a child learns two or more languages. Being bilingual or multilingual is very positive. However, some people see bilingual skills differently depending on which languages are being spoken. For example, a person who speaks English and French may be viewed more positively than a person who speaks English and Amharic. Children will develop fluency in both languages, although they may at times switch between languages in the same sentence. This is called code-switching. Children may also use the languages they speak in different situations – for example, English in the setting and their home, or first language at home. Being able to speak more than one language is extremely advantageous. It can enhance an individual's sense of self-esteem and identity (which will be discussed later in this chapter), as well as developing and enhancing cognitive and thinking skills. When the child becomes an adult, being able to speak more than one language may even have an economic advantage.

Children can develop bi-lingual skills in two ways, either simultaneously or successively. Simultaneous bilingualism is when children learn both languages at the same time from birth. Successive bilingualism is when children learn one language first and then learn a second language.

Simultaneous bilingualism

Children learning two languages at the same time have the same pattern of language development as children learning one language. The rate at which they learn the languages may be different from that for a child learning one language as they have two different languages to learn. At first children may use both vocabularies together as one language, but gradually they begin to separate them and use them as two languages. Children then begin to recognize which adults or settings speak which language, and begin to use the languages in the correct situation. In order to be able to do this, children need to hear languages being used consistently. They also need opportunities to practise their language skills and encouragement to do so.

Successive bilingualism

In successive bilingualism the same patterns or stages of development occur as in learning a second language. Children learn one language first and then a second. Children learning a second language need help and encouragement. Workers in many settings may be in a position where they are caring for children who speak one language at home, and then have to learn English or another language when they come to the setting. A child between 18 and 24 months who goes to a setting where workers do not speak his or her home language may have a period where development in both languages becomes frozen. Some children have a silent period when they do not speak the language they are learning, but they are taking in the language and begin to understand it. Suddenly, when they feel confident in how to use the language, they begin speaking it.

A Chance to Think 2

Alexandra, a 2½-year-old Spanish child, is due to start in your setting. Alexandra's first language is Spanish and she does not speak any English. Her mother has arranged to take a few days off work to help settle her into the setting, but then she has to return to work. You are going to be Alexandra's key worker.

What could you do before Alexandra starts in the setting to prepare yourself for her arrival?

When Alexandra starts in the setting, how will you help her to feel welcome and to settle?

How will you prepare Alexandra and her mother, and support them both when she has to return to work?

Compare your answers with the sample answers in Appendix 6.

Special needs

Some children have special needs that affect their language and communication skills. They may be using systems to communicate that do not involve a spoken language, such as sign or symbol languages or a form of communication that is individual to a particular child, or a variety of forms of communication used by other children as well. Some children use a spoken language, but, whatever form of communication is being used, it is important that workers recognize it, value it and support children in it. Ways of supporting language and communication development are discussed later in this chapter.

Hearing impairment

There are different degrees of hearing impairment that affect the way children hear and communicate. A child may be born with a hearing impairment or may develop a hearing impairment later on in life. Sometimes this may be due to an injury or illness (e.g. meningitis or 'glue ear'). If a child has a hearing impairment, this must be recognized as early as possible, so that help and support can be provided for both child and parents. Children may have mild, moderate or severe hearing loss. A child with mild hearing loss may find it hard to hear people speaking. He or she might develop spoken language, but it might be delayed. A child with a moderate hearing loss might need some help with language development. Some children have to wear hearing aids. Children with severe hearing loss need help with language development and, because they are unable to hear spoken language, they may use sign language.

Speech impairment

Some children do not develop speech or speak in their own individual language. Children with autism or cerebral palsy may not develop spoken language. Children with Downs' syndrome may be slow to develop language, but often understand more than they can put into words. All children are individuals and workers should not make assumptions about their language development, or lack of it. Workers should observe children's language and communication skills and base their knowledge on that, and then encourage children to develop.

Some children develop a stutter. This may be because a child is in a hurry to talk, and his or her brain gets ahead of the language coming out. A stutter often disappears, but if it does not, a child may need the specialist help of a speech therapist.

Body language

Body language is just what it says it is: the way we communicate with our bodies. Many messages can be given with the body silently. Some workers, when they see children doing something they are not supposed to, can just look at them in a particular way and the children will alter their behaviour. Children learn to 'read' body language. Just as language alters according to the situation people find themselves in, so does body language and the distance people stand apart from one another. Edward Hall, a psychologist, discovered that there are four zones of proximity. The zone of intimacy is where people who know each other well stand. This can be from as close as bodily contact to about eighteen inches away. Personal distance is for friends, people we trust or people we have something in common with. This is from eighteen inches to four feet. The third zone is that of social distance, which is from four to twelve feet. The last zone is the public zone, which is anything over twelve feet. The distances alter across cultures. In some cultures standing close to someone is considered impolite, and in other cultures it is quite acceptable to stand very close to people and have bodily contact with them. Likewise, in some cultures it is considered impolite for children to look at adults when they are talking to them. Workers need to consider body language when they are working with children, parents and colleagues.

Supporting children's language and communication skills

All children need support and encouragement in order to help their language and communication use and development. This support needs to meet the individual needs of each child. All children need the chance to practise their language skills in a non-threatening environment, with both their peer group and adults. It is important for workers to listen to what children are saying and to respond to them. As well as listening to children, workers need to provide them with opportunities to develop listening skills. Children developing language and communication skills will make mistakes in the way they say things and in the vocabulary they use. When this happens, it is important that workers do not

Figure 6.1 Books help children to develop language and communication skills.

ridicule them, draw everybody's attention to their mistake, or laugh at them. Children should not be expected to 'perform' or 'show off' their language skills in front of others. One effective way of helping children's language development is to say things back to children rephrased correctly rather than saying, "That is wrong. Say it like this.'

Children need opportunities to practise their language and communication skills in a positive and supportive environment. They need to feel secure in themselves and the environment, and trust the workers in the setting. Children need to hear language spoken naturally and be able to use language in many different situations and with a variety of people. Children benefit from hearing language and vocabulary used consistently. It can be very confusing when there are so many words for the same thing. For example, some people may describe a drinking vessel as a 'cup', others as a 'mug' and yet others as a 'beaker'. It also helps children if workers communicate with parents and share information about language and communication development. Parents can tell workers what vocabulary they use at home and whether they have any special words for particular things.

Workers should use a variety of activities that enable children to hear and practise language, including stories, rhymes, songs and music. Poems, drama, role-play and props, as well as conversations and listening games undertaken in a sensitive and supportive way, can all help a child to develop confidence in themselves and their language. Workers should provide a natural environment that is rich in both verbal and written language and communication. This should include languages other than English, and can include welcome posters, labelling of objects in the environment, interest tables, books in single languages other than English, as well as dual-language books and books in English. It should also have a place for children to write and make marks. Chapter 5 gave ideas for other activities that workers can do that will help develop and enhance language and communication skills.

Children who speak more than one language

Workers who speak only one language can support and facilitate all children's language and communication development. Workers should acknowledge and respect children's skills in speaking more than one language. Sometimes workers can feel threatened when children talk in a language they don't understand, and ask them to speak in English. If children are speaking to each other in their home language, or first language, in the setting this should not be discouraged, as otherwise children may feel that only English is valued in the setting.

Many children will not speak in the setting until they are confident in their language skills. They may go through a silent period, as discussed earlier in this chapter. Children should not be forced to speak or be told off if they don't get it right when they do speak. Workers should speak to children naturally in normal English. It is important not to speak in 'pidgin English' or baby talk, or to talk slowly and loudly, as this will not help a child's language development. Tone, gesture, facial expressions and visual clues help a child to understand what is being said.

Workers should ensure that they know how to pronounce and spell all children's names and that they are using the child's correct name. Some children may use their second name. Names should not be shortened, or altered, to make it easier for workers to say them, as this is not valuing the person. A person's name is important; it is part of his or her identity. Asking parents is the only way to ensure that the correct name is being used. Workers could also begin to keep a record of common words used by children in their language (e.g. toilet, drink, hello and goodbye). If this is done each time a child with a 'new' language to the setting begins attending, the setting will soon have a useful reference tool that can be added to. This ensures that even if staff who speak a variety of languages leave the setting, it still has the information it needs. It is possible to add words that can be used for displays or notices, such as 'welcome', and the names of colours or numbers. Children should see and hear examples of their own language and a variety of languages. This can be done through dual-language books, displays and music tapes. Chapter 5 gave more examples of activities that support and encourage language development.

Children with special needs

It is important not to make assumptions about the language and communication skills of children with special needs. Workers should observe children to ensure that they are aware of the individual language and communication skills of each child. Often, a child will start in a setting and parents and workers are not aware that he or she has any special needs; it is only by observation that this becomes apparent. If this is so, parents must be informed sensitively so that appropriate help can be obtained (for example, a child may develop a hearing problem or may require specialist help with speech from a speech therapist).

Figure 6.2 My name is Sue.

Children who have a hearing impairment will need particular help depending on the amount of hearing loss they have. Workers need to face children, as they may lip-read. Children also need to sit 'face on' to workers or other children, so that their lips can be clearly seen. In school this might mean their sitting at the front of the group. This should always be done in a sensitive way so as not to make a child feel stupid or embarrassed. The other children in the setting will generally respond positively if workers explain why a child with a hearing impairment needs to sit near the front. Children with a hearing impairment may also need non-verbal cues, such as a gentle touch, to gain their attention or to encourage them to look and listen at the same time. If workers say a child's name before they start a sentence, then the child will be aware that it is they who are being spoken to and not anyone else. Listening games, such as sound lotto, will help a child to develop listening skills. One of the most important things to remember is to speak clearly with hands away from the mouth. If a child is wearing a hearing aid it will pick up all the sounds around, not just the sounds he or she wants to hear. If the environment is noisy to workers it will be doubly noisy to children wearing a hearing aid.

Children with other special needs should also be encouraged in their language and communication skills. Some children may be able to vocalize, even if they cannot say particular words. Workers should encourage children to use their voice and praise them for it. Workers may need to learn sign or symbol languages in order to communicate with children. This may mean workers attending training courses. Once signs are being used regularly in the setting, it is possible for other children in the setting to learn some of them. It is important that workers acknowledge and respect the different ways children have of communicating and do not make derogatory remarks about them in front of the children. It is also important that workers talk to children in natural language, and sing songs, speak rhymes and tell stories. It is now possible to get books in Bliss symbols as well as other symbol and sign languages.

A Chance to Think 3

David, a little boy with Down's syndrome, attends your setting. He has been attending for some time and is very settled. David is very independent. He has some speech that those who are close to him understand, and he uses sign language. Amanda, a student, has recently started in the setting. Amanda does not understand David's speech or sign language. You have noticed that she is actively avoiding David, and when she does have contact with him she laughs at his attempts to communicate with her and tells you she can't understand him. David is beginning to lose his confidence and the other children are beginning to notice this and starting to laugh at David.

What will you do about this situation?

How will you ensure that David regains his confidence and communication skills?

Compare your answers with the sample answers in Appendix 6.

Attitudes towards language and communication

We saw in Chapter 1 that we all possess attitudes towards a whole variety of things. People may also have attitudes towards language and communication strategies. Some people feel that some languages are 'better' than others and have greater value. In particular, English and European languages are often seen as 'better' languages to speak than African or Asian languages. However, all languages are important and linguistically are of equal value. The same can also be said for dialects and accents. Some accents are seen as 'better' than others and some people make judgements about individuals based on the accent they speak with. Workers need to be aware of their own attitudes towards languages and communication strategies.

The way language is used can also shape people's attitudes. Words can be used, sometimes unintentionally, in an oppressive or discriminatory way. The word 'black' is often used in a negative way, e.g. 'blackleg', 'black mood', etc. Phrases can be used that exclude people with a disability, e.g. 'Stand on your own two feet'. English is, at present, a very male-dominated language. For example, textbooks are often written using the male gender, and people still use words and phrases such as 'mankind', 'chairman', 'fireman', 'all things to all men', etc. The way words and phrases are used can, either intentionally or unintentionally, marginalize, exclude, oppress and stereotype individuals and groups. Workers need to constantly think about, and evaluate, how they use language and the messages it conveys.

Language and communication strategies are not static implements. They are constantly evolving and changing. Some words and phrases that were used without thought at one time are now considered offensive or inappropriate. New words are constantly entering our vocabulary, and individuals and groups are now thinking about how language is used and the impact it has on individuals and groups. Words and phrases that are used today will change and evolve; new words will come into being and people's attitudes towards language will change. Workers need to discuss the use of language, its effects and their own attitudes to it within the team.

Child protection

Child protection or child abuse matters can raise many varying emotions and issues for workers. It is not easy to think that other people can deliberately harm children, or fail to prevent harm coming to them. This section looks at child protection issues within an anti-discriminatory framework. It gives an overview of child abuse. It looks at indicators that may lead workers to suspect that a child is being abused, and who is abusing. A list of publications is given at the end of this chapter for workers needing further information and support.

It is important to remember that abused children grow into adults. It is possible that someone reading this book has been abused or that people are working with parents or colleagues who have been abused. Some childcare workers may never have to deal with child protection issues during the whole of their professional career, some workers may deal with child protection issues occasionally, and others may be working with child protection issues regularly. Workers must receive help and support when they are dealing with child abuse issues. For workers in a group setting this can be from line managers or colleagues. Workers in isolated settings also need to find sources of support, and this may be through, social services or any of the organizations working in the child protection field. Local authorities have a legally binding duty under the Children Act 1989 and the Care Standards Act 2000 to investigate any cause for concern they may have relating to child protection issues. Childcare workers have a responsibility to protect the children in their care. The Care Standards Act 2000 resulted in the issuing of National Standards for Under Eights Day Care and Childminding. Standard 13 concerns Child Protection and says, 'The registered person complies with local child protection procedures approved by the Area Child Protection Committee and ensures all adults working and looking after children in the provision are able to put the procedures into practice.' The focus for Standard 13 goes on to say:

> The welfare, safety and protection of children are paramount. Where the registered person and staff recognise their responsibilities towards those in their care, they will be aware of their individual roles and understand the procedures they must follow if they have concerns about the welfare of a child.

Settings will need to work with local authorities if they have concerns about children. Workers must be familiar with the child protection policies of the setting in which they work and be aware of whom to go to if they have concerns about a child in the setting.

What is child abuse?

Child abuse takes place when an adult harms a child, either deliberately or by not keeping the child safe from harm. Local authorities and agencies working in the child protection field have many technical definitions of what child abuse is. Abuse can be defined under four headings:

- physical abuse;
- sexual abuse;
- emotional abuse;
- neglect.

Physical abuse

Physical abuse is what it says it is, an adult physically hurting or injuring a child. This includes adults hitting, burning, biting or shaking children. Workers often worry about recognizing abuse. In the case of physical abuse, workers need to be aware of how children naturally or accidentally injure themselves when playing or in their day-to-day activities. This depends on the age and stage of a child's development. For example, children running around and learning to ride bikes will have bumps, bruises and grazes around their knees and lower legs. Once workers are aware of this they will begin to recognize where it is unusual for children to hurt or injure themselves. Physical abuse is often called 'non-accidental injury', as a child has not been injured accidentally. A child's behaviour may also change. Workers need to know the children in their care, so that they can recognize any changes in behaviour. Some changes in behaviour will be for reasons other than physical abuse (e.g. moving home or the arrival of a new baby). Physical abuse takes place in cities, towns and villages, on boys and girls of all ages, in all classes, colours, cultures, incomes and religions, and among working and non-working families alike. It does not just happen in families on a low income living in the inner city.

The following list shows some possible signs of physical abuse. It is not an exhaustive list, but a list of some possible signs of physical abuse of which workers need to be aware.

- bruises in places where children do not naturally injure themselves and bruises of different ages;
- outline bruises, such as fingertip bruises, hand marks or marks made by objects such as a strap;
- burns and scalds that have a regular shape, such as cigarette burns or burns from irons or fires;
- bite marks (adult bite marks are larger than children's bites);

- broken skin, scratches and grazes;
- broken bones;
- changes in children's behaviour.

All children bruise themselves, and workers should be able to recognize bruises and how they age on different skin colours and tones. A bruise will look different on a child with white skin and on a child with black skin. If you are not sure how bruises age and what bruises of different ages look like, it is a good idea to watch one age next time you are bruised. Some black and mixed-race children may have a birthmark that looks like a bruise. This is called a Mongolian blue spot. It is a naturally occurring mark, and is sometimes found at the base of the spine. It is useful for workers to know whether children have any birthmarks, as sometimes they may wonder what they are when they first see them. Parents will be able to provide workers with this information.

There are many variations in how parents discipline children. These are linked to child-rearing practices and vary across cultures and between families. Some families feel that smacking children with the palm of the hand is an acceptable form of discipline. Other parents believe that using a strap or stick is acceptable. Sometimes the edges begin to blur between discipline and abuse. It can be hard to tell when discipline turns into child abuse. A child who has some sort of injury that can be seen and measured is said to have a significant injury.

There are no laws in Britain to prevent parents disciplining or punishing their children, but local authorities have guidelines as to what are considered to be acceptable forms of discipline. Many childcare settings have guidelines on disciplining children, which include a 'no smacking policy', as it is not considered good practice to smack or physically punish children.

Sexual abuse

Sexual abuse occurs when adults use children to gain sexual pleasure. This may include adults involving children in sexual activities such as masturbation, oral and penetrative sex (anal and vaginal) and other sexual behaviour, or involving them in pornography. Both boys and girls can be sexually abused. Sexual abuse also occurs on young babies and may continue over a period of time. Like physical abuse, sexual abuse takes place in cities, towns and villages, among all classes, colours, cultures, incomes and religions, and in working and non-working families.

Company magazine published an article in the summer of 1995 on sexual abuse in the Asian community, in which a spokeswoman from the Asian Women's Advisory Service said:

> There's no doubt there is sexual abuse going on in the Asian community. But what is changing is that more women are coming forward to deal with it. As more organizations for counselling and assistance are set up, Asian women will hopefully feel safer about seeking help.

The article interviewed an Asian girl who had been sexually abused by her father from the age of 6. She said, 'I didn't ask questions. I just did what he told me like the good little Asian girl I was.'

Like physical abuse, sexual abuse may result in physical injuries and changes in a child's behaviour. Some workers may find sexual abuse particularly difficult to deal with, as it is distressing to think that adults can deliberately harm children in this way. It is important for workers to get support in dealing with the emotional issues this may raise for them. The following list gives some possible signs of sexual abuse of which workers need to be aware. Sexual abuse may also be accompanied by physical and emotional abuse.

- pain, discomfort, soreness, cuts or bruising around the genital area;
- pain on going to the toilet, urinary tract infections;
- difficulty or pain in sitting down or walking;
- frequent masturbation;
- changes in children's behaviour, with their becoming withdrawn, regressing or in a state of 'frozen watchfulness';
- sexual knowledge, behaviour and play that is inappropriate for the age or stage of development.

Workers need to be aware of what bruises and cuts look like on different skin colours and tones. Workers also need to be aware of some cultural traditions that are considered to be abuse and are illegal in Britain. One of these is female genital mutilation, also known, incorrectly, as female circumcision. Female genital mutilation is practised by some groups in over twenty African countries as well as in Arabic countries and some Muslim groups. Female genital mutilation is carried out for cultural and religious reasons. In their publication *Child Protection and Female Genital Mutilation* (1992), Hedley and Dorkenoo, addressing whether communities practising it will resent action and intervention, say, 'Preventing mutilation may seem like an attack on the community . . . Always be clear that it is a matter of child protection: it is not racist' (p. 15). Although it is illegal in Britain, some girls are still at risk. It may take place in Britain and girls may be taken abroad to be circumcised, often with no anaesthetic and with basic instruments. Three types of female genital mutilation are described by Hedley and Dorkenoo: circumcision, the cutting of the hood of the clitoris; excision, the cutting of the clitoris and the labia minora; and infibulation, the cutting of the clitoris, labia minora and much of the labia major. The two remaining sides of the vulva are then sown up. This is a sensitive subject and workers should discuss any concerns they have with their line manager or a relevant professional.

Emotional abuse

Emotional abuse can be very damaging to children. The old nursery rhyme, 'Sticks and stones may break my bones but words will never hurt me', is very wrong. Words are powerful, and can affect children greatly. Emotional abuse can include adults teasing children, ridiculing them, withdrawing love as a punishment and ignoring children. Like physical and sexual abuse, emotional abuse takes place in all parts of the country and among all groups.

One child in a family may be singled out for emotional abuse. This is known as 'scapegoating'. Emotional abuse can be harder to detect than, for example, physical abuse, as there are generally few physical signs, but an abundance of behavioural ones. The following is a non-exhaustive list of signs of emotional abuse of which workers need to be aware:

- withdrawing or regressing;
- emotional outbursts;
- aggression;
- attention-seeking behaviour;
- low self-esteem.

Children who are emotionally abused may be experiencing other forms of abuse as well. They may feel unloved and unwanted. Emotional abuse may be used as a form of discipline – for example, 'I won't love you if you aren't good', 'Why can't you be good like your brother?', 'You were never wanted anyway!' This may often be said in the heat of the moment as a 'one off' and not be meant, but it becomes emotional abuse when it constantly happens. This is an unacceptable form of discipline and can leave a child psychologically damaged.

Neglect

Neglect happens when adults fail to care for children appropriately and to meet their essential needs. This is often difficult to define, as everyone has different standards of care. These may be influenced by the way people themselves were brought up, their parenting skills, cultural expectations, level of income and the environment in which they live.

Neglect can include not washing children, or not keeping them and their clothes clean; or not providing an adequate, or balanced, diet and clothing suitable for the prevailing weather conditions. Parents may not be deliberately neglecting their children. They may not have adequate resources to keep clothes clean. For example, homeless families living in bed-and-breakfast accommodation may have to share a bathroom with several other families and not have access to a washing machine. Parents on a low income may find it difficult to provide clothing and shoes. Neglect may also be deliberate and not due simply to poor parenting. It can include all of the above as well as leaving children alone to look after themselves, locking them in ('home alone' children) or even locking them out of the home.

The following non-exhaustive list gives some possible signs of neglect of which workers need to be aware:

- failure to thrive;
- poor hygiene;
- regular illness;
- tiredness, listlessness and hunger;
- unresponsiveness and low self-esteem.

Just as parents have different standards of care, so do childcare workers. Workers should try not to judge everyone by the standards they may hold.

Children who are suffering neglect may, or may not, also suffer other forms of abuse.

Who abuses?

It is possible for any adult to abuse a child. Child abuse is often portrayed in the media as something men do to children. Women are generally portrayed as the people who care for children. This is not always the case. Women can and do abuse children. Michele Elliott has discussed the issue of women abusers in her book *Female Sexual Abuse of Children: The Ultimate Taboo.*

Abusers also manage to gain access to children. As much as we don't like to think about it, it is possible for childcare workers to abuse children. Male workers often meet comments from parents wondering why they want to work with children. Many male workers feel they have to justify working in the childcare field. Abusers can be people in positions of responsibility, such as police and probation officers, clergy and volunteers in any group that involves children. Abuse can be carried out by parents, siblings, people known to the children, such as members of the immediate family, and people in positions of trust, as well as complete strangers to the children.

Workers with concerns about children

All settings should have a set of policies and procedures for dealing with child protection. It is important for workers to know what these are and with whom to discuss any concerns they may have about a particular child. Policies will vary between settings but they should all reflect local authority guidelines.

As a general rule, if workers have concerns about a child, talking to a colleague usually helps. Workers should always act within their work roles. It is generally not the role of workers, other than managers or perhaps childminders, to have to make a decision to report child protection issues to the local authority. If workers have a line manager, any concerns should be discussed with him or her. Workers must be aware of and work within confidentiality policies.

Once workers have passed on concerns to a line manager, the policies and procedures of the setting should be followed. These will generally involve discussing concerns with parents and keeping records. Some workers may have concerns about keeping records, owing to their inadequate literacy skills or lack of knowledge about correct terminology. Records should be factual and legible. They do not have to be written in jargon, and people reading them need to be able to understand them. All records should be dated and signed. It needs to be remembered that parents have the right to see records kept about their children.

Support systems and training

Settings need to put in place systems that support workers with issues relating to child protection. We saw at the beginning of this section that child protection can be an emotive issue for individuals. It is therefore essential that workers are able to access support appertaining to this. Male workers may feel particularly vulnerable with this area of work. Employers may feel that male workers should not be employed in this area in order to protect children from abuse by men. This is a sensitive area and one that needs careful thought by all involved. Workers may also need to take part in training and development in order to feel comfortable and confident with child protection issues and also to keep themselves up to date with developments in this area and changes in legislation.

A Chance to Think 4

Child protection work can be unsettling and raise many emotions in childcare workers. We have seen that there are four main types of abuse and that abusers can be male or female.

What other issues do workers need to be aware of when thinking about anti-discriminatory practices in child protection work?

Compare your answers with the sample answers in Appendix 6.

Development of identity and self-esteem

The final section of this chapter examines the development of identity and self-esteem. Workers should understand how children develop their own self-identity and self-esteem, and try to ensure that the development is positive. They also need to be able to recognize if, and when, children are suffering from low self-esteem (for example, a child who is, or has been, suffering abuse may have low self-esteem). In this section we look at some of the signs of low self-esteem and examine the worker's role in the development of identity and self-esteem.

The *Concise Oxford Dictionary* defines 'identity' as 'the quality or condition of being a specified person or thing; individuality, personality'. 'Esteem' is defined as meaning 'have a high regard for; greatly respect'. Gergen and Gergen, in their book *Social Psychology*, state that 'self esteem refers to an individual's perception of his or her own adequacy, competence or goodness as a person'.

Psychologists and sociologists both agree that people are not born with any idea of who they are. A sense of self and identity is not innate. People learn who they are and start to develop a sense of identity as they grow, because they start to interact with other people. Babies interact with people from their own families as well as people from society at large. It is only by interacting with others from the moment they are born that individuals develop

A Chance to Think 5

Every individual has his or her own identity. This identity has to be formed, so that people know who they are. Once individuals have developed their identity, they also develop feelings about that identity. Some people feel good about themselves. This is known as having high self-esteem. Some people do not feel good about themselves. This is known as having low self-esteem.

What factors play a part in how people develop their sense of identity?

Why do some people have high self-esteem?

Why do some people have low self-esteem?

Compare your answers with the sample answers in Appendix 6.

a sense of self and identity. Individuals begin to become aware of who they are, and how they fit into the world, by the way people respond and react to them. Children are aware that people are reacting to them. People 'goo' and 'coo' at babies, talk to them, interact with them and respond to them. In the feature film *Nell*, starring Jodie Foster, the character Nell had been brought up without contact with other people. She developed her own language and sense of identity, which changed when she began to interact with other people.

Babies begin to learn that they are separate people with their own identities. They learn that they are not physically attached to their mothers or to any other person. Babies learn very quickly that if they cry, people will respond to them. They learn that they are part of a group of people (i.e. family and society) and that they have a particular place in that group. This may be a single-parent family, a gay or lesbian family, an extended family or any other group of people. We have seen that babies soon begin to learn language and that they respond to language. Language has a very powerful part to play in how children develop their identity and self-esteem. People talk to babies and children. They tell them they are loved, beautiful, cute, clever, silly, naughty, bad, ugly and many other things. Children soon learn that these words mean something and that they have a value attached to them. If children are constantly told that they are beautiful or loved by people around them, then they will believe that they are beautiful and loved. If children are constantly told they are bad or naughty and unloved, they will believe it.

Children learn that they have a name and a language and they respond to that name and language. A person's name is very important. It can be central to their identity: how a person sees themselves as well as how others see them. A name can say a lot about a person's culture or even their religion. For some individuals it may provide a link to their family history. Naming traditions and systems may vary between cultures, religions and places. For example, in Tigray in Ethiopia, Christian children are given a name at birth and then a Christian or saint's name when they are later baptized. Surnames are not used; children take the name of their father as their last name. In the Sikh religion some children get their names in a naming ceremony that takes place in the gurudwara, the Sikh religious building. They then take the Sikh family name, with boys taking the name Singh and girls the name Kaur. Some given names are associated with religions; for example, Christian names come from the Bible, and many Jewish names from the Old Testament of the Bible. Some Muslim names come from the Qur'an. In some cultures, such as the Arabic one, some names are everyday words; in other cultures, names come from particular traditions associated with that culture. It is important that workers understand the naming systems used by the children and families they work with. Some families do not use surnames. Other families may have a child where the two parents have different surnames or they may share the same surname. It is also important that workers are clear about how to pronounce and spell names. If necessary, workers should check with parents about pronunciation and spelling. Workers should not shorten or change names, but use the name the child is given. Some families may use the second name they have given their child and not the one that is written first. Other children may have a 'given name' but be called by a derivative of it; for example, Henry may be known as Harry.

Workers should also check with parents about how they would like to be addressed. Some parents like to be addressed formally by their title and surname, e.g. 'Mrs Kaur'. Other parents prefer to be addressed informally by their first name. The same is true of colleagues. Workers should not change or shorten colleagues' names, or use nicknames for them, unless they are invited to.

Sometimes there may be children, workers or parents in the setting with the same name. It is possible to identify individuals in this situation without taking away from each person their identity. Names should not be changed if there happen to be two people with the same name in a setting, nor should anything be added that might be derogatory to the person, e.g. 'Old Jane'.

Workers should not make assumptions about an individual's name and what they are called. An individual's name plays an important part in the development of their identity and workers should recognize and respect names and what they may mean to people.

The development of identity is a complex process. A baby is not born with a sense of identity, but it is built up from birth from all that they experience. Identity changes over time. It is not something that is static, but is constantly changing and growing. It can be influenced by many things, including age, culture, family background, religion, achievement, disability, self-esteem, country of residence, sexuality, gender, political beliefs, legal status, other people's perceptions, as well as all the life experiences a person has. Amin Maalouf in his book *On Identity* (2000), when describing his identity, says:

> So am I half French or half Lebanese? Of course not. Identity can't be compartmentalised. You can't divide it up into halves or thirds or any other separate segments. I haven't got several identities: I've got just one, made up of many components combined together in a mixture that is unique to every individual.

While it is important not to compartmentalize identity, or put a label or type on a person, we will now examine how identity can be influenced or shaped. When discussing identity it is important to remember that every person is an individual, and no two people are the same. Some people may have many things in common, say as a result of their gender. They may even undergo the same experiences, but each person will react to them in their own way and these influences will be different for each individual. Even twins, who genetically have the most in common, will develop their own identity and sense of self. Everyone is unique and has their own identity.

It is essential that workers recognize the importance of children developing a positive sense of their own identity and a strong sense of self-esteem. Workers have an important part to play in this, and their very presence in a child's life will have an influence on this development, as will other people whom children have contact with, together with the environment in which they live. Some children may receive many positive messages about themselves, which will help them develop a positive sense of identity and strong sense of self-esteem. Other children may receive negative, stereotypical, discriminatory or oppressive messages, which may result in their developing low self-esteem and a poor sense of identity. Developing positive self-esteem and a strong sense of identity depends in part on children's feeling accepted, valued and respected by others as worthwhile individuals. Discrimination, prejudice, stereotyping and oppression all hurt people and may harm the development of a positive sense of self-identity and self-esteem.

Language identity and self-esteem

We saw earlier on in this chapter the importance of language and communication strategies. Language and identity are closely linked. We have seen how language can be used to stereotype individuals and groups. We have also seen how language can be very male oriented, with the use of male pronouns in books and words being ascribed to male occupations. For example, when the word 'nurse' is used, most people tend to think about this as a female profession, where the word 'doctor' suggests a male profession. The publication *Women and Language* from the European Commission (Niedzwiecki, 1993) reports, 'as a result, in language as in the social environment, women are rendered transparent, non-existent, invisible and there is an indirect message that they should keep quiet'.

We saw how the language, accent or dialect spoken by individuals may influence the way they are perceived by others and that people make judgements about individuals depending on the way they speak. Individuals who do not use a spoken language, but who may 'sign' or use technology as a means of communication, may often miss out on 'everyday' communication and conversation. They may feel isolated by this. Workers need to be aware how the use of language and communication can impact on identity. They need to think about how they use and respond to language, and the messages thus portrayed. Workers also need to ensure they are valuing and respecting an individual's first language and that all children are able to use their first language. If people are unable to use their first language they may feel that their language is not valued and in consequence feel that they are not valued. Workers may therefore need to learn to sign or to use technology in order to communicate. Children also need to hear and see their language used and reflected in the environment. It needs to be accessible to them and valued and respected by workers at all times.

Abused children's identity and self-esteem

We saw earlier in this chapter what constitutes child abuse. A child who has been abused may have low self-esteem and have issues concerning identity. A child who has been abused may feel they are to blame for the abuse or that being abused is a part of life. Such feelings can have a profound effect on a child's sense of identity. Greff and Stuart say in *The RHP Companion to Foster Care*, (Wheal, 1999):

> The abuse can leave a child with feelings of having been damaged, of somehow being responsible for the fact that the abuse happened, of guilt, of shame and so on. All of this will of course have a major impact on their sense of their own value and worth. (Section 1.4, p. 37)

Workers need to work with children in a sensitive manner and may need to seek help and advice when working with children who have been abused. Children need to be told that the abuse was not their fault and that they are not 'bad'. Some children may need the help of other professionals when working through issues relating to the abuse.

'Looked-after' children's identity and self-esteem

Not all children live with their birth family. Some children may be adopted, some may spend some time in short-term foster care and then return to live with their family. Some children may spend a longer period with foster carers and then be adopted, and some children may spend time in a residential setting. Children who are 'looked after' will have different experiences of family and being cared for from those children who live with their birth families. Some children may know their birth families, others may not. This in itself may have a deep impact on an individual's sense of self and identity. Some children may feel a sense of loss, some may feel rejected and confused, others may wonder about their origins and background. An awareness of, and acknowledgement of, a person's origin is an important part of that individual's development of identity. Greff and Stuart in *The Companion to Foster Care* quote The Who Cares? Group, which said that young people in the care system should be given 'the right to know who we are . . . to have factual information about our family origins and background . . . [We must] make sure every young person really understands [their] situation and why [they] cannot live with [their] family.' Some children who were born in one country and then adopted and subsequently come to live in a different country may experience a name change. We have already seen how important a person's name is in the development of identity. Some children may not speak English, or they may be bilingual and living in a monolingual household or care setting. This has implications for the development of the children's first language, and we have seen how important it is for individuals to be able to use their first language and take pride in it. Some children may have limited personal possessions or limited space they can call their own. Children who are 'looked after' may have several different professionals involved in, and knowing about, their lives and making decisions about them. They may regularly experience situations in their lives that other children do not – for example, moves between care settings and people, regular reviews, medicals, and involvement with a variety of professionals and a wider number of people having personal information about them.

Workers may or may not know that a child is 'looked after' or adopted. They should work equally with all children to develop a positive sense of self and identity. If workers are aware that a child is 'looked after' or adopted, they should not make assumptions or judgements about why that is the case, or label children. Some children may have contact with their birth family, some may be involved in life story work and workers need to participate sensitively in that with them. Workers need to be alert to the needs of individual children and work with them sensitively and accordingly.

Achievement of identity and self-esteem

In Chapter 1 we discuss research into teachers' perceptions of children at school and how they could be stereotypical. We also saw how teachers' expectations of children can influence them and act as a self-fulfilling prophecy. Teachers and all individuals who work with children are in a very powerful position. They are in a position of trust and influence. A child's achievements, or their sense of achievement, may have a great effect on the development of their identity and their self-esteem.

The document *Education of Young People in Public Care* identified that children who are 'looked after' experience barriers to educational success, including the fact that 'schools and carers display lower expectations of young people in public care, which contribute to under achievement and failure' and the fact that 'they experience unnecessary moves out of school or are out of school for prolonged periods'.

Workers' assessments of children may also influence the way they behave towards them and consequently affect a child's achievements. Workers and parents are continually assessing children both formally and informally. Parents may judge their child, either intentionally or unintentionally, in relation to things written in books or to test scores, e.g. developmental tests, or compare them with other children. Workers and parents will then talk to one another and compare information. This in turn influences workers because they learn information about children that they might not otherwise have known. This information is then used to make decisions about a child and their abilities. This informal assessment can be very subjective and may be based on a worker's personal beliefs and cultural 'norms'. This may lead workers to be biased towards an individual child or a group of children, particularly if workers are not aware of how their own personal frames of reference can influence their assessment of children. Indeed, Murphy (1999) said that there are 'no assessments that are culture fair or culture blind'.

Formal assessment can include many aspects such as profiles, exams, SATs, etc. Profiles are becoming more widely used, particularly in education settings. They may show where a child is at any given moment in time. Depending on the format used, a profile may include the skills and attitudes that an individual has developed, as well as what that child has learnt or knows. Because profiles are individual to each child, and children may be involved in helping to compile them, they give a greater understanding of where a child has started from, and what they have achieved. Individuals are being compared not with others, but against themselves. This is extremely positive for children, as their achievements are being recognized, acknowledged and valued for what they are. Children can see and have an input into this process, which will help develop a sense of achievement and self-esteem. A child with a sense of self and self-esteem may be motivated to learn and participate, for then they can see what precisely they are achieving and that their individual efforts are therefore important.

Norm-referenced assessment compares the achievements of individuals with those of other individuals – for example, it will rank class scores and there will be a first and a last. This can have a particularly strong influence on an individual's motivations and self-esteem. There always has to be a 'number one' and also an individual who comes last. For some individuals, no matter how hard they try, or what they learn or achieve, they will never come 'top of the class'. They may then become demotivated, or start to see themselves as 'not able to learn', which leads us back to the self-fulfilling prophecy. The individual who comes 'top of the class' may also be influenced by the results. They may feel they do not have to try, and consequently may acquire a false sense of themselves and of what they are capable. Norm-referenced assessments may also give workers a false sense of children's achievements. For example, the individual who comes last may have actually learnt a great deal since the last assessment, but this may not be recognized in the result. They may feel they have put in a great deal of effort and it is not being recognized. As Murphy (1999) said, 'for effective learning, it makes a difference if pupils believe that effort is more important than ability, that mistakes are an inevitable part of learning, and that they have control over their own learning'.

Even the way workers work together and the records they make and keep can influence both themselves and the achievements of a child. As Drummond says, 'I like to make up my own mind, I like to start with a clean slate, children can be too easily labelled, teachers are always biased. I leave the records alone until I have had a chance to see for myself' (1997, p. 176).

We can see that achievement can, and does, play a part in the development of self-esteem and identity. Workers need to be aware of the large role they play in this and how their day-to-day work and behaviour can have a huge impact on children and their achievements. Workers need to communicate with one another and constantly evaluate their own actions, behaviour, assessment methods, assumptions and biases. They need to recognize the achievements and efforts of all individual children and to praise, encourage and value the efforts and achievements of each child. They need to know where a child started from so that they are clear about what a child has achieved.

Gender identity and self-esteem

In Chapter 1 we saw how gender can influence and affect identity development. There are differences between men and women. What they are, how they came about and how they influence identity has long been debated. Cohen, in *Essential Psychology* (1990, p. 202), says:

An enormous literature has tried to establish the psychological differences (if any) between males and females. There are three broad positions. First, sociobiologists believe in profound biological differences: men were 'made' to hunt; women were 'made' to look after the babies, and this ancient 'truth' continues to affect behaviour deeply. Second, there is the feminist view which claims that men have exaggerated such differences for their own patriarchal advantage: the best way to keep women in their place is to persuade them that they are less able and less dynamic than men. Biological differences actually mean much less than has been believed: any woman can drive a tank or become prime minister like Mrs Thatcher. A third view argues that, although differences have been exaggerated, there is some biological validity to them.

Gender identity and the behaviour of males and females may also be influenced by cultural expectations. The book *Child Development* by Sharma and Kaushik (published in New Delhi in 1994) starts by saying:

> High school girls like to play with babies and small children. They enjoy caring for children . . . Out of the experiences provided in the area of child development, the natural eagerness in girls to nurture, to protect, to educate and to love children will be enhanced.

If girls and boys are expected to behave in a particular way, then that will have an influence on the development of their identity and their behaviour.

We saw earlier in this chapter how language has a significant influence on gender and the development of identity. We also saw how achievement can influence self-esteem and identity. We saw in Chapter 1 how boys and girls are treated differently, and every year when the GCSE and A level results are announced there is great debate in the media about the grades and differing gender achievements. Are there any gender differences in educational performance? It appears there are. Girls appear to be ahead in examination results for all subjects except physics.

Female and male genders are equally important and there are differences between the genders. Children learn about gender, and what they learn affects their identity and self-esteem. As we have seen, attitudes and values also develop towards gender, and stereotypes and discrimination occur. Workers need to consider their own values and attitudes towards gender. They need to consider their own behaviour and how this affects the identity development and self-esteem of the children they work with. For example, they need to consider the language they use, the resources provided and how they are used, the images seen and not seen in the environment and the messages they give, the roles children are expected to conform to, and the expectations of parents and how workers communicate with parents.

Racial identity and self-esteem

We have seen that children receive messages about their identity from many sources. Jocelyn Emama Maximé (1993), in the book *How and Why Children Hate*, says that in order for children to develop a positive identity they need to be aware of their racial identity and have a positive image of it. She argues that some aspects of identity are common to all children, such as self-esteem, self-concept, pride and social awareness, but that racial identity is not the same for all children. Children come from different racial backgrounds and need to have a positive image of their racial background in order to develop a strong personal identity and self-esteem. This is particularly true for black children who grow up experiencing prejudice, discrimination and stereotyping. Maximé writes, 'I have argued that the nurturance of black children's development of racial identity is fundamental to sound psychological well being' (p. 96).

This point is well illustrated by a piece of research undertaken by Clarke and Clarke in 1947 into self-hatred. They showed a pair of dolls to black children between the ages of 3 and 7. One doll had a dark brown skin tone and one had a light brown skin tone. They asked the children questions, including which doll they wanted to play with, which doll was the nicest and which doll looked bad. Two-thirds of the children favoured the doll with the lighter skin tone. They appeared to dislike the doll that most resembled them in appearance. These children had assimilated the message received from society about the value placed on race and colour. We saw in Chapter 1 that children do notice skin colour and make value judgements about it. We also saw that teachers make judgements and treat children differently depending on their background and colour.

Workers need to recognize that individuals and groups are discriminated against on account of their colour or perceived racial identity. Very young children can experience racism. This may lead to those children having a low sense of self-esteem and a damaged sense of identity. Workers need to challenge their own perceptions and values as well as those of others. They also need constantly to review and evaluate their own practice to ensure that they are not being discriminatory and that they are enabling children to develop a strong and positive sense of identity.

Identity in children of mixed parentage/dual heritage

We have just seen how race and colour may influence and affect a child's identity. As we saw at the beginning of this section, every individual has many components that go to make up their identity, every one of which is important. Children who have two parents from different backgrounds may have different issues that affect the development of their identity and self-esteem from children who have parents of the same background. We have seen how powerful language is and how it can affect people's perceptions. This is particularly true when using words describing children who have parents from two different backgrounds. Children of dual heritage need to feel that the heritage of both parents is valued and respected. We saw in Chapter 1, and also above, that children may be discriminated against and that there are stereotypes of many individuals and groups. Dual heritage children may also suffer from discrimination and stereotypes that can be damaging. It is important to recognize that these stereotypes are not accurate, and being of dual heritage is indeed very positive, as seen in the titles of two publications on the subject: *The Colour of Love: Mixed Race Relationships* (Alibhai-Brown and Montague, 1992) and *The Best of Both Worlds: Celebrating Mixed Parentage* (Early Years Anti-Racist Network, n.d.).

Tizard and Phoenix, in their book *Black, White or Mixed Race?* (1995), reported the research they had undertaken. Parents with dual heritage children, when interviewed, felt that they needed to provide a strong sense of identity for their children and to encourage confidence and self-esteem. One parent said, 'I have always said to x, "It is not that the world is divided into black and white people, that is not the conflict, it is divided into prejudiced and non-prejudiced people, and they can be any colour."'

Workers need to recognize that children need to develop a positive sense of their own identity and the components that go together to make them the person they are. As we saw earlier in this chapter, identity is made up of many parts and all need to be recognized and valued. Dual heritage children should be able to recognize, value and feel proud of all the various facets of their heritage. Workers need to talk to parents so that all are working together to enhance children's self-esteem and identity.

Effects of family composition on identity and self-esteem

Families are made up of many different permutations, as we saw in Chapter 1. Some children are being brought up in lone-parent families. The Gingerbread report for 2000, *The Future for Lone Parent Families*, cites the statistic that one in four families is now being headed by a lone parent, and says that for many of these families poverty is a very real issue. Both lone parenthood and poverty can raise identity and self-esteem issues for children. Children want to 'belong', and in these days of ever-growing commercialization, having and owning items is becoming important for more and more individuals, be it the latest trainers or other items that children in their peer group possess. Children have peer groups to which they 'belong'. Peer pressure is likely be influential in how individuals feel about themselves and how they see themselves as fitting into or belonging to a group. Being part of a lone-parent family can also influence a child's identity and self-esteem. Some people often make assumptions about lone parents and their circumstances. As with all assumptions, these may be wrong. The reasons why a family is headed by a lone parent are as many and various as reasons for other family structures. A person may have made a decision to be a lone parent, like for example Jodie Foster, the Hollywood film star. Two parents may have lived together and then separated, with a child living with one parent and seeing the other parent. A parent may have died, leaving the remaining parent to bring up any child alone. A child may be brought up by a lone foster parent. In every case the lone parent may be either female or male. Each of these differing situations may have a different impact on the life of a child. Families may also be made up of two heterosexual parents, or one or both parents may be gay or lesbian. Some workers may not have considered this family composition and may feel uncomfortable with it, depending on their own values and feelings concerning sexuality. Other families attending the setting may be discriminatory or not approve as they might feel homosexuality is wrong, or contrary to their religious beliefs. Children may ask questions about why someone has two mothers or two fathers and workers need to think about how they would respond to these situations. We have seen that not all families are 'nuclear' families made up of mother, father and 2.4 children. Children may also be brought up in reconstituted or extended families.

This whole book is about the issues that affect and influence a child's development. How a child is brought up, and by whom, is one of the major influences that will shape that child's identity and self-esteem. Workers need to provide images of various family structures and compositions. They need to be prepared to discuss and respond to comments and questions about families in a sensitive and non-discriminatory manner.

Identity and self-esteem in children with disabilities or special needs

There are many types of disability. The type and influence of the disability on an individual's life may have differing effects on the development of that person's identity and self-esteem. Some people see children with disabilities as 'sad' or to be 'pitied' as they will never 'get well'. This in itself may influence how someone with a disability is perceived and consequently how they then may perceive themselves. A child will pick up messages they

receive from people and their surroundings about themselves.

If an individual is unable to gain access to particular places, they may feel marginalized. If a child is unable to communicate with others who do not understand, or use the same communication system as they use, they may feel frustrated or rejected. Some individuals may have a mild form of disability that is not immediately obvious or hardly affects their day-to-day life. It is therefore important for workers not to make assumptions about a child, their disability or their identity. Some disabled children may be very confident, outgoing and have a strong sense of identity; others may be lacking in confidence, and have low self-esteem or a poor sense of identity. Often children react to people whose appearance is different from theirs. This can be true if a child sees an individual with a disability that makes them look 'different' from the child who notices them. Children often ask questions that embarrass the adults accompanying them. The reaction of an adult in this situation will have an effect on the identity and self-esteem of both the child asking the question and the person with the disability. A child who has a disability may find it hard to develop a positive identity and self-esteem. Often people see the disability first before they see the individual; or perhaps the identity of the individual gets caught up with the disability, and that is all people focus on.

We have already seen how powerful language can be. Being referred to as a 'disabled person' means that the disability comes first and that is how an individual is perceived. Terms such as 'the disabled' depersonalize people. As with all issues concerning identity, it is important to recognize that disability is only one area that may affect how an individual sees themself. A child with a disability will also have other areas that will affect their identity, such as gender, family composition, colour and culture. Each will overlap and make a contribution as to how an individual perceives themself and their identity. Workers need to build on what a child can do and not what they cannot do. Children need to feel secure, loved, respected and valued. As we saw in Chapter 1, the Care Standards Act 2000 brought forth the National Standards for Under Eights Day Care and Childminding. Standard 10, Special needs (including special educational needs and disabilities), states:

> The registered person is aware that some children may have special needs and is proactive in ensuring that appropriate action can be taken when such a child is identified or admitted to the provision. Steps are taken to promote the welfare and development of the child within the setting in partnership with parents and other relevant parties.

This is further qualified in the guidance documents that are issued for each area. The guidance for sessional day care states:

> Children with special needs are most likely to have their needs met where the registered person and staff have secure knowledge and understanding of individual needs of every child in their care. Staff work together with parents and other relevant parties to organise the environment and plan activities to ensure all children take part at an appropriate level to their needs.

Refugee children's identity and self-esteem

The United Nations paper *Working Far from Home: Migration and Discrimination* (2001) says that 'some 150 million men, women and even children, about three percent of the world's population, are outside their country of origin, coming as strangers to the country where they reside'. It goes on to say, 'Women and children account for more than half the refugees and internally displaced persons.' Many refugees will have experienced war or violence, spent time in hiding and had a long and dangerous journey to safety. The magazine *Eve*, in an article entitled 'Prejudice' published in August 2001, told the history of a woman and her children. She and her husband had been arrested, beaten and tortured. A few years later her husband and two of her sons were arrested and tortured. A bribe was paid to release the boys, but the husband was destroyed mentally. The woman fled the country with her children, a four-month journey to safety during which she had a stroke. She eventually ended her journey in England. This, and experiences like it, will have an effect on a child's self-esteem and identity. Children who are refugees may be experiencing discrimination, have physical and mental health issues, feel isolated, and not be able to understand the language or the day-to-day systems. They may have had to leave family members behind, resulting in worry or guilt. Another issue that the family may have to deal with is the uncertainty about their legal status. Will they be granted refugee status or leave to remain, or will they face the fear of having to return to the country from which they fled?

Tina Hyder, in an article in *Nursery World* (2001) described 'STOP – a framework for working with refugee children: S – space and structure, T – trust and talking, O – opportunities to play, P – Partnership with parents (and other carers)'. Workers following this framework will be able to begin working with children and families in a supportive way. Some children may need specialist help in dealing with what has happened to them and their family, while other children may need time and support to help them to develop and resolve issues concerning their identity. Workers themselves may need to seek support, time, knowledge and help in working with children who are refugees.

Traveller children's identity and self-esteem

Travellers are classed as a racial group, and therefore the contents of the Race Relations Act 1996 and Race Relations (Amendment) Act 2000 apply. Children of traveller families may experience discrimination, which may in turn affect their self-esteem and development of identity. Some travellers may have a nomadic lifestyle, others may live on sites, and yet others in houses.

Mental health in relation to identity and self-esteem

Mental health is an area about which some workers feel uncomfortable as they may know little about it, or may have had personal experience of mental health issues or are unsure about what it is and what it means. The Department for Education and Skills document *Promoting Children's Mental Health within Early Years and School Settings* (2001) says:

> Mental health is about maintaining a good level of personal and social functioning. For children and young people, this means getting on with others, both peers and adults, participating in educative and other social

activities, and having a positive self esteem. Mental health is about coping and adjusting to the demands of growing up. It does not all happen at one point in time, and appears to result from an interactive process to which we can all contribute, based on the child's environmental, social and cultural context.

Children who are experiencing poor mental health may have low self-esteem. It may affect the development of their identity, as people may see and label 'the problem' before they see the child. Such children may be bullied or teased. They may feel rejected and isolated, and some may self-harm. Workers may need to seek advice from relevant professionals as to how best to support and work with children experiencing difficulties with their mental health.

Other factors that may affect identity and self-esteem

While we have looked at some issues that may affect a child's identity and self-esteem, it is important to remember that this is not an exhaustive list. Identity can also be influenced by sexuality, religion, culture, class, age, economic status, etc. As we saw at the beginning of this section on identity, each child is an individual. Some children may have several facets to their identity that overlap and change and develop over time. Identity and its development is not static. It is important for workers not to make assumptions about children or fit them into categories – for example, to assume that all children with a disability, all children who live in a lone-parent household will . . .

Signs of low self-esteem

Workers must acknowledge that not all children feel good about themselves, and that some children in the setting may be suffering from low self-esteem. Children who have been abused may have low self-esteem. Children who consider themselves not valued and respected because of the way they look or because of their colour, culture, race, religion, language, abilities or disabilities may also suffer from low self-esteem.

Signs of low self-esteem in children's behaviour include:

- not mixing with other children, or wanting to be by themselves;
- not wanting to be cuddled and avoiding physical contact;
- withdrawn or aggressive behaviour;
- not trying to do things in case they get it wrong;
- saying that they are no good at anything, that they are ugly or bad;
- harming themselves (for example, cutting, or trying to remove skin colour by bleaching or burning themselves);
- not having any pride in their appearance;
- antisocial behaviour, e.g. disrupting other children;
- poor concentration;
- lack of confidence;
- issues around food, e.g. overeating, not eating.

A Chance to Think 6

So far in this section we have talked about children's identity and self-esteem. It is also possible for adults to suffer from low self-esteem. Workers may know colleagues or parents who have low self-esteem.

What effect might a parent with low self-esteem have on his or her children?

Compare your answers with the sample answers in Appendix 6.

The worker's role

Much has been written about the worker's role in working with children to develop a positive sense of identity and self-esteem. Standard 9 of the National Standards for Under Eights Day Care and Childminding covers 'equal opportunities'. It says, 'The registered person and staff actively promote equality of opportunity and anti discriminatory practice for all children.' The focus for Standard 9, *Out of School Care: Guidance to the National*

Standards, says, 'Children need to feel valued and be free from discrimination. Where the registered person and staff are committed to equality they recognise that children's attitudes toward others are established in these early years.'

Workers have a vital role to play in their day-to-day contact with children. Siraj-Blatchford and Clarke (2000) identify six stages of equality-oriented practice that they have seen. Stage 1 is the least desirable and stage 6 the most desirable. They are: stage 1 – discriminatory practice; stage 2 – inadequate practice; stage 3 – well-meaning but poorly informed practice; stage 4 – practice that values diversity generally; stage 5 – practice that values diversity and challenges discrimination; stage 6 – practice that challenges inequality and promotes equality. Workers often do not recognize the level of practice they are providing and need to use staff meetings and training as a way to review and evaluate their own practice.

We have seen all the way through this section, and all the way through this book, that adults have an important part to play in the way children grow and develop. Nowhere is this more important than in the development of identity and self-esteem. People who work with children have a particularly important part to play, as they are seen as role models by both children and parents. Childcare workers have a role to play in the development of identity and self-esteem in all the children in their care, not just those who have the same cultural, racial, religious or linguistic background, abilities or disabilities as themselves.

It is often not possible for workers to represent the backgrounds of all the children in the setting. Workers will then need to ensure that they are providing positive adult role models by inviting other adults to visit the setting (for example, inviting parents to come in and help, or other adults to come in to be with the children and talk to them). If this is not possible, workers could take children out into the community to see positive role models.

Workers need to take a proactive approach to ensure that all children are developing a positive sense of identity and self-esteem. There are times when workers may need to ask other professionals for help and advice in this area. This should be seen not as a sign of weakness or failure, but as a gap that other people may be more

Figure 6.3 Children and workers interacting together.

qualified to fill. By talking to other professionals, workers will enhance their knowledge in this area.

Things that workers can undertake to develop a child's identity and self-esteem include:

- respecting and valuing children as individuals and all the things that go to make them individuals (their colour, disability, language and all the other factors that go to make them who they are);
- respecting and valuing the parents and families of children in the setting;
- providing opportunities for children to explore their identities;
- not using derogatory, discriminatory or negative language, or talking about individuals or groups in a negative way;

- providing children with opportunities to grow and develop as individuals, but not consciously or subconsciously setting them up to fail;
- praising children's achievements;
- allowing children to make mistakes and learn from them;
- not doing everything for children, but encouraging them to do things for themselves;
- providing resources and activities with positive images of all groups in society;
- spelling and pronouncing names correctly;
- acknowledging that discrimination, oppression and stereotypes exist and challenging them;
- having policies and procedures that are implemented, reviewed and evaluated;
- starting with what children can do, not what they cannot do;
- ensuring that the physical environment is accessible as possible;
- recognizing that language is powerful and thinking about how it is used;
- not categorizing or labelling children;
- working with colleagues to discuss and evaluate practice;
- attending training sessions and keeping up to date with issues, knowledge and new developments;
- recognizing that one person cannot do or know everything;
- learning from their own mistakes;
- listening to children and allowing them to share their experiences;
- communicating with parents effectively and providing explanations;
- working with parents;
- working with other professionals;
- ensuring that there is specialist equipment and resources for those who need it;
- being a positive role model.

Useful publications

Language development and communication

Arnberg, L. (1987) *Raising Children Bilingually: The Pre-school Years*. Multilingual Matters.

Brown, B. (1999) *Unlearning Discrimination in the Early Years*. Trentham Books.

Elliott, M. (1993) *Female Sexual Abuse of Children*. Guilford Press.

Kersner, M. and Wright, J. A. (1993) *How to Manage Communication Problems in Young Children*. Winslow Press.

Konner, M. (1991) *Childhood*. Little, Brown.

Lindon, J. and Lindon, L. (1993) *Caring for the Under Eights*. Macmillan.

Minet, P. (1989) *Child Care and Development*. John Murray.

National Society for the Prevention of Cruelty to Children (1997) *Turning Points: A Resource Pack for Communicating with Children*. NSPCC.

Niedzwiecki, P. (1993) *Women and Language*. Cahier de Femmes d'Europe no. 40. European Commission.

O'Hagan, M. (1997) *Geraghty's Caring for Children*. Baillière Tindall.

O'Hagan, M. and Smith, M. (1999) *Early Years Child Care and Education: Key Issues*. Baillière Tindall.

Siraj-Blatchford, I. (1994) *The Early Years: Laying the Foundations for Racial Equality*. Trentham Books.

Siraj-Blatchford, I. and Clarke, P. (2000) *Supporting Identity, Diversity and Language in the Early Years*. Open University Press.

Syder, D. (1992) *An Introduction to Communication Disorders*. Chapman & Hall.

Vygotsky, L. S. (1962) *Thought and Language*. John Wiley.

Wales Pre-school Playgroups Association and Mudiad Ysgolion Meithrin (n.d.) *Playing Together*. NES Arnold.

Child protection

Albany Video (n.d.) *A Case for Concern*. Video, for sale or hire from Albany Video, Film and Distribution, Battersea Studios TV Centre, Thackeray Road, London SW8 3TW.

Albany Video (n.d.) *Kids Can Say No!* Video, for sale or hire from Albany Video, Film and Distribution, Battersea Studios TV Centre, Thackeray Road, London SW8 3TW.

Children's Legal Centre (1988) *Child Abuse Procedures: The Children's Viewpoint*. Children's Legal Centre.

Department of Health (1991) *Working Together*. Consultation Paper no. 22. HMSO.

Elliot, M. (1985) *Preventing Child Sexual Assault*. Bedford Square Press/ NCVO.

Hedley, R. and Dorkenoo, E. (1992) *Child Protection and Female Genital Mutilation.* Forward.

National Society for the Prevention of Cruelty to Children (1997) *Turning Points: A Resource Pack for Communicating with Children.* NSPCC.

O'Hagan, M. (1997) *Geraghty's Caring for Children.* Baillière Tindall.

O'Hagan, M. and Smith, M. (1999) *Early Years Child Care and Education: Key Issues.* Baillière Tindall.

Owen, C., Cameron, C. and Moss, P. (1998) *Men as Workers in Services for Young Children: Issues for a Mixed Gender Workforce.* Institute of Education.

Wheal, A. (1999) *The RHP Companion to Foster Care.* Russell House Publishing.

White, D. and Woodlett, A. (1992) *Families: A Context for Development.* Falmer Press.

Development of identity and self-esteem

Albany Video (n.d.) *Coffee Coloured Children.* Video, for sale or hire from Albany Video, Film and Distribution, Battersea Studios TV Centre, Thackeray Road, London SW8 3TW.

Alibhai-Brown, Y. and Montague, A. (1992) *The Colour of Love: Mixed Race Relationships.* Virago.

BBC Education (1994) *Children without Prejudice: Equal Opportunities and the Children Act* (video). BBC.

Brown, B. (1999) *Unlearning Discrimination in the Early Years.* Trentham Books.

Centre for Studies on Inclusive Education (1996) *Developing an Inclusion Policy for Your School.* CSIE.

Chakrabarti, M. and Hill, M. (2000) *Residential Child Care: International Perspectives on Links with Families and Peers.* Jessica Kingsley.

Chambers, C., Funge, S., Harris, G. and Williams, C. (1996) *Celebrating Identity: A Resource Manual.* Trentham Books.

Clarke, K. B. and Clarke, M. P. (1947) Racial identification and preferences in negro children, in T. M. Newcomb and E. L. Hartley (eds) *Readings in Social Psychology.* Holt, Rinehart & Winston.

Cohen, D. (1990) *Essential Psychology.* Bloomsbury.

Department for Education (1994) *Code of Practice for Identification and Assessment of Special Educational Needs.* Department for Education. (Being revised.)

Department for Education and Skills (2001) *Promoting Children's Mental Health within Early Years and School Settings.* DfES.

Derman Sparks, L. (1989) *Anti-bias Curriculum: Tools for Empowering Young Children.* National Early Years Network.

Drummond, M. (1997) *Assessing Children's Learning.* David Fulton.

Early Years Training Anti Racist Network (n.d.) *The Best of Both Worlds: Celebrating Mixed Parentage.* EYTARN.

Elliott, M. (1993) *Female Sexual Abuse of Children: The Ultimate Taboo.* Longman

Gergen, K. J. and Gergen, M. M. (1981) *Social Psychology*. Harcourt Brace Jovanovich.

Gipps, C. and Murphy, P. (1999) *A Fair Test? Assessment, Achievement, and Equality*. Open University Press.

Hyder, T. (2001) Safe haven. *Nursery World*, 23 August.

Katz, I. (2001) *The Construction of Racial Identity in Children of Mixed Parentage. Mixed Metaphors*. Jessica Kingsley.

Kindersley, A. and Kindersley, B. (1999) *Children of Britain Just Like Me*. Dorling Kindersley.

Konner, M. (1991) *Childhood*. Little, Brown.

Lane, J. (1990) *From Cradle to School*. Commission for Racial Equality.

Lloyd, B. and Duveen, G. (1992) *Gender Identity and Education: The Impact of Starting School*. Harvester Wheatsheaf.

Maalouf, A. (2000) *On Identity*. Harvill Press.

Maccoby, E. E. (1998) *The Two Sexes Growing Up Apart Coming Together Again*. Belknap Harvard.

Maclean, S. and Maclean, I. (2000) *Understanding the NVQ Value Base: A Reference Guide for Foster Carers*. Kerwin Maclean Associates.

Maximé, J. E. (1993) The therapeutic importance of racial identity in working with black children who hate, in V. Varma (ed.) *How and Why Children Hate: A Study of Conscious and Unconscious Sources*. Jessica Kingsley.

Maximé, J. E. (n.d.) *Black Like Me*. Emani Publications.

Millner, D. (1983) *Children and Race Ten Years On*. Ward Lock.

Murphy, P. (1999) *Learners, Learning and Assessment*. Paul Chapman.

National Society for the Prevention of Cruelty for Children (1977) *Turning Points: A Resource Pack for Communicating with Children*. NSPCC.

Niedzwiecki, P. (1993) *Women and Language*. Cahier de Femmes d'Europe no. 40. European Commission.

Save the Children and Early Years Training Anti Racist Network (n.d.) *Equality in Practice: A Conference Report*. Save the Children and EYTARN.

Singh Ghuman, P. A. (1994) *Coping with Two Cultures*. Multilingual Matters.

Siraj-Blatchford, I. (1994) *The Early Years: Laying the Foundations for Racial Equality*. Trentham Books.

Siraj-Blatchford, I. and Clarke, P. (2000) *Supporting Identity, Diversity and Language in the Early Years*. Open University Press.

Tizard, B. and Phoenix, A. (1995) *Black, White or Mixed Race?* Routledge.

Tomlinson, S. (1984) *Home and School in Multicultural Britain*. Batsford.

United Nations (2001) *Working Far from Home: Migration and Discrimination*. <www.un.org/WCAR/e-kit/migration.htm>.

Varma, V. (1993) *How and Why Children Hate: A Study of Conscious and Unconscious Sources*. Jessica Kingsley.

Wheal, A. (ed.) (1999) *The RHP Companion to Foster Care*. Russell House Publishing.

Yelland, N. (1998) *Gender in Early Childhood*. Routledge.

Appendix 1

Sample answers for Chapter 1

A Chance to Think 3

Children may have attitudes that are racist, prejudicial, discriminatory. They may feel superior, feel inferior, have low self-esteem or have pride in skin colour.

Children may get their attitudes from their parents, other adults, television, books or comics, the toys or equipment they play with, the environment around them.

Children's behaviour can include white children using derogatory language about skin colour; children not wanting to play with children who have a different background to themselves; black children suffering from low self-esteem or poor self-image; white children feeling that they are superior to or better than black children.

A Chance to Think 7

The situation seems not to reflect the true mix of the local environment. It is a false situation.

It may be happening genuinely by accident; the admissions policy may be at fault; it may be for racial reasons; parents may be asking for a particular session.

The things that could be done about it are: ask the manager again; discuss it with the owner or management committee, and ask them to look at the admissions policy; monitor admissions over the next few months to see why it may be happening.

A Chance to Think 8

Providing resources and activities that contain positive visual images, e.g. jigsaws, posters, wall displays, books, dressing-up clothes, a home corner representing a variety of homes, skin tone paints. Providing diets that meet the needs of all children. Ensuring that notices are translated and that languages other than English are used in the setting, e.g. tapes, books, labelling. Working closely with all parents to find out what their needs and the children's needs are. Acknowledging festivals. Planning activities around a topic web. Inviting people from different groups in on an everyday basis. Visits out into the community. Evaluating policies and procedures. Ongoing training for all staff, on religion, race, culture and language. Challenging discriminatory behaviour. Talking with children. Respecting dress codes. Ensuring that hair and skin care is provided for.

A Chance to Think 9

Multicultural. Recognizing that children have different cultural backgrounds, and, through planning, trying to meet the needs of the children; involving and recognizing everyone's culture; accepting and respecting people's cultural backgrounds; celebrating festivals and cultural events; providing resources that show people's culture.

Anti-racist/anti-sexist. Providing an anti-racist, anti-sexist environment; allowing boys and girls to have equal access to experiences; treating people as individuals, not on the basis of race or sex; not stereotyping because of race or sex; being aware of the language used.

Anti-discriminatory practice. Incorporates and recognizes all groups in society, so is anti-racist, anti-sexist and also anti-ageist, etc.; recognizes race, culture, disabilities, language, sexual orientation, etc.; sees people as individuals and of equal value and concern; recognizes all groups in society and provides positive images, resources and attitudes for them all; does not just provide equipment, but explains about injustices in society.

Anti-discriminatory practice ensures that all groups in society are reflected. The other two are making a start, but both have things missing.

A Chance to Think 10

Feelings might include embarrassment, feeling awkward, being unsure what to do, wanting to get the children to be quiet, feeling unable to handle the situation.

Explain to the children about Down's Syndrome using language appropriate to their understanding; explain how hurtful their remarks are making the father and child feel; ask the father and child to join the group for a story if appropriate; find a book or books to take back to the setting to use with the children.

A Chance to Think 12

Feelings might include embarrassment, no particular strong feelings, not like it but be professional about it, feel it is positive for Claire as she is wanted and loved, put feelings to one side and work in partnership for the benefit of Claire.

In the same way as when working with all the other parents: communication; welcoming Claire's mother and partner into the setting; inviting them to be involved in the setting.

That some children have a mum and dad, some have only one parent and some children have two mums or two dads, step-families, etc.; get books about families from the library.

A Chance to Think 13

Before Fasil and his parents start, contact an interpreter for a few words; arrange for an interpreter to be present on the first day; smile; body language; gestures; welcoming atmosphere; say 'hello' in Amharic if possible.

Try to get an interpreter; use other parents who speak Amharic if the information is not confidential; do not use an interpreter the family are not happy with.

A Chance to Think 14

Allow Jane to reply if she wants to; deal with the outcome of that;
sensitively try to find out what the mother means by that remark
and whether she understands what she has said; explain that the
remark is offensive and why; explain the ethos of the setting and
why the remark may have hurt Jane's feelings; try to deal with the
hurt feelings and any other feelings that may be around; look for
literature that will support the setting's point of view.

Appendix 2

Sample answers for Chapter 2

A Chance to Think 3

The statement is incorrect and shows a narrow view of race issues; the setting is not complying with the Children Act; all children are not the same and should not be treated the same (this is not treating all children equally).

All workers and settings need to be addressing the issue of race.

By recognizing the need to address the issue; by realizing that there is a legal duty to do so under the Children Act; getting training to help deal with their own feelings; incorporating activities that acknowledge and reflect individuals' backgrounds in a positive way.

A Chance to Think 4

By asking if they realized that the word 'half-caste' was offensive and explaining what it meant.

Talking to colleagues about the meaning of the word and asking what they meant by it; talking about the positive benefits of being of mixed race; asking the manager for training if appropriate; bringing in literature to support the positive factors of being of mixed race.

Provide positive images of mixed-race children and adults; talk to Jason about his background and how he sees himself; talk to Jason's parents; provide resources and activities so that Jason can feel positive about himself.

A Chance to Think 5

Things that might be included in a person's culture are dress, language, diet and food, way of eating, music, art, literature, hygiene, jewellery, traditions, discipline.

The setting needs to be aware of these so that it can acknowledge them and provide for them: appropriate diets, hair and skin care; providing positive images, resources and activities that reflect cultural backgrounds; not using negative or derogatory language when discussing religions.

A Chance to Think 6

Appropriate diets, hair and skin care; providing positive images, resources and activities that reflect cultural backgrounds; not using negative or derogatory language when discussing religions.

A Chance to Think 7

By providing activities, resources and positive images relating to religions; providing for dietary requirements; acknowledging festivals; respecting dress codes; not using negative or derogatory language when discussing religions.

Appendix 3

Sample answers for Chapter 3

A Chance to Think 1

Ask colleagues if they have any information or know anything about the Buddhist religion; visit the library to get information; ask the family, when the child starts, about her needs.

A Chance to Think 2

It is a good idea.

Some parents may not want their children to visit a church, so it is important to talk to them about the outing, the reasons for it and where else you are visiting; get parents' permission; talk to the vicar about the reason for the trip and what you want the children to get out of it; take photos during the visit; ensure that workers are dressed appropriately for the visit.

Talk to the children about where they are going, what the building is, what they are going to see, who they are going to meet; get books from the library about churches and different buildings; answer their questions.

Talk with the children about where they went, what they saw, etc., and answer their questions; do art work and create an interest table; develop photos; talk to parents about the visit.

A Chance to Think 3

Find out about Diwali; some parents may object to this, so talk to them about it, what you will be doing and why.

Make diva lights; tell or act out the story of Rama and Sita; ask parents to come in and help; cook Diwali food or have a Diwali meal; make Diwali cards with appropriate scripts; visit a Hindu temple; make pictures, colourings and art of Rama and Sita; get some Hindu art to display; create a Hindu interest table; play Hindu music; make a wall picture or display; turn the home corner into a Hindu home.

A Chance to Think 4

It depends on the times at which Fatma has to pray; it might be disruptive but it should have no effect on the running of the setting; it will be good for the children and broaden their experience.

The setting will have to alter its routine slightly, and workers may have to take different breaks; talk to all the workers so that they are aware of the situation; Fatma can do the shifts that allow for greatest flexibility for her; provide a quiet private space for her to pray.

A Chance to Think 5

Be pleased that Elizabeth feels able to come into the setting and glad that she has offered.

Elizabeth will get to see the setting and the children; she will, it is to be hoped, feel valued and respected; the children will benefit from having another adult to tell them stories; they will learn about Hanukah and Elizabeth will be able to answer their questions; the staff may see Elizabeth in a different way, as they will have a chance to talk to her in the setting; they may learn more about Hanukah.

A Chance to Think 6

Sensitively take the member of staff to one side and explain that Tafari keeps his hat on indoors and why.

A Chance to Think 7

Sensitively explain what the five Ks are, and that the dagger is one of them and not a symbol of violence; ask them if they would like Rajinder to talk to them about the five Ks.

Appendix 4

Sample answers for Chapter 4

A Chance to Think 3

Say to the group something like, 'That isn't worms, it's spaghetti, and we like to eat it'; talk to Fred away from the children, to see if he realized what he had said; explain to him that what he said was not appropriate and tell him why.

A Chance to Think 4

Go to the library before Yasmin starts to find information that will give an overview of Muslim dietary requirements; talk to the person who cooks the meals in the setting; when Yasmin starts ask her parents what her needs are.

A Chance to Think 6

Experiencing eating food with fingers; introducing thali dishes and using them correctly; introducing new skills and vocabulary; recognizing, acknowledging and respecting cultural variations in the eating of food.

A Chance to Think 7

It depends on the level of Kevin's dyspraxia: providing space for Kevin; providing appropriate cutlery and equipment; allowing him to be as independent and autonomous as possible; supporting him as appropriate to his needs.

A Chance to Think 9

Lakshmidevi's jewellery should not be removed, as it is not dangerous; workers should discuss why they want to do this; the manager should explain that the jewellery should not be removed and why.

Lakshmidevi might be upset; the other children might see her as different; Lakshmidevi's parents could be very upset.

A Chance to Think 10

Upset that no one had been consulted, as other workers and parents may have views on taking the children swimming; that Shelan should go to the pool to help with the children but not go in; if staffing is tight, Shelan could stay in the setting and cover there, to allow another worker to go swimming with the children.

Support Shelan as much as possible by offering to go to the pool instead of her.

A Chance to Think 11

Feelings may include anger after having tried to reassure parents; being upset at the parents' attitude; understanding how parents feel and trying to think about their rights.

The manager could talk to James and the parents separately; James should be supported, as he is a worker and changing children is part of his job; the manager should also discuss with James why he or she thinks the parent does not want him to change Lalita; discuss the rights of James and the rights of the parents; the parents should have had this explained to them before they started in the setting; try to find out what the parents' concerns are and reassure them.

A Chance to Think 12

Feelings might include shock, embarrassment, surprise, empathy, understanding; it might be appropriate not to say anything at the time but to go away and plan what to say.

The supervisor could talk to George about why he wants to wear a dress to the setting; ask him whether he thinks it is appropriate; take time to think about it and discuss it with others as appropriate; discuss it with the staff team to see how they feel; if not agreeing to let George wear a dress, explain why; if agreeing, discuss the dress code and what is appropriate and what is not; work out how questions from parents and children will be handled; talk to George's tutors if appropriate to see what he is being told by them.

A Chance to Think 14

Talk sensitively to the parents, explaining the importance of washing and changing Tom, as he is uncomfortable and may develop nappy rash; try to find out sensitively why this is happening and how the setting can support Tom's parents.

A Chance to Think 16

Put back the cloth as well as possible; comfort Amarjit; explain to the children that it is possible for boys to have long hair; explain why Amarjit has long hair; explain that his feelings have been hurt and that this needs to be put right; find pictures of other boys and men with long hair to show the children.

Sample answers for Chapter 5

A Chance to Think 2

Feelings could include: feeling OK; slightly nervous owing to never having worked with a child with cerebral palsy before; anxiety. You might try to find out as much about cerebral palsy before Magdy started in order to be prepared.

Treat Magdy as an individual, not making assumptions about his physical skills; he may have difficulty being able to control movements or may be unable to control movements depending on the severity of the cerebral palsy; may be floppy; have poor balance; muscle stiffness; may have difficulty in feeding himself.

Talk to his parents to ensure that the setting has all the information it needs; get support from other agencies as appropriate; introduce Magdy to the children and the staff; involve Magdy in activities with the other children; take him to activities and carry him round; treat him as an individual; talk to him; provide any equipment he may need to join in; adapt equipment as appropriate; find equipment that he likes to use; give him the opportunity to try things and support him when needed; answer any questions from the other children honestly.

A Chance to Think 3

Eurocentric means a white European viewpoint.

The setting needs to address the issue, as children are being given incorrect messages about the world and the people in it.

Staff may need training to begin to address why the setting needs to change and to address issues, attitudes and feelings around this; visit other settings recommended by the inspection officer to see their approach; talk to the inspection officer and ask for his or her opinion and recommendations; evaluate the equipment and resources being used in the setting and, if necessary, get rid of the ones that are not appropriate and recommend buying new ones; advise staff on how to use equipment and resources and the importance of language; introduce new menus and foods to the setting.

A Chance to Think 4

Girls are not getting a chance to use the water tray.

Ensure that the girls are given the opportunity to use the water tray, and explain to the boys that as they played yesterday and the day before it is someone else's turn; talk sensitively to the member of staff about what has been happening, as he or she may not realize what is happening.

A Chance to Think 5

Sabrina may feel hurt, sad, upset, confused. She might understand why the children said that and feel not valued as a person.

Intervene sensitively; go into the home corner to play and take Sabrina in; talk to the children about their remark and how it makes Sabrina feel; talk to the parents when they arrive about the remark and why it is hurtful and unacceptable in the setting; continue to address the issue as appropriate through activities and discussion.

A Chance to Think 6

Go to the library; talk to colleagues and parents; contact relevant organizations and ask for information.

The setting could label things in a variety of languages; dual-language books; songs and rhymes in a variety of languages; music tapes; ensuring that children see and hear a variety of languages; acknowledging and talking about languages positively; doing activities that involve languages.

A Chance to Think 9

See Figure A.1.

A Chance to Think 11

You need to think about seating and the layout of the activity; the type of activity; the type of resources being used.

A collage with bright-coloured materials with different textures.

Only have a few children; ensure there is enough space to do the activity; ensure that there is enough equipment for the number of children; sit them so they can reach things; help them, but do not do it for them; talk about what is happening and facilitate conversation; ensure they are all participating but do not force participation; show things to Veronique as appropriate.

A Chance to Think 12

Think about the needs of the individuals taking part; have a selection of songs and rhymes ready; organize the instruments; organize a quiet place for it to take place, so there is no background noise; think about how long it is going to last.

Finger rhymes; nursery rhymes; action songs with parts of the body; quiet and loud songs; playing instruments loudly and quietly.

Ensure that there is no background noise or distraction; sit facing the children; do things individually so that all the children get a turn; do things at different volumes.

A Chance to Think 13

Talk to the children about what the interest table and display is going to be on; ask them for ideas; talk about what types of homes they live in and how they can be incorporated in the display; talk about the types of homes they do not live in; talk about animal homes; talk about people who do not have a home; build homes from construction toys, junk, etc.; paint pictures of homes; visit different homes if possible; help with putting the display together.

Planning web

Communication, language and literacy

① Food interest table labelled and with cookery books (ask parents to help with labelling in various languages).

② Story tapes, stories, rhymes e.g. hungry caterpillar, chapatis not chips, five little peas in a pea pod pressed.

Creative development

① Drama – the hungry caterpillar.

② Printing using fruit and vegetables, e.g. apple, mango, kiwi fruit, plantain, potato.

Physical development

① Eating food with different types of implements, e.g. knife and fork, chopsticks, fingers.

② Opening food containers, e.g. bags, tins, jars and measuring out food with spoons, knives.

Mathematical development

① Weighing ingredients for cooking, and following a recipe.

② Matching food, e.g. colour, length weight, shape.

FOOD

Knowledge and understanding of the world

① Growing food, e.g. mung beans, cress.

② Using senses to identify food whilst blindfolded.

③ Examining cooking equipment and seeing how it works, e.g. fridge, cooker, whisk, etc.

Personal, social and emotional development

① Discussion about where food comes from and how it is distributed.

② Turn home corner into a food shop or Chinese restaurant.

③ Invite a parent to come in to cook food with the children.

Figure A.1 Planning for the theme of food.

Children's work: their pictures, and homes they make from construction toys or other resources; posters and photographs of homes; books; labelling; an animal home, such as a bird's nest, if possible.

A Chance to Think 15

Sand play; water play; matching; shapes; sorting; number rhymes and songs; puzzles.

Number rhymes; stories with numbers, e.g. the three bears; malleable play; making things of different sizes; posting boxes; sorting games; puzzles; stacking beakers; matching games; sand and water play.

A Chance to Think 16

Talk to the student sensitively about what has been observed; ask him if he realizes that this is what is happening.

Talk to him about the importance of girls doing science and technology activities; bring in research to back this up; explain the ethos of the setting and that, even if he thinks it is wrong, the setting has a policy of anti-discriminatory practice; if necessary talk to the student's tutors, so that this attitude can be monitored; bring in literature to back up what has been said (e.g. research findings).

All the children are getting messages that are gender stereotyped.

Appendix 6

Sample answers for Chapter 6

A Chance to Think 2

Try to learn a few Spanish words, such as hello, toilet and drink.

Smile; talk to her mother so that Alexandra can see that the setting is friendly and that her mother trusts it; show her round; introduce her to children and staff; start her in the setting gradually, so that she gets used to spending more time each day without her mum.

Reassure Alexandra's mother and give her the phone number of the setting so that she can phone to see how Alexandra is; ask her to write down some words that may be useful; ask her to explain to Alexandra what is happening; ensure that the setting has the mother's work phone number and emergency numbers in case Alexandra becomes very upset; comfort Alexandra as appropriate, and encourage her to join in with the other children.

A Chance to Think 3

Talk to Amanda on her own and find out why this is happening; explain how damaging it is to David and the other children; explain to her how to communicate with David; discuss her feelings about working with David; talk to her tutors if necessary; if this continues, remove her from the situation and inform her tutors why.

Work with David and support him; develop situations where he can regain his confidence; praise his communication skills; talk to the other children and explain how David feels when they laugh at him.

A Chance to Think 4

Recognizing that people have different ways of disciplining children, and that some of these may not be appropriate; cultural and religious variations in child-rearing practices; what bruises and injuries look like on different skin colours and tones; Mongolian blue spot is a naturally occurring mark; different economic situations may mean that people have different standards of care; child abuse can occur in any race, religion, culture, class and economic group; and in cities, towns and villages; men and women can abuse children.

A Chance to Think 5

The images they see around them; what they hear being said about them; how people react to them.

Because they have a positive sense of who they are; they feel good about themselves; they get positive reassurance about themselves from other people and/or society at large.

Because they have a poor self-identity; they do not feel good about themselves; they may be being abused; they get negative messages about themselves from other people and/or society at large.

A Chance to Think 6

Parents with low self-esteem will not be able to give their children the positive reassurance and images they need to develop their self-esteem; their children may also have low self-esteem.

Useful Addresses

Ability Net
PO Box 94, Warwick,
CV34 5WS
www.abilitynet.co.uk

Action for Blind People
14–16 Verney Road, London,
SE16 3DZ
www.deon.co.uk/afbp

Adoption UK
Lower Boddington, Daventry,
Northants, NN11 6YB

Advisory Conciliation and
Arbitration Service (ACAS),
27 Wilton Street, London,
SW16 4ER
www.acas.org.uk

Advisory Council for the
Education of Romany and
Other Travellers
Mary Ward Centre, 42 Queen
Square, London, WC1N 3AJ

Afro-Caribbean Education
Recource Project (ACER)
Acer Centre, Wyvil School,
Wyvil Road, London, SW8 2TJ

Anti-Bullying Campaign
185 Tower Bridge Road,
London, SE1 2UF

ASBAH (Spina Bifida
and Hydrocephalus)
42 Park Road, Peterborough,
PE1 2UQ
www.asbah.demon.co.uk

Association for All Speech
Impaired Children (AFASIC)
347 Central Markets,
Smithfield, London,
EC1A 9NH
www.afasicorg.uk

Board of Deputies of British
Jews
Woburn House, Tavistock
Square, London, WC1H 0EZ

British Association for
Adoption and Fostering
Skyline House, 200 Union
Street, London, SE1 0LX

British Association for Early
Childhood Education
(BAECE)
111 City View House, 463
Bethnal Green Road, London,
E2 9QH

British Association for the
Study and Prevention of Child
Abuse and Neglect
10 Priory Street, York,
YO1 6EZ

British Diabetic Association
(Diabetes UK)
10 Queen Anne Street,
London, W1M 0BD
www.diabetes.org.uk

British Deaf Association
1-3 Worship Street, London,
EC2A 2AB

British Epilepsy Association
New Anstey House, Gate Way
Drive, Yeadon, Leeds,
LS19 7XY
www.epilepsy@bea.org.uk

British Humanist Society
47 Theobalds Road, London,
WC1X 8SP

British Institute of Human
Rights
Kings College London, 8th
Floor, 75-9 York Road,
London, SE1 7AW
www.bihr.org

British Institute of Learning
Disabilties
Wolverhampton Rd,
Kidderminster, Worcs,
DY10 3PP
www.bild.org.uk

Centre for Accessible
Environments
Nutmeg House, Gainsford
Street, London, SE1 2NY
www.cae.org.uk

Centre for Studies on
Intergration in Education
415 Edgware Road, London,
NW2 6NB

Child Poverty Action Group
94 White Lion Street, London,
N1 9PF
www.cpag.org.uk

Children First
41 Polwarth Terrace,
Edinburgh, EH11 1NU

Children in Scotland
Princes House, 5 Shandwick
Place, Edinburgh, EH2 4RG
www.childreninscotland.org.uk

Children in Wales
25 Windsor Place, Cardiff,
CF10 3BZ

Children's Legal Centre
The University of Essex,
Wivenhoe Park, Colchester,
Essex, CO4 3SQ
www.2.essex.ac.uk/clc

City and Guilds of London
Institute
1 Giltspur Street, London,
EC1A 9DD
www.city-and-guilds.co.uk

Commission for Racial
Equality (CRE)
Elliot House, 10–12 Allington
Street, London, SE1E 5EH
www.cre.gov.uk

Council for Awards in
Children's Care and Education
(CACHE)
8 Chequer Street, St Albans,
Hertfordshire, AL1 3XZ
www.cache.org.uk

Council for Disabled Children
National Children's Bureau,
8 Wakley Street, London,
EC1V 7QE

Cruse – Bereavement Care
Head Office, Cruse House,
126 Sheen Road, Richmond,
Surrey, TW9 1UR

Cystic Fibrosis Trust
11 London Road, Bromley,
Kent, BR1 1BY
www.cftrust.org.uk

Daycare Trust
21 St Georges Road, London,
SE1 6ES
www.daycaretrust.org.uk

Department for Education and
Skills (DfES formally DfEE)
DfES Publications, PO Box
5050, Sherwood Park,
Annesley, Nottingham,
NG15 0DJ
www.dfes.gov.uk

Department of Health (DOH)
Publications Centre, PO Box
276, London, SW8 5DT
www.doh.gov.uk

Disability Information Trust
Mary Marlborough Centre,
Nuffield Orthopaedic Centre,
Headington, Oxford,
OX3 7LD
www.home.btconnect.co/
ditrust/home.htm

Disabled Living
Redbank House, 4 St Chad's
Street, Cheetham, Manchester,
M8 8QA
www.disabledliving.co.uk

Down's Syndrome Association
155 Micham Road, London,
SW17 9PG
www.downs-syndrome.org.uk

Early Years National
Training Organisation
Pilgrims Lodge, Holywell Hill,
St Albans, Herts, AL1 1ER
www.early-years-nto.org.uk

Early Years Trainers Anti-Racist
Network (EYTARN)
1 The Lyden, 51 Granville
Road, London, N12 0JH

Equal Opportunties
Commission
Overseas House, Quay Street,
Manchester, M3 3HN

Equality Learning Centre
356 Holloway Road, London,
N7 6PA

Ethnic Minorities Advice
Bureau
1109–1111 London Road,
London, SW16 4XD

Families Need Fathers
134 Curtain Road, London,
EC2A 3AR
www.fnf.org.uk

Family Rights Group
The Print House, 18 Ashwin
Street, London, E8 3DL

Gender Trust
PO Box 3192, Brighton,
BN1 3WR
www.3.mistral.co.uk.gentrust

Gingerbread
16–17 Clerkenwell Close,
London, EC1R 0AN
www.gingerbread.org.uk

Gypsy Council for Education,
Culture, Welfare and Civil
Rights
8 Hall Road, Aveley, Romford,
Essex, RM15 4HD

Handicapped Adventure
Playground Association
(HAPA)
Pryor's Bank, Bishops Park,
London, SW6 3LA

Home Office
Public Enquiry Team,
Room 856, 50 Queen
Anne's Gate, London,
SW1H 9AT
www.homeoffice.gov.uk

Hyperactive Children's
Support Group
71 Whyte Lane, Chichester,
West Sussex, PO19 2LD

Immigration and Nationality
Directorate
Lunar House, 40 Wellesley
Road, Croydon, CR9 2BY

Jewish Care
Stuart Young House, 221
Golders Green Road, London,
NW11 9DQ

Kidsactive
Pryor's Bank, Bishops Park,
London, SW6 3LA
www.kidsactive.org.uk

Kids' Clubs Network
279–281 Whitechapel Road,
London, E1 1BY
www.kidsclubs.co.uk

Kidscape
152 Buckingham Palace Road,
London, SW1W 9TR

Letterbox Library
Unit 2D, Leroy House, 432
Essex Road, London, N1 3QP

London Lesbian and Gay
Switchboard
PO Box 7324, London, N1 9QS
www.llgs.org.uk

Mental Health and NHS
Community Care Division
Wellington House, 133–155
Waterloo Road, London,
SE1 8UG

Mencap
123 Golden Lane, London,
E1 1BY
www.mencap.org.uk

Mind (National Association for
Mental Health)
Granta House, 15–19
Broadway, Stratford, London,
E15 4BQ

Minority Rights Group
379 Brixton Road, London,
SW9 7DE

National Asthma Campaign
Providence House, Providence
Place, London, N1 0NT
www.asthma.org.uk

National Association for Gifted
Children
Elder House, Milton Keynes,
MK9 1LR
www.rmplc.co.uk/orgs/nagc/
index.html

National Association for Gifted
Children in Scotland
12 Woodside Place, Glasgow,
G3 7QW

National Association of
Toy and Leisure Libraries
(NATLL)
68 Churchway, London,
NW1 1LT
www.charitynet.org/~NATLL

National Autistic Society
393 City Road, London,
EC1V 1NG
www.oneworld.org/autism-uk/

National Childminding
Association (NCMA)
8 Mason's Hill, Bromley, Kent,
BR2 9EY
www.ncma.org.uk

National Children's Bureau
(NCB)
8 Wakley Street, London,
EC1V 7QE
www.ncb.org.uk

National Council for One
Parent Families
255 Kentish Town Road,
London, NW5 2LX

National Day Nurseries
Association (NDNA)
16 New North Parade,
Huddersfield, HD1 5JP
www.ndna.org.uk

National Early Years Network
77 Holloway Road,
London, N7 8JZ

National Eczema Society
163 Eversholt Street,
London, NW1 1BU
www.eczema.org

National Foster Care
Association
87 Blackfriars Road,
London, SE1 8HA

National Foster Care
Association Scotland
1 Melrose Street, off Queen's
Crescent, Glasgow,
G4 9BJ

National Library for the
Handicapped Child
Reach Resources Centre,
Wellington House, Wellington
Road, Wokingham, Berkshire,
RG11 2AG

National Playbus Association
AMS House, Whitby Road,
Brislington, Bristol, BS4 3QF

National Portage Association
12 Monks Dale, Yeovil,
Somerset, BA21 3JE

National Society's RE Centre
36 Causton Street, London,
SW1P 4AU

National Society for Epilepsy
Chesham Lane, Chalfont St
Peter, Bucks, SL9 0RJ
www.epilepsynse.org.uk

National Society for
Mentally Handicapped
People in Residential Care
(RESCARE)
Rayner House, 23 Higher
Hillgate, Stockport, Cheshire,
SK1 3ER

National Society for the
Prevention of Cruelty
to Children (NSPCC)
NSPCC National Centre,
42 Curtain Road, London,
EC2A 3NH

National Training
Organisation for Sport,
Recreation and Allied
Occupations
Playwork Unit,
24 Stephenson Way,
London, NW1 2HD
www.playwork.org.uk

Northern Ireland Pre-School
Playgroups Association
Enterprise House, Boucher
Cresent, Boucher Road,
Belfast, BT12 6HU

One Parent Families Scotland
6th Floor, 7 Buchanan Street,
Glasgow, G1 3HL

Office for Standards in
Education (OFSTED)
Early Years Directorate,
Alexandra House,
33 Kingsway, London,
WC2B 6SE
www.ofsted.gov.uk

Pali Text Society
73 Lime Walk, Headington,
Oxford, OX3 7AD

Parentline Plus (incorporating
Parentline and The National
Stepfamily Association)
Unit 520 Highgate Studios,
53–57 Highgate Road,
London, NW5 1TL
www.parentlineplus.org.uk

PHAB (Physically Disabled and
Able Bodied)Phab England
Office, Summit House, Wandle
Road, Croydon, CRO 1DF

PHAB Northern Ireland
Mourne Villa, Knockbracken
Healthcare Park, Saintfield
Road, Belfast, BT8 8BH

PHAB Scotland
5a Warriston Road,
Edinburgh, EH3 5LQ

PHAB Wales
2nd Floor, St David's House.
Wood Street, Cardiff,
CF10 1ES

Play Leisure Advice Network
(PLANET)
Cambridge House, Cambridge
Grove, London, W6 0LE

Prader-Willi Syndrome
Association (UK)
2 Wheatsheaf Close, Horsell,
Woking, Surrey, GU21 4BD
www.pswa-uk.demon.co.uk

Pre-School Learning Alliance
69 Kings Cross Road, London,
WC1X 9LL
www.pre-schoool.org.uk

Qualifications and Curriculum
Authority (QCA)
QCA Publications,
PO Box 99, Sudbury, Suffolk,
CO10 6SN
www.qca.org.uk

Quaker International Social
Projects
Friends Meeting House,
6 Mount Street, Manchester,
M2 5NS

Refugee Council
3 Bondway, London SW8 1SJ
www.refugeecouncil.demon.
co.uk

Royal Institute for the Blind
(RNIB)
224 Great Portland Street,
London, W1N 6AA

Royal Society for Mentally
Handicapped Children
and Adults (MENCAP)
117–123 Golden Lane,
London, EC1Y 0RF

SSAFA Forces Help
19 Queen Elizabeth Street,
London, SE1 2LP

Scottish Pre-School Playgroups
Association
14 Elliot Place, Glasgow,
G3 8EP

Sickle Cell Society
54 Station Road, Harlesden,
London, NW10 4BO

SCOPE
The Old School House, Main
Road, Kingsley, Bordon,
Hampshire, GU35 9ND

Standing Committee on
Sexually Abused Children
(SCOSAC)
73 Charlie Square, London,
W10 6EJ

TALK Adoption
12 Chapel Street,
Manchester,
M3 7NN

Terence Higgins Trust
52–54 Gray's Inn Road,
London, WC1X 8JU

UNICEF
12 Lincoln's Inn Fields,
Holborn, London, WC2B 6NB

Vegetarian Society
The Vegetarian Centre,
53 Marloes Road, Kensington,
London, W8 6LD

Website addresses

www.barnados.org.uk – Barnado's

www.bbc.co.uk – BBC

www.blink.org.uk – Black information link

www.childline.org.uk – Childline

www.community-care.co.uk – Community Care magazine

www.earlyyearseducator.co.uk – Early Years Educator magazine

www.echr.int – European Court of Human Rights

www.education.guardian.co.uk – the Education Guardian

www.guardian.co.uk – the Guardian newspaper

www.ioe.ac.uk – Institute of Education

www.legislation.hmso.gov.uk – website of legislation

www.nursery-world.com – Nursery World magazine

www.nspcc.org.uk – NSPCC

www.parents.dfee.gov.uk – parents information site

www.tes.co.uk – Times Educational Supplement

www.un.org – United Nations

www.underfives.co.uk – under fives website

Voice for the Child in Care
Unit 4 Pride Court, 80–82
White Lion Street, London,
N1 9PF

Wales Pre-School Playgroup
Association
2A Chester Street, Wrexham,
Clywd, LL13 8BD

Working Group Against
Racism in Children's
Resources (WGARCR)
460 Wandsworth Road,
London, SW8 3LK

World Health Organisation
(WHO)
20 Avenue Appier, Geneva,
Switzerland
www.who.int

World Organisation in Early
Childhood Education (OMEP)
C/o Thomas Coram
Foundation, 40 Brunswick
Square, London, WC1N 1AU

Index